Criminal Justi

Providing a comprehensive and up-to-date introduction to the contemporary Scottish criminal justice system, this book focuses on its key processes (from arrest to post-sentence) and institutions, as well as its history and some of the key challenges and critical issues facing Scottish criminal justice today.

Highly attentive to procedural and institutional detail, this book is underpinned by a critical sociological perspective. The opening chapter considers Scotland in its post-devolutionary context within the UK, setting the scene for Scottish criminal justice institutions. Subsequent chapters deal in turn with different institutions and processes of Scottish criminal justice: surveillance and crime prevention, policing, prosecution and the courts, criminal fines and other financial penalties, community justice, electronic monitoring, prisons, youth justice, and parole and post-sentence reintegration and supervision. The final chapter draws on comparative and international criminology to look at Scottish criminal justice in changing international contexts and its response to new global crimes.

Designed to support learning, it includes the following:

- Key ideas at the start of each chapter, outlining expectations and providing a very high-level summary of the most important points.
- Text boxes covering key issues, controversies and/or key populations in focus.
- Critical questions to challenge students to develop their own thinking and ideas about key issues in Scottish criminal justice.
- Short, informal interviews with key practitioners and researchers.
- Essential readings and key resources at the end of each chapter.

Criminal Justice in Scotland is a key text for students of criminology and criminal justice, particularly those with an interest in the Scottish criminal justice system. It will also be of value to students of law, social work and social policy.

Jamie Buchan is an Associate Professor in Criminology at Edinburgh Napier University. His research centres on penal policy in Scotland, with a particular emphasis on community penalties and restorative justice.

Sarah Anderson is a Lecturer in Criminology at Edinburgh Napier University. Her research has focused on desistance from crime, the intersection of health and justice, and the harms of the criminal justice system.

Katrina Morrison is an Associate Professor in Criminology at Edinburgh Napier University and an Associate Director at the Scottish Centre for Crime and Justice Research (SCCJR). Her work focuses on penal politics and penal change, imprisonment, prison workforces and cultures and healthcare in prisons, with a focus on Scotland.

Criminal Justice in Scotland

Jamie Buchan, Sarah Anderson
and Katrina Morrison

Routledge
Taylor & Francis Group
LONDON AND NEW YORK

Designed cover image: Jamie Buchan, Sarah Anderson and Katrina Morrison

First published 2026
by Routledge
4 Park Square, Milton Park, Abingdon, Oxon OX14 4RN

and by Routledge
605 Third Avenue, New York, NY 10158

Routledge is an imprint of the Taylor & Francis Group, an informa business

British Library Cataloguing-in-Publication Data
A catalogue record for this book is available from the British Library

ISBN: 9781032445816 (hbk)
ISBN: 9781032445809 (pbk)
ISBN: 9781003372882 (ebk)

DOI: 10.4324/9781003372882

Typeset in Sabon LT Pro
by codeMantra

Contents

Preface

Why we think this book is required

Scotland is part of the UK, but many people do not realise that it has its own criminal law and justice system and that this was not created by devolution but evolved separately within a distinct political landscape. This system is a primary focus for students of (especially) criminology in Scotland.

As lecturers who teach these students, we have noticed that they often struggle to find accurate information on the distinct features of the Scottish system. UK textbooks tend to focus on the English/Welsh system, with Scotland confined to a single chapter or ignored entirely. Although targeted at an undergraduate readership, our book should also be relevant to postgraduate students – and to *anyone* starting to get to grips with the Scottish criminal justice system.

There are other excellent books on Scottish criminal justice, which we encourage readers to seek out – notably *Criminal Justice in Scotland* (Duff and Hutton, 1999) *Criminal Justice in Scotland* (Croall et al., 2010) and *Crime, Justice and Society in Scotland* (Croall et al., 2016). But a lot has happened since the most recent of these – including the end of child imprisonment in Scotland, the UK's exit from the European Union, and events internationally prompting greater engagement with institutional racism and misogyny. A global pandemic disrupted criminal justice and raised questions about how (or whether) criminal justice should be used to achieve public health aims. Other things have remained stubbornly the same: high imprisonment rates alongside a rise in other forms of criminal justice supervision, and a crisis of drugs deaths with devastating effects across Scotland.

The limits of 'criminal justice'

We approach criminal justice from a sociology of punishment perspective, focused on how changing understandings of offending, justice and social life generally have shaped the development of criminal justice, its role in the social construction of crime, and related questions of (in)equality and fairness.

Critical criminologists and social harm theorists might rightly say that by focusing on the criminal justice system, we are implicitly accepting some highly contested premises. In particular, we are *necessarily* looking at responses to those harms that are defined legally as crimes. While there are significant harms associated with (some) crime, most people who go through the criminal justice system have *not* committed serious harm. In our social construction of crime, minor harms are often criminalised, while exceptions are made for the often far greater harms of the powerful (for example, the involvement of companies based in Scotland in the global arms trade). We encourage students to engage with social harm critiques – a good starting point for undergraduates is *Criminal obsessions: Why harm matters more than crime* (Dorling et al., 2008).

We still think our book is important, not least because criminal justice is arguably *itself* enmeshed in perpetrating social harm. We aim to encourage critical thinking about Scottish criminal justice – but to critique a system, you need to understand it.

How to use this book

This book is a comprehensive, up-to-date introduction to the Scottish criminal justice system – its key processes, institutions, history, and some contemporary challenges and critical issues. Chapter 1 considers Scotland's post-devolutionary context, setting the scene for Chapters 2–10 which deal in turn with different institutions and processes. Chapter 11 considers Scottish criminal justice in changing international contexts and its response to transnational crimes. Finally, Chapter 12 considers the question of how distinctive Scottish criminal justice really is.

These are designed to work as standalone chapters, but we encourage you to read across them – to consider links between parts of the system and how ideas and narratives surface in different places. For this reason, we also encourage you not to skip the first and last chapters. More advanced students will benefit from critical examination of challenges facing Scottish criminal justice, along with signposting to further reading. Other features include critical questions for discussion, as well as conversations with practitioners and researchers (with extended and additional conversations published online as accompanying podcasts).

This book is just a starting point – and writing it entailed difficult decisions about what to leave out. We encourage you to follow up our references and identify your own further reading. In the time since we have written this, Scottish criminal justice will continue to change in important ways, and you may need to seek updated information from academic research, justice agencies, and governmental and inspectorate reports. Textbooks are static, but – as we will see – criminal justice is not.

Jamie Buchan, Sarah Anderson and Katrina Morrison
Edinburgh Napier University and Scottish Centre
for Crime and Justice Research

References

Croall, H., Mooney, G. and Munro, M. (eds) (2010) *Criminal Justice in Scotland*. Routledge.

Croall, H., Mooney, G. and Munro, M. (eds) (2016) *Crime, Justice and Society in Scotland*. Routledge.

Dorling, D., Gordon, D., Hillyard, P., Pantazis, C., Pemberton, S. and Tombs, S. (2008) *Criminal Obsessions: Why Harm Matters More than Crime*. Centre for Crime and Justice Studies. https://www.crimeandjustice.org.uk//sites/default/files/Criminal%20obsessions.pdf

Duff, P. and Hutton, N. (eds) (1999) *Criminal Justice in Scotland*. Routledge.

Acknowledgements

We are extremely grateful to the publisher's peer reviewers for their constructive suggestions in shaping this book. We are also enormously thankful to the chapter peer reviewers who provided helpful and supportive comments (often at short notice): Alistair Henry, Estelle Clayton, Cyrus Tata, Margaret Malloch, Beth Weaver, Hannah Graham, Kirstin Anderson, Fern Gillon, Cara Jardine, Ben Collier and Shane Horgan. Any errors that remain are of course our own.

Cameron McCartney and Sheriff Kenneth Campbell provided vital legal expertise on children's hearings, criminal procedure and fine default. Fern Gillon provided helpful advice on the SVRU. We are also grateful to Gabrielle Watson and Grant Barclay (Edinburgh Law School), Nicola Ceesay (University of Glasgow), and Andrew Wooff (Edinburgh Napier University) for their assistance on key points.

Thanks also to Fiona and Duncan Collier for the use of their house in Aberdeenshire, where significant parts of this book came together.

We are also grateful to a number of our students for their feedback, including the 2022–23 cohort of the Youth, Crime and Deviance module, and to Gerda-Liis Nurmjoe and Feodorea Abifarin for their work on the 'Blethers'. Laurie Bowman, technician at the School of Arts and Creative Industries, provided vital technical help with recording.

Many thanks to our Blethers interviewees, who very kindly gave up their time and expertise to speak to us; their contributions have helped to bring these issues to life. We have benefited from the institutional support of Edinburgh Napier University and the Scottish Centre for Crime and Justice Research (SCCJR).

And finally, thank you to Ben, Fabrice, Si, Breagha and Anders for your support throughout.

1 What is distinctive about Scotland?

Key ideas

- In Scotland, as elsewhere, the practice of criminal justice is deeply shaped by social, historical and political context.
- Scotland has always had a separate criminal law and justice system from the rest of the UK. With devolution, Scotland regained a measure of autonomy over policy as well as practice.
- Key political roles and institutions involved in shaping criminal justice include the Scottish Government, the Cabinet Secretary for Justice, the Scottish Parliament and its Justice Committee, and the Lord Advocate.
- Scotland is sometimes understood as more egalitarian than the rest of the UK, particularly in relation to class and ethnicity. However, research evidence calls this self-image into question.
- This feeds into a pervasive discourse that Scotland is somehow exceptional, and that Scottish criminal justice is better than that of England and Wales – a discourse we critically question throughout this book.

Introduction

In common with many criminologists, we understand crime as **socially constructed**. That means that 'crime' is only real because it is understood *as crime* within the societies in which it happens and that this changes across time and place, affected by historical, social and political factors. A key argument in favour of this understanding is the changing nature of crime across different countries and time periods. Some actions, such as murder, are treated as crimes nearly everywhere, but even for this most 'obvious' of crimes, there is significant variation: for instance, killings by police officers or indirectly by corporate negligence are rarely prosecuted as murders. Other activities (e.g. homosexuality, drug or alcohol use, protesting against the government, sexual and physical violence within a marriage) have been criminalised in some places or historical periods but not others. The same goes for the systems and institutions put in place to respond to, prevent and punish offending; as comparative criminology shows, countries differ in how they *respond to* crime.

DOI: 10.4324/9781003372882-1

Criminal justice systems and institutions do not simply emerge naturally – but are not usually planned from scratch either. Instead, they are shaped by social and political context – so to understand criminal justice, it is essential to understand this context. This is not a comparative criminology textbook, but we *do* look at Scotland through a comparative 'lens' – things are more easily understood with reference to something else. Scotland is of particular interest as a jurisdiction within a larger nation state that is dominated (economically and politically) by England.

The Scottish criminal justice 'system' is a patchwork of complex institutions. While some of these, such as the criminal trial (Chapter 4), have existed for centuries, others such as justice social work (Chapter 6) are relatively recent developments. In this chapter, we outline some key elements of the Scottish social and political context which have shaped – and continue to shape – developments in criminal justice and which we will refer to often throughout this book.

1.1 The political and policymaking landscape of Scotland

1.1.1 Political identity

Scotland's political identity reflects the unique contours of Scottish national identity and distinctive institutional arrangements, though it has often been mythologised (particularly by those on the left). The distinctiveness of the Scottish landscape is perhaps more recent than people might first think. Apart from the postwar elections which brought in a Labour government in the UK (leading to a significant expansion of the welfare state), Scotland voted mostly Conservative until the 1970s (Cairney and McGarvey, 2013). Conservative support in Scotland had been declining for some time, but (as in much of the North of England) collapsed completely during the premiership of Margaret Thatcher (1979–90), due partly to the rapid pace of deindustrialisation, which cut through communities leaving generations of unemployment and associated hardships in its wake.

Scottish political views diverged from England during the 1980s, driven by a 'democratic deficit' – the fact that Scotland was consistently voting Labour, but (because of the union) getting Conservative governments. This divergence increased further with devolution (see Section 1.1.2) and the political ascendancy of the Scottish National Party (SNP) early in the 21st century. The SNP is a broadly socially democratic party, albeit a broad church united around Scottish independence from the UK; it has won the biggest voting share in Scotland from 2007 to the present day. From 2016 to 2025 the Scottish Conservatives have been the second biggest party in Scotland, followed by Scottish Labour and the Scottish Greens.

In 2014, with the agreement of the UK government, a referendum was held on making Scotland independent. Although Scotland voted to remain in the union, the independence issue remains prominent a decade later. Thus,

Scottish political identity is complex, with (at least) two key axes: left and right, and pro- and anti-independence. These do not always map onto each other neatly (though there are many more pro-independence views on the left than the right). Given that Scotland's criminal justice has long operated largely autonomously (see below) the independence debate did not centre on criminal justice – but it did speak to important wider questions of distinctiveness, progressiveness and welfarism.

Scottish support for more left-leaning parties feeds into a strong national narrative about Scottish identity aligned with principles of egalitarianism (see below). However, the reality is rather more complicated (Cairney and McGarvey, 2013), not least with parties of the populist (arguably, far) right projected to have stronger sway in Scotland from 2025 onwards.

Although Scottish New Labour had also sought to project Scotland as a 'left-leaning' nation in the early days of devolution (Scott and Mooney, 2009), this idea was especially promoted by the SNP. This connects with a wider SNP project of 'nation building' – the effort to construct (a new) national identity through public policy and other state action. Seen this way, the SNP's more left-leaning policy initiatives (e.g. greater support for low-income parents, no university tuition fees, free NHS prescriptions, etc.) are an attempt to coalesce a strong political identity around socially democratic values (Bond, 2024).

This has reached criminal justice too; the SNP Government has attempted to 'cleanse itself' of problematic aspects of Scottish identity, for example, through introducing minimum unit pricing to tackle high levels of alcohol consumption (Section 2.2), legislation against hate speech, and legislation aimed at tackling sectarian singing and behaviour at football matches. The Offensive Behaviour at Football and Threatening Communications (Scotland) Act was introduced in 2012 but was repealed four years later after campaigners highlighted its criminalisation of working-class young people and football fans, with wider questions of the extent to which social problems can be solved by the criminal justice system (McBride, 2022). For criminal justice policy and practice, the effects of a more left-leaning politics have resulted in a *discourse* which is more moderate than the (frequently) more populist crime and justice rhetoric in Westminster. However, we caution against thinking this translates neatly into more moderate policy, or a 'better' experience for those involved in the justice system (McAra, 2017) – indeed, in this book, we provide ample evidence of the sustained harm caused by the system.

1.1.2 *Devolution and political structures*

In the late 1990s, the UK government delegated political powers from Westminster to the new government and Parliamentary institutions in Scotland, Wales and Northern Ireland, in a process known as **devolution**. Scotland's devolutionary settlements are different to the other two (for these, see McAlinden and Dwyer, 2015; Jones and Wyn Jones, 2022), partly because of a long legacy of autonomy. Before devolution, Scots law and criminal justice institutions were distinct, while much of Scottish policy – including criminal justice – was organised by the Scottish Office (part of the UK Government which sat in Edinburgh, with relative freedom from Westminster).

With the creation of the Scottish Parliament and the then-Scottish Executive in 1999, devolution meant key areas of domestic policy (including health, education, criminal justice, and transport) would be governed and held accountable, by Scottish institutions (with some exceptions which remained 'reserved' to Westminster – notably drugs policy, discussed in Box 1.1). The key national institutions involved in the politics and governance of Scottish criminal justice are:

- The *Scottish Government* (named the 'Scottish Executive' from 1999 to 2007) – made up of Ministers and Cabinet Secretaries chosen by the First Minister from the party/parties with the most Members of the Scottish Parliament (MSPs), responsible for setting the legislative agenda according to their manifesto commitments.
- The *Cabinet Secretary for Justice and Home Affairs* – the main member of the Scottish Government responsible for criminal justice policy.
- The *Scottish Parliament* – made up of MSPs of all parties, who scrutinise proposed legislation and can propose their own legislation and who hold the Government to account through questions, debates and votes.
- The *Justice Committee* – a committee of the Scottish Parliament that scrutinises all proposed Scottish justice legislation and amendments, as well as holding its own enquiries into chosen priorities.
- The *Lord Advocate* – Scotland's chief law officer, a minister of the Scottish Government who advises the Scottish Government on all legal matters and is also the head of the Crown Office and Procurator Fiscal Service (see Chapter 4).

The Scottish Parliament is elected with the Additional Member System, a form of 'mixed' voting system that uses Westminster-style 'first past the post' to elect 73 constituency MSPs, with the remaining 56 elected in regions by proportional representation (more in line with European norms). In theory, this is supposed to prevent single-party majorities, which should make governments more likely to compromise (Cairney and McGarvey, 2013), although the SNP succeeded in forming a majority government between 2011 and 2016. The need for compromise in proportional representation has been argued to lead to more moderate forms of criminal justice, which may be one contributing factor to the more moderate rhetoric of Scottish penal politics, compared to Westminster (Lacey, 2012).

1.1.3 *Local governance*

Scotland is noted for its diverse geography and a particularly sharp contrast between dense urban areas in the 'Central Belt' and sparsely populated areas (including large parts of the Highlands and Islands). This poses various challenges, including for criminal justice (see for instance Section 3.4.4 on rural policing). Due in part to this varied geography, Scotland has a tradition (if not always practice) of localism (the political approach which favours 'the local'), despite its relatively small overall size.

The Scottish approach to localism is underpinned by the fragmentation of local government over 32 local authority areas, and the 'community empowerment' agenda supported by the Community Empowerment (Scotland) Act 2015 (see Section 2.1.3). However, localism has tended to be understood in terms of the political power of local (as opposed to central) government, which is not necessarily the same thing as control by local people and communities. A report from the think tank Our Scottish Future (Dickson and Barnes, 2024) argues that Scotland is in fact extremely politically centralised by European standards.

Local authorities have historically played a role in the governance of policing (Chapter 3) and continue to do so as members of Community Safety Partnerships (Chapter 2). As providers of social work and as political actors, they remain important in community penalties, youth justice and supervision on licence (Chapters 6, 9 and 10). Proponents of localised approaches argue that such an approach means that services can be tailored and responsive to local issues and needs. Opponents, however, argue that such an approach is wasteful and inefficient, with the replication of bureaucracy 32 times over Scotland (arguments which underpinned the eventual creation of Police Scotland in 2013), and raises concerns about inequalities between local government areas.

1.2 Scottish demographics

The proportion of the Scottish population in relative poverty fell since the late 1990s but has been increasing again since 2009–12, with a widening gap between the lowest and middle-income households (but has not yet quite returned to 1990s levels); in the period 2020–23, 21% of the Scottish population had a household income (after housing costs) less than 60% of the current UK median income (Scottish Government, 2024a). While Scotland had previously experienced greater deprivation than England, the gap narrowed in the 1980s; by 2016, England and Scotland had similar levels of deprivation (Abel et al., 2016). Moreover, 2021/22 data suggested average poverty rates in Scotland are similar to those in England and Wales, although higher than in Northern Ireland. Nearly a quarter of children (24%) in Scotland were living in relative poverty (after housing costs). Probably due to Scottish Government policies, child poverty – while still exceeding the Scottish Government's targets – is much lower in Scotland than in England and Wales and only slightly higher than the Northern Ireland (Joseph Rowntree Foundation, 2024).

Scotland's population is predominantly white Scottish or other British, but census data show that the proportion of people from a minority ethnic background has been steadily increasing from 4.5% in 2001, to 8.2% in 2011, and to 12.9% in 2022 (Office for National Statistics, 2022). Christianity remains the largest religious affiliation (20.4% Church of Scotland; 13.3% Roman Catholic), but like the rest of the UK, Scotland is becoming more secular over time (the majority now identify as having no religion). Relative poverty is substantially higher among Asian, Black, Mixed and Other ethnic groups (around 50%), and higher still among Muslims (60%), a difference only partly explained by differing age profiles for these groups (Scottish Government, 2024a).

Census data confirm that Scotland is also ageing, now with more people aged over 65 than under 15. The age profile is different for different ethnic groups, with non-White groups, and people born outside of Scotland more likely to be younger. This is important for thinking about the criminal justice system in Scotland since the types of harms and offences responded to by the criminal justice system are most often committed by young men. Famously, Houchin (2005) identified a link between imprisonment rates and neighbourhood deprivation, reconfirmed in Matthews' (2019) analysis of 2014 data. Rather than endorsing the idea that poverty causes crime or that poor people are inherently more criminal, Houchin's analysis suggests that imprisonment disproportionately affects the most disadvantaged communities.

Box 1.1 The Scottish drug deaths crisis

Scotland has the worst rate of drug-related deaths (DRD) recorded in Europe by some margin, over three times the next highest national rate (Ireland), 2.7 times as many DRDs as England and Northern Ireland, and 2.1 times as many as in Wales; 1,172 people died due to 'drug misuse' in 2023 (National Records of Scotland, 2024). Part of the explanation lies in the ageing of a generation of people who grew up in the 1980s, a time of industrial decline and associated socioeconomic worsening in parts of Scotland – the average age of people dying in this way has risen over the years to 45. The biggest determinant of DRD is socioeconomic: a person from the most deprived areas of Scotland is 15 times more likely to die from drug use than one from the least deprived areas.

Efforts to address this crisis raise questions of Scottish distinctiveness in criminal (and social) justice and Scotland's evolving relationship with UK political structures. The Scottish Government has been vocal in support of safe consumption rooms – places where people can take illegal drugs with clean needles and under the supervision of medical staff. However, because drugs policy is reserved (meaning control of it lies with Westminster, not Holyrood), the creation of safe consumption rooms would have been contrary to the 1971 Misuse of Drugs Act; the

UK government has rejected SNP calls to decriminalise drug possession in Scotland. This created a potential standoff where people seeking to create such facilities ran the risk of arrest, and opposition parties criticised the Scottish Government of trying to make the issue about independence rather than helping those in need. One factor in generating support was campaigning by the drug policy activist Peter Krykant, who ran an 'unofficial' safe consumption facility (mostly with the tacit toleration of the authorities) from his van in Glasgow.

A way through this standoff came when the Lord Advocate issued guidance in 2023 saying it would not be in 'the public interest' to prosecute those using such facilities for possession of drugs, a stance supported by Police Scotland. As a result, the Scottish Government announced that it would support a three-year pilot for a safe consumption room in Glasgow, which finally opened in early 2025. As well as indicating the tensions between a **public health** approach (emphasising harm reduction and prevention) and a criminal justice approach (emphasising a reactive enforcement approach), this illustrates the challenge of responding to problems caused by deep structural inequalities in Scotland, and tensions between the 'reach' of devolved politics in Scotland and relations with the UK Government (Fotopoulou and Malloch, forthcoming).

Questions to consider

- Does it make sense for drugs policy to remain 'reserved' to Westminster? Why/why not?
- Is it inevitable that, in a devolved political structure, some areas of Scottish policy will lie 'in between' control of Holyrood and Westminster?
- What other public health-based approaches might reduce DRDs and other harms associated with drug use in Scotland?

1.3 Social and cultural context

1.3.1 Welfarism, egalitarianism and neoliberalism

In accounts of the history of punishment (most prominently Garland, 2001), the mid-20th century is typically characterised as an era of **penal welfarism** – an approach which understands offending as a symptom of a psychological or social problem that can be diagnosed and 'cured' by trained professionals like social workers or psychiatrists. This is associated with the rise of 'social democracies' – where the state, including criminal justice, is used to reduce or mitigate socioeconomic inequalities.

In the 1970s, amid pervasive global economic and social crisis, social democracy in many Western countries gave way to **neoliberalism** – associated with an emphasis on economic growth over full employment, and scepticism about the state as a provider of services, favouring instead the free market as the means of meeting social needs. The exception to this retreat of the state is in matters of security, since in neoliberal thinking, one important function of a government is to protect the operation of markets. Hence, neoliberalism has been associated with a shift across the West towards more intensive policing and surveillance, the growth of private security, and harsher punishment, including huge increases in imprisonment (often called the 'punitive turn').

Economically, Scotland remains part of a neoliberal polity, though its justice system is sometimes portrayed as a holdout of penal welfarism (e.g. Muncie, 2011), especially compared with England and Wales. Some institutional aspects of Scottish criminal justice resonate with this, especially arrangements under the 1968 Social Work (Scotland) Act, which established the use of social work (not a probation service) for community penalties, and the Children's Hearings System (Chapters 6 and 9). A narrative of Scotland as a welfarist holdout, or an 'exceptional' outlier from the punitive turn, fits well with an understanding of Scotland as essentially egalitarian – and with a Scottish Nationalist 'nation-building' political agenda emphasising Scottish distinctiveness and commitment to social democratic values (Bond, 2024).

Yet criminal justice in Scotland is in many ways no less punitive than elsewhere; Scotland's rate of imprisonment is high by European standards, sometimes exceeding that of England and Wales. Furthermore, as discussed throughout this book, there are deep-seated and longstanding relationships between social inequalities and punishment. At best, the burden of punishment falls most heavily on people already experiencing deprivation and social marginalisation; at worst, it plays an active role in perpetuating these inequalities.

1.3.2 *Social attitudes*

As with the discussion about political identity, there is an inescapable tendency to make sense of Scotland's social attitudes both in themselves and by comparison with England and Wales. Robust and comparable data exist about these three nations, and much of Scottish nationalism (and discourses around criminal justice) also views these issues comparatively. Although we do the same in the following section, we nonetheless return to, and critically assess, these tendencies in Chapter 12. Data from social attitudes surveys suggest that Scotland is more socially democratic in some key areas of social attitudes, but that the differences are less significant than sometimes claimed (Curtice et al., 2020); for instance, there is only marginally more support for increased progressive taxation in Scotland than in England and Wales.

In relation to racism in Scotland, there has been a "powerful myth that there is 'no problem here'" (Davidson and Virdee, 2018: 9); the narrative that Scotland is less racist, and more welcoming towards migrants, has been pushed strongly by SNP-led governments. There is evidence that *overt* racism is less commonly expressed in Scotland (Meer, 2018). However, this sits at odds with self-reported data on prejudice towards different racialised minorities, which reveal a sizeable minority of the population expresses negativity towards particular minority communities or people of colour, especially Gypsy, Roma and Traveller people (Abrams et al., 2018).

The idea that racism is absent in Scotland does not reflect the lived experience of many people from minority communities and people of colour in Scotland, as reported by Meer (2018). It has been argued that racism is not absent but simply manifests in different ways, and there is a need to "wrestle with the geo-cultural and socio-political traits that are particular to Scotland" (Sobande and Hill, 2022: 16). Experiences of racism may vary significantly between different groups and communities (see Box 3.1), in ways not always well-captured by official statistics – where terms like 'Black, Asian and Minority Ethnic' (BAME) can mask (arguably deny) significant diversity of experience.

In recent years, Scotland – and Scottish nationalism – have had to revisit Scotland's role as an oppressor within the British imperial project (not a victim of English colonialism). There is a need to critically engage with the legacies of our colonial history in the structural racism facing the descendants of people from former colonies in Scotland (Sobande and Hill, 2022) and related experiences of and inequalities within criminal justice. As yet, little work has been done by criminal justice institutions or criminologists to engage with these issues. This remains an important project for the future.

In relation to criminal justice, social attitudes data reveal that only 19% of people in Scotland agree that those who experience problem drug use 'only have themselves to blame', and there is growing acceptance that "many people who use heroin come from difficult backgrounds" (50% in 2021/22, up from 29% in 2009) (Scottish Government, 2022a). Data on social attitudes around sexual violence against women and girls reveal some improvement over time, but in 2019, 3 out of 10 people still thought a woman was 'at least partly to blame' for being raped if she wore revealing clothing, and over a quarter believed rape results from men's inability to control their need for sex (Scottish Government, 2020).

In relation to punishment, the Scottish Crime and Justice Survey 2021–22 found that 54% of adults believe only those who have committed the most serious crimes should be imprisoned, with the vast majority believing prisons should help change behaviour rather than just punish (90%). For minor crimes, there is also substantial support (82%) for community sentences over short prison sentences (Scottish Government, 2022b).

Box 1.2 Crime trends in Scotland

There are two main ways of recording crime in Scotland: police-recorded data and data on victimisation. Police-recorded crime data tend to be taken as the definitive picture of crime trends, but only around 29% of crime in Scotland is reported to the police (Scottish Government, 2024b). It is therefore imperative that these figures are understood as being a *partial* view of crimes which occur in Scotland – they represent institutional activity rather than patterns of offending; and (taking a **zemiological** position) do not match onto patterns of social harm, much of which is not legally or practically criminalised.

With this (substantial) caveat in mind, however, police-recorded crime trends in Scotland have, similar to England and Wales, decreased overall over 30 years from a peak in the early 1990s and remained relatively stable between 2013 and 2023. Although there has been an overall reduction in police-recorded crime, it is important to note that within this overall trend, some types of recorded crime have increased. The most striking example of this is sexual crimes, which have risen by 52% over the past nine years – a pattern broadly reflected in the key Scottish victimisation survey, the **Scottish Crime and Justice Survey** (Scottish Government, 2022b). Much of this increase is likely to result from changing societal views towards the reporting of (especially non-recent) sexual violence. Moreover, 24% of sexual crimes recorded by the police were for crimes which occurred longer than 12 months prior, with 8% occurring before 2010. There have also been legislative changes which mean that crimes which would have previously been recorded as something else are now recorded as sexual crimes. Sexual crimes are therefore an example of how police-recorded data may reflect changing social views and institutional decisions, as much as actual increases in these forms of harm.

Questions to consider

- Are you surprised that overall crime trends in Scotland are very similar to trends in England and Wales? Why/why not?
- Why do you think crime rates overall have decreased since the 1990s?
- What would be other ways of measuring crime *and harm* which would compensate for the limitations of official data?

1.3.3 Influential discourses and myths in Scottish criminal justice

As you read this book, you will see there are recurring discourses – ideas communicated through language – which run through Scottish criminal justice. These are often found in policy documents or official statements from the Scottish Government or criminal justice agencies, and – reflecting comments above about nation building – these discourses both reflect and promote ideas relating to Scottish identities and culture.

These discourses suggest something benign about the Scottish approach. They include 'Scottish exceptionalism' (the idea there is something 'exceptional' – and 'better' about the Scottish approach) and the related narrative of Scotland as a penal welfarist holdout. Within these are narratives about 'desistance' (a theory about how people move away from crime – see especially Chapter 6), and being 'trauma informed' (a set of ideas about how to reduce the inevitable trauma inflicted by the justice system, though one which sees itself as being able to ameliorate these pains). We merely highlight these discourses here, but we critically examine them in practice in our concluding chapter.

Conclusion

Criminal justice in any jurisdiction is an inherently political project which also reflects wider social, cultural and historical currents. This chapter has outlined the political and social contexts which give shape to Scottish criminal justice, and the historical and institutional arrangements which have given rise to the devolved political landscape, political identity and institutional structures. We have also seen how the powerful myths of welfarism and egalitarianism in Scotland sit at odds with the strong and persistent currents of social and economic inequalities in the population, and, relatedly, even though voting behaviour has been more left-leaning in Scotland than in England and Wales, social attitudes are not that markedly different. In the rest of this book, we see how these factors have shaped criminal justice, beginning in Chapter 2 with community safety.

Key resources

Davidson, N., Liinpää, M., McBride, M. and Virdee, S. (eds) (2018) *No Problem Here: Understanding Racism in Scotland*. Luath Press.

An essential edited collection on racism in Scotland.

McCrone, D. (2017) *The New Sociology of Scotland*. SAGE.

A comprehensive sociological overview of Scotland.

Scottish Government – Crime and Justice Statistics. https://www.gov.scot/collections/crime-and-justice-statistics/

A collection of official statistics covering recorded crime and criminal justice in Scotland – not perfect (as we discuss in Box 1.2*) but still likely to be useful for study of criminal justice in Scotland.*

References

Abel, G.A., Barclay, M.E. and Payne, R.A. (2016) Adjusted indices of multiple deprivation to enable comparisons within and between constituent countries of the UK including an illustration using mortality rates. *BMJ Open* 6: e012750.

Abrams, D., Swift, H. and Houston, D. (2018) *Developing a national barometer of prejudice and discrimination in Britain*. Equality and Human Rights Commission. https://www.equalityhumanrights.com/our-work/our-research/developing-national-barometer-prejudice-and-discrimination-britain-0#document-download

Bond, R. (2024) National identities, migration histories and attitudes to independence in Scotland. *Scottish Affairs* 33(4): 431–464.

Cairney, P. and McGarvey, N. (2013) *Scottish Politics*. Second edition. Red Globe Press.

Curtice, J., Hudson, N. and Montagu, I. (eds.) (2020) *British Social Attitudes: The 37th Report*. The National Centre for Social Research.

Davidson, N. and Virdee, S. (2018) Introduction: Understanding racism in Scotland. In Davidson, N., Liinpää, M., McBride, M. and Virdee, S. (eds) *No Problem Here: Understanding Racism in Scotland*. Luath Press. 9–12.

Dickson, S. and Barnes, E. (2024) *Rewiring Scotland*. Our Scottish Future.

Fotopoulou, M. and Malloch, M. (forthcoming) Why are we still debating Safer Drug Consumption Facilities (SDCFs): A critical analysis of the drug policy constellation of power and its impact on the introduction of SDCFs in Scotland. *British Journal of Community Justice*, forthcoming issue.

Garland, D. (2001) *The Culture of Control: Crime and Social Order in Contemporary Society*. Oxford University Press.

Houchin, R. (2005) *Social Exclusion and Imprisonment in Scotland: A Report*. Glasgow Caledonian University.

Jones, R. and Wyn Jones, R. (2022) *The Welsh Criminal Justice System: On the Jagged Edge*. University of Wales Press.

Joseph Rowntree Foundation (2024) *UK Poverty 2024: The Essential Guide to Understanding Poverty in the UK*. JRF. https://www.jrf.org.uk/uk-poverty-2024-the-essential-guide-to-understanding-poverty-in-the-uk

Lacey, N. (2012) Political systems and criminal justice: The prisoners' dilemma after the coalition. *Current Legal Problems* 65(1): 203–239.

Matthews, B. (2019) Is the relationship between imprisonment and deprivation in Scotland at its most pronounced in Glasgow? *Howard League ECAN Bulletin* 41: 51–58.

McAlinden, A.M. and Dwyer, C. (eds) (2015) *Criminal Justice in Transition: The Northern Ireland Context*. Bloomsbury.

McAra, L. (2017) Can criminologists change the world? Critical reflections on the politics, performance and effects of criminal justice. *British Journal of Criminology* 57(4): 767–788.

McBride, M. (2022) Tackling offensive behaviour in Scottish football: A how (not) to guide to developing criminal justice policy? *Criminology & Criminal Justice* 22(1): 24–42.

Meer, N. (2018) What do we know about BAME self-reported racial discrimination in Scotland. In Davidson, N., Liinpää, M., McBride, M. and Virdee, S. (eds) *No Problem Here: Understanding Racism in Scotland*. Luath Press. 104–118.

Muncie, J. (2011) Illusions of difference: Comparative youth justice in the devolved United Kingdom. *British Journal of Criminology* 51(1): 40–57.

National Records of Scotland (2024) *Drug-Related Deaths in Scotland in 2023*. National Records of Scotland. https://www.nrscotland.gov.uk/publications/drug-related-deaths-in-scotland-in-2023/

Office for National Statistics (2022) *Scotland's Census 2022 Results*. ONS. https://www.scotlandscensus.gov.uk/2022-results/

Scott, G. and Mooney, G. (2009) Poverty and social justice in the devolved Scotland: Neoliberalism meets social democracy? *Social Policy and Society* 8(3): 379–389.

Scottish Government (2020) *Scottish Social Attitudes Survey 2019: Attitudes to Violence against Women*. Scottish Government.

Scottish Government (2022a) *Scottish Social Attitudes Survey 2021/22: Public Attitudes towards People with Problem Drug Use*. Scottish Government.

Scottish Government (2022b) *Scottish Crime and Justice Survey 2021/22: Main Findings*. Scottish Government.

Scottish Government (2024a) *Poverty and Income Inequality in Scotland 2020–23*. Scottish Government. https://data.gov.scot/poverty/2024/

Scottish Government (2024b) *Recorded Crime in Scotland, 2023–24*. Scottish Government.

Sobande, F. and Hill, L.-R. (2022) *Black Oot Here: Black Lives in Scotland*. Bloomsbury.

2 Community safety and crime prevention in Scotland

Key ideas

- Crime prevention and 'community safety' are not the preserve of any single agency or of the criminal justice system; they involve local government among other bodies.
- Community safety in Scotland is shaped by changing ideas about urban life and social housing, deindustrialisation and associated social inequality.
- While largely similar to developments elsewhere in the UK, Scottish community safety has been characterised as having a more holistic conception of community safety, though it remains heavily focused on crime and antisocial behaviour.
- Contemporary crime prevention also takes place in the context of efforts to reorient Scottish public services towards prevention of adverse outcomes, following the recommendation of the 2011 Christie Commission.
- Post-devolutionary Scotland has tried to reduce alcohol-related harms (including crime) by restricting the sale and consumption of alcohol.
- A significant drop in violent crime in Scotland is often attributed to the Scottish Violence Reduction Unit (SVRU) and its 'public health approach' to violence. However, the meaning of this approach in practice is not straightforward, while evidence for its role in reducing violence is limited; the application of concepts and methods from public health to criminal justice may need to be treated with caution.

Introduction

Prevention, supposedly, is better than cure. For the last few decades, responses to crime have been characterised by a so-called 'preventive turn' – a shift away from dealing with crime after it has occurred to preventing it from happening in the first place. Crime prevention has long been an important police function, but over the last few decades, a set of specialist prevention bodies and practices, under the 'community safety' banner, has developed in communities across Scotland and the wider UK.

DOI: 10.4324/9781003372882-2

The most widely used Scottish definition of community safety is an endeavour to ensure that:

> People are safe from crime, disorder, danger, and free from injury and harm; communities are socially cohesive and tolerant; and are resilient and able to support individuals to take responsibility for their well-being.
>
> (Bannister et al., 2011: 238)

The practical remit of this work tends to centre on specific forms of injury, harm and 'safety'; arguably the ways in which harm is understood by those working in this field reflect the interests of more powerful groups in society (see Box 2.1). Although community safety is not straightforwardly a criminal justice matter, much activity centres on preventing crime and antisocial behaviour, the latter of which is not necessarily criminal.

There is no single community safety agency. The most relevant formal bodies are the **Community Safety Partnerships (CSPs)** – multiagency partnerships operating within each of Scotland's 32 local authorities, supported nationally by the **Scottish Community Safety Network (SCSN)**. CSPs vary between local areas but always include the local authority and the police, the latter of whom carry out crime prevention work and share local intelligence. Some CSPs include local or national charities as members, alongside other public sector and justice agencies. CSPs provide advice and guidance to local communities on safety issues (e.g. road safety, smoke alarm testing) as well as developing strategy on crime and antisocial behaviour. As well as CSPs (and the community justice partners – see Section 6.1.5), several other types of local partnerships are involved in the complex task of preventing crime. Security is increasingly understood not as the preserve of the police but as governed through a network of 'nodes' that also includes local authorities, private security, and informal groupings (Johnston and Shearing, 2002).

One way of understanding prevention is to divide it between situational and social forms. **Situational crime prevention (SCP)** is underpinned by (neo-) classical criminological theories which see crime as a choice, in which people weigh the benefits and downsides of offending. **Social crime prevention,** on the other hand, claims to address underlying causes of crime, such as poverty or unemployment. Similarly, Ekblom (1994) differentiates between 'proximal' mechanisms of prevention, closely linked to the event in time and space (hence usually situational), and 'distal' measures centred on longer-term causes. In much of the policy implementation of crime prevention since the 1980s, situational and proximal measures have tended to predominate.

Another approach common in Scottish policy, imported from public health, is to divide prevention into **primary, secondary and tertiary** forms (Brantingham and Faust, 1976). In this model, primary prevention centres on addressing possible criminogenic factors across the general population.

Secondary prevention targets specifically those people and places thought to be at risk. Tertiary prevention is more in line with the traditional aims of criminal justice, responding to incidents that have already occurred and seeking to prevent reoccurrence.

These frameworks fit with a mainstream view popular in policy and practice circles, which you are likely to encounter in your reading about the topic. Criminal justice policymakers – and many students new to the discipline – often find them helpful, because they fit everyday explanations about the causes of crime and are relatively free of abstract theorising or overt ideology. But just because these theories have been highly influential, doesn't mean that they are the best explanations for how crime occurs and there have been significant critiques of these approaches.

Ostensibly, 'community safety' promises a less harsh, socially oriented approach in which prevention of crime and harm takes precedence over punishment. But despite the communitarian language, activity under the 'community safety' label entails the state exerting power over people and places (see e.g. Hughes, 2007). A key critical source which guided our thinking here is Cohen's (1985) book *Visions of Social Control*, which argues that apparently preventive and community-oriented schemes represent a 'dispersal of discipline' – the insidious creep of social control and surveillance out of institutions and into the community.

In this chapter, we outline the historical development of Scottish community safety measures. We then discuss how Scotland has tried to reduce harm (including crime) related to alcohol through criminal justice and health measures, before considering the rise of public health approaches to preventing violence, with a focus on the much-publicised success story of the Scottish Violence Reduction Unit (SVRU).

2.1 From Greenock to Google: the development of crime prevention and community safety in Scotland

The wide acceptance of multiagency crime prevention and community safety in policy circles is a relatively recent phenomenon. The history of community safety shows how today's policy and practitioner common sense has been shaped by wider factors and specific understandings of community and harm.

Because prevention and community safety are diffuse, the way they have developed in Scotland is shaped by factors largely outwith criminal justice: changes in housing policy and urban planning after the Second World War, the effects of deindustrialisation in Scottish cities, rising concern over crime and 'antisocial behaviour', the responsibilisation and 'empowerment' of local communities under neoliberalism, and two specifically Scottish factors: the development of our devolutionary settlement, and the sometimes difficult relationship between central and local government. This section makes particularly extensive use of Monaghan (1997) and Henry (2009).

The origins of Scottish community safety are typically sited in the 1950s (Henry, 2009; Fyfe, 2010) in Greenock, an industrial town near Glasgow, where experiments with preventive policing appeared to produce a dramatic decline in housebreaking (Mackenzie and Henry, 2009). These included situational measures like targeted police patrols and installing credit electrical and gas meters in homes to replace prepayment meters (which in those days took coins, so were an easy target for theft). Alongside this came social measures, including local arts projects as well as police supervision of local young people thought to be 'at risk' of offending (Fyfe, 2010).

Many Scottish police forces followed suit by creating 'community involvement' departments, with Scotland seen by the 1970s as a leader in community policing (Monaghan, 1997 and Section 3.4.1). These developments sometimes ran up against the ingrained tendency of police culture to emphasise 'crime fighting' over prevention and 'social work' tasks (Monaghan, 1997; Henry, 2009). Furthermore, such approaches involve the police in disciplining young people who in some cases had not been convicted of any crime.

2.1.1 Deindustrialisation, design and Dundee

The postwar expansion of the welfare state saw major shifts in urban life, as huge numbers of mostly working-class people were relocated from inner cities to new social housing in towers, low-rise flats, planned suburbs or sometimes entire 'New Towns' (notably Cumbernauld). Although it replaced often overcrowded and unsanitary housing, this process uprooted many working-class communities – and the new 'schemes' were not without social problems of their own, due partly to their cheap construction and designs inadequately adapted to the Scottish context.

A backlash followed against high-density social housing and modern architecture generally. In reporting, politics, and even popular culture, the very *look* of these estates would come to be associated (not always fairly) with poverty and crime (Coleman, 1985). This was reflected in criminological theory; Newman's (1972) *Defensible Space* argued that 'traditional' streets afforded natural informal surveillance and social control that prevented crime. Situational ideas like these (often grouped as 'Crime Prevention Through Environmental Design' or CPTED) influenced an understanding of crime as a problem of urban social housing (Monaghan, 1997).

From the 1970s onwards, the UK underwent 'deindustrialisation' – a dramatic shift from a manufacturing- to a service-based economy. The closure of hundreds of mines and factories brought a sharp rise in unemployment, deprivation and ill-health in much of Scotland. Alongside this, chiming with the prevailing neoliberal politics of the time, was declining trust in the ability of the state and its institutions to address crime. The first British victim surveys highlighted the scale of crime that never came to the attention of the police (and which they anyway lacked the resources to deal with).

These developments fuelled an interest in engaging local communities in preventing crime – as did policymakers' interest in 'regenerating' the places hardest hit by deindustrialisation. It was decided that this would be done by attracting business to Scottish towns and cities, but to attract investment, these places needed lower crime rates. Politically, it was convenient to make local government responsible for crime prevention, under the label of 'empowering' communities.

In 1989, the Scottish Office (of the UK government) announced the Safer Cities programme as part of a wider agenda of 'urban regeneration' in post-industrial cities. This included four local partnerships, centred on social housing 'schemes' in Scottish cities. One of these was developed in Dundee; Scotland's fourth-largest city had been particularly hard-hit by deindustrialisation in the early 1980s and acquired a reputation for drug use and violent crime. Dundee's Whitfield estate was reconstructed along 'defensible space' and CPTED principles, its forbidding concrete blocks replaced by low individual houses looking out onto gardens and streets (Dundee City Council, 2015). At the same time, Dundee generally was pioneering partnership approaches to urban regeneration, in which a range of public sector and community stakeholders, including ordinary citizens, were enlisted in formal partnership structures.

2.1.2 *Devolution, New Labour and antisocial behaviour*

These developments generally tracked wider changes in the UK, with partnership approaches to crime control becoming popular, especially under the UK New Labour governments of 1997–2010 (Hughes, 2007). It came to be accepted that complex social problems like crime and safety were beyond the power of any single agency to address, so required agencies to make arrangements to work together rather than in separate 'silos'.

The 1990s also saw a sharp increase in the use of CCTV in public spaces, operated mainly by local authorities (Scottish Government, 2011), despite ambiguous evidence for its efficacy (Welsh and Farrington, 2008). Neighbourhood Watch schemes had been introduced in Scotland in 1986 but took off during the 1990s, although somewhat unevenly (Figure 2.1). Efforts to engage local authorities further in preventing crime were disrupted by the Scottish local government reorganisation in the 1990s. However, the 'regeneration' agenda developed in places like Whitfield was becoming increasingly organised, formalised and spread across Scotland.

At this point, the Scottish approach diverged from England and Wales (Henry, 2009). The 1998 Crime and Disorder Act required every English and Welsh local authority to establish a Crime and Disorder Reduction Partnership. However, with devolution now on the horizon, Scotland was left to develop its own approach, in which crime prevention merged with a wider 'Community Planning' agenda. Thus, the systematic development of CSPs across Scotland occurred on a non-statutory basis. However, Community

Figure 2.1 A neighbourhood watch sign in Edinburgh.

Planning Partnerships (CPPs) were made mandatory for Scottish local authorities in 2003.

The 1990s and 2000s saw a wave of concern about 'antisocial behaviour' – a vague term encompassing a range of activities that might or might not be illegal, but could be annoying or unpleasant. Much of this centred on the activities of young people (see Chapter 9), and especially so-called 'neds' – a stigmatising, classist term for young people presumed to be uneducated and deviant, often associated with particular forms of dress (e.g. tracksuits).

For many in the UK, antisocial behaviour is synonymous with the **Antisocial Behaviour Order (ASBO)** – a court order which places certain requirements on a person, e.g. not going to a particular place. These were introduced across the UK by the 1998 Act, although Scottish ASBOs cannot be imposed by the police, only by local authorities or housing providers. The Scottish Executive (2004) defined ASBOs in terms of prevention – the prevention of further antisocial behaviour and crime, since the person under the order would be incentivised to comply.

Crucially, an ASBO is a *civil* order, and does not itself imply legal guilt or criminal punishment – but breach of an ASBO is a criminal offence. ASBOs were extended to children aged 12–16 in the 2004 Antisocial Behaviour etc. (Scotland) Act, which required all police forces and local authorities to develop local antisocial behaviour strategies (Henry, 2009). The Act introduced Fixed Penalty Notices (see Chapter 5) for antisocial behaviour, as well as 'dispersal orders', granting the police powers to disperse groups of people in an area, and parenting orders (but see Section 9.3.1). The advancement of a Scottish antisocial behaviour agenda, alongside related developments in youth justice, was sometimes seen as evidence that Scotland (then also under a New Labour government) was converging with punitive practices in England – sometimes known as 'detartanisation' (McAra, 2006).

ASBOs did not really 'take off' in Scotland to the same extent as in England and Wales. Between 1999 and 2005, only 559 ASBOs were granted in Scotland, compared to nearly 10,000 in England and Wales (Donoghue, 2010), although this difference is less marked once the population difference is taken into account. Despite the 2004 Act, very few ASBOs were imposed on under-16s in Scotland, with children's hearings (Chapter 9) remaining the main forum for dealing with young people's misbehaviour.

Research by the Scottish Community Safety Network (2020) suggests that local authorities in Scotland tend to prefer diversionary and less formal measures. It is therefore surprising that ASBOs remain in law in Scotland when England and Wales abolished them in 2014 (though only to replace them with a range of similar orders). Henry (2009) suggests that while the then-Scottish Executive preferred an emphasis on situational measures to control antisocial behaviour, local government tended to emphasise social welfare and did not always agree with the characterisation of young people as antisocial.

While the development of community partnership approaches to crime prevention in Scotland has certainly included antisocial behaviour as a key concern, it has arguably taken a more holistic view of community safety, and a less punitive approach to antisocial behaviour, than in England and Wales (Henry, 2012) – despite the significant funding priority attached to antisocial behaviour by the 2004 Act. The 2000s also saw renewed preventive efforts specifically targeting knife and gang crime (see Section 2.3).

2.1.3 *The SNP, safer communities and prevention*

The 2007 election produced a minority government led by the nationalist Scottish National Party (SNP), which has been in power ever since. The Scottish Government (as it was now called) established a Community Safety Unit and funded the SCSN, which carries out research and provides guidance to local community safety practitioners. These new organisations centred on promoting good practice and consistency across CSPs and developing a programme of research to support 'evidence-based' community safety interventions practice (Bannister et al., 2011). Much of the most prominent crime prevention work in this period centred on the development of 'public health' approaches, particularly in reducing rates of violence, discussed in Section 2.3.

Following the 2007–08 global financial crisis, the response of the Conservative-led coalition UK Government (2010–15) was to enact a programme of 'austerity' – major spending cuts across the public sector, ostensibly with the intention of reducing government borrowing and debt, which is widely thought to have contributed to rising inequalities and deprivation across the UK. Austerity created a political problem for the SNP which had taken power in Scotland in 2007, because its governance might have to be shaped by the spending cuts required by UK economic policy, while it simultaneously wished to assert a distinctly Scottish approach by not following a right-wing agenda of shrinking the state.

The Christie Commission (2011) – officially the *Commission on the Future Delivery of Public Services* – seemed to provide a way forward. It recommended that public services must cut costs not by reducing the level of services, but by realising efficiencies from closer partnership working, sharing resources between agencies, and by reorienting towards prevention (the 'prevention principle'). This led to a renewed focus on community planning and empowerment for local communities under the 2015 Community Empowerment (Scotland) Act, and a further emphasis on partnership working across the public sector and local government. The prevention principle continues to inform much community safety work.

Box 2.1 Whose communities, whose safety?

When we discuss prevention and community safety it is worth considering what we actually mean by these terms. While Scottish community safety work may entail a somewhat more holistic conception of safety and harm than the English model, crime and antisocial behaviour (ASB) still occupy prominent roles, and there tends to be an emphasis on interpersonal harms. A critical criminological or zemiological perspective would suggest that these harms, although not unimportant, are not as significant as the harms of state or corporate forms of violence.

A related question is what exactly constitutes 'safety', and how it is achieved. Recorded crime figures suggest that overall, we are safer from crime now than we were 30 years ago. But behind this is considerable complexity; some people and communities may be (or feel) less safe (from crime or other harms). Some recorded crime (particularly sexual offences) has risen, while much is missed by recorded crime figures, now and historically.

Elsewhere in this chapter, we have seen how the community safety agenda has been shaped by neoliberal capitalism: the process of deindustrialisation itself, then a model of community development which centres private-sector investment and urban renewal (or gentrification) as solutions to the impacts of deindustrialisation.

Another view might position capitalism itself as implicated in or even causative of these problems, and hence damaging to communities. Smith and Stewart (2024), discussing experiences of poverty in Glasgow, note the role of 'profiteers' (including exploitative landlords) in compounding and entrenching deprivation. Problems like these are sometimes discussed as though they 'just happen', but they result from specific political choices and might also be understood as a form of 'political attack' on its population (Smith and Stewart, 2024). One view might see this, too, as a form of violence.

Questions to consider

- Who is included and excluded within the 'community' in community safety?
- How could community safety include a wider range of communities?
- What do you think a version of community safety work focused on larger structural harms (like environmental pollution or state corruption) could look like?

2.1.4 *Changing attitudes? Policing, data and advertising*

In recent years, some national crime prevention approaches have concerned not only crime itself but also cultural aspects thought to be implicated in it. Much of this has centred on harms where there is a power imbalance – hate crime and various gender-based and sexual harms – which also tend to be under-reported but also have been brought to greater prominence by activism from the 2010s onwards.

Some of this work has been led by the Scottish Government and some by the police; many of the prevention and awareness-raising campaigns have taken place partly or entirely online. Much of this is ostensibly inspired by feminist and antiracist thinking; although in some ways outside the scope of usual police work, this type of 'cultural' awareness-raising work has been seen by Police Scotland as part of their wider remit to promote wellbeing.

The 'That Guy' campaign (2021 onwards) aims to address sexism and male sexual entitlement, encouraging men to challenge friends who used sexist or objectifying language; it was widely praised particularly in light of controversy surrounding English forces' responses to the murder of Sarah Everard. Recent qualitative research (McQueen, 2024) suggests that young men who see this material generally agree with its message but might feel uncertain about what they can really do or that they are targeted unfairly.

Horgan et al. (2024) have identified campaigns like this as part of a wider trend in the UK towards 'influence policing', in which governments seek to change behaviour by shifting cultural narratives alongside more targeted 'nudges'. Although ostensibly grounded in understandings of inequality, discrimination and harm as structural, these measures tend to focus on individuals and arguably miss the wider picture (e.g. the disproportionate effect of poverty on women). Related to this is the question of whether the criminal justice category of 'hate crime' is adequate to address structural forms of discrimination (or even the reality of hate crime).

In the rise of the community safety agenda in Scotland, we can see wider political and cultural developments playing out in ways shaped by the local context and politics of Scotland. We turn now to an issue of particular prominence in post-devolutionary Scotland – preventing crime and other harm related to alcohol.

2.2 Regulating alcohol

In the popular imagination, Scotland is sometimes stereotyped as a culture of high alcohol use. Much preventive activity has centred on harms associated with alcohol, including confrontational violence, drink-driving and antisocial behaviour. For these reasons, Scotland has made significant efforts to reduce drinking and alcohol-related harm, with local work paralleling developments in community safety, alongside a series of national policies.

At the local level, local authorities and partnerships play a significant role in preventing crime and other harms related to alcohol. The 2005 Licensing (Scotland) Act created Licensing Boards in each local authority, which decide whether to grant or deny licences to taxi drivers, restaurants, pubs and entertainment venues. The Act explicitly links licensing to questions of crime prevention and public health through its list of 'licensing objectives':

- a Preventing crime and disorder;
- b Securing public safety;
- c Preventing public nuisance;
- d Protecting and improving public health and
- e Protecting children from harm.

Alcohol licensing is particularly significant among the Board's responsibilities. For instance, if a local pub is frequently the scene of violent altercations which lead to the police being called and the landlord/owner does not take measures to address this, the Licensing Board can restrict their operating hours or withdraw their licence altogether. Most local authorities in Scotland also use **byelaws** (local laws made by councils that apply to specific places) to prohibit public drinking in certain areas to prevent crime and antisocial behaviour. Glasgow City Council makes particularly extensive use of this power, forbidding outdoor drinking in almost the whole city – a measure which has been criticised as excessively wide-ranging in scope and discriminatory in its effect on people less able to afford to drink in licensed premises. Some support for the ban has (perhaps unsurprisingly) come from the Scottish Licensed Trade Association, a body representing the interests of pubs, hotels and others in hospitality.

Local approaches to alcohol also include partnerships similar to those discussed above. **Alcohol and Drug Partnerships (ADPs)** seek to reduce alcohol- and drug-related harms and help people with excessive or dependent use of alcohol and drugs, working alongside CSPs and other partnerships. ADPs commission residential recovery services and group work programmes as well as 'primary' prevention work, such as public information campaigns about the criminal consequences of buying alcohol for children. In 2021, the Scottish Government funded the Residential Rehabilitation Programme to improve access to residential rehabilitation for people with dependent substance use (including alcohol), working with ADPs as part of a wider effort to address the drug deaths crisis (see Box 1.1). An evaluation of the programme (Public Health Scotland, 2024) found it had had some effect but that only 24% of practitioners agreed that residential rehab was easily accessible.

The most visible efforts to change Scotland's relationship with alcohol have been progressively stronger restrictions on its sale. Since the 2005 Act, shops in Scotland have only been permitted to sell alcohol between 10 am and 10 pm. Further legislation restricted, then banned altogether, 'happy hours' and most other drinks promotions, as well as making 'Challenge 25' effectively mandatory. In 201–, the drink-drive limit was lowered to be stricter than in the rest of the UK. This was followed, in May 2018, by the introduction of 'minimum unit pricing', initially set at 50p then raised to 65p per unit of alcohol (so for instance, a 750-ml bottle of vodka at 40% abv must cost at least £19.50). Although welcomed by public health groups, there is mixed evidence for the effect of this on alcohol-related harms, and it inevitably affects those with the least money to pay.

Political concern about alcohol has often centred on sporting events, especially football. The 1980 Criminal Justice (Scotland) Act, passed in response to several high-profile incidents of alcohol-fuelled football violence, prohibits the sale of alcohol at football games (unlike in England and Wales). The Act may, however, be counterproductive in incentivising supporters to pre-drink large quantities shortly before arrival (Martin et al., 2022). Furthermore, it does not apply in designated hospitality areas, so those with the (considerable) resources to pay for the 'VIP experience' can escape it. There has also been significant concern about a supposed relationship between alcohol, football and domestic violence, despite very limited evidence for this (Brooks-Hay and Lombard, 2018).

The issue of class hangs over much of this discussion. Problematic and dependent alcohol use is arguably constructed in the policy narrative as a working-class issue, and policy responses have tended (intentionally or otherwise) to target those with less money. Even where successful, these policies have often centred on pricing people out of drinking rather than understanding why they drink. This implies a proximal (Ekblom, 1994) way of thinking about causation, in which problem drinking is the result of individual irresponsibility and excess money. Equally or more important causal factors may lie in forms of deprivation rooted in the structure of society itself – but these are more distant and perhaps a less politically expedient focal point.

Recent victim survey figures (Scottish Government, 2023) suggest that the proportion of violent crime that is alcohol-related has fallen. Evidence also suggests that excess drinking and alcohol use generally have also fallen (SHAAP, 2022). It is not straightforward to attribute this to Scottish Government policy – there have been significant shifts in how alcohol is marketed, bought and consumed, with young people in particular increasingly likely not to drink.

In November 2022, the Scottish Government began a consultation on restricting advertising and promotion of alcohol, similar to the progressively stronger restrictions on tobacco advertising over the last few decades. These plans met resistance from the alcohol industry, which noted the cultural significance of whisky and the economic importance of alcohol production (although this is arguably outweighed by the economic impact of alcohol-related harms). As of May 2025, the plans are on hold and it is unclear if or when the Scottish Government will re-engage with this problem.

Having discussed the development of crime prevention policy in Scotland and the efforts to reduce alcohol use, we turn now to something linked to both: the development of a 'public health' approach to preventing violence.

2.3 Violence reduction and public health

Glasgow is Scotland's largest city, famous in the Victorian era as 'the Second City of the Empire' for its rapid growth as an industrial centre. However, deindustrialisation had a sharp impact on Glasgow, feeding wider socioeconomic deprivation including complex health problems. Glasgow became increasingly associated with gang violence and knife crime through much of the 20th century. By the 2000s, it accounted for about a third of the homicides in Scotland and attracted considerable political concern.

Without denying these problems and the ways in which they have disproportionately affected greater Glasgow, it is important to avoid slipping into a stigmatising narrative in which Glasgow comes to be seen as a 'problem' in itself – since this may serve to entrench social and geographic inequalities, even as it seems to support a narrative of miraculous recovery.

A new approach to addressing violent crime, using ideas from the field of public health, would become one of Scotland's most widely regarded criminal justice success stories (Fraser and Gillon, 2024). Inspired by the World Health Organisation and similar initiatives to tackle gang violence in the

USA, this 'public health' model entails understanding interpersonal violence as like a disease that can be prevented. This includes the identification of specific risk and protective factors thought to influence levels of violence (e.g. local rates of unemployment), but also the idea of violence as like a disease that can 'spread' from one person to the next (see Slutkin, 2013 for a proponent of this idea). In this theory, by targeting specific factors and preventing transmission, violence can be prevented rather than treated. It is not the same as considering the *individual health consequences* of violence (injuries, disability, trauma, etc.) – but policy discussions have sometimes conflated the two.

This was driven especially by the **Scottish Violence Reduction Unit (SVRU)**, a partnership organisation officially part of Police Scotland but funded directly by the Scottish Government. The SVRU was founded in 2004–05 by Detective Superintendent John Carnochan and police analyst Karyn McCluskey; this section draws extensively from Carnochan and McCluskey's (2010) history, but we explore some issues from a critical academic standpoint. Initially focused on Glasgow (and known simply as the VRU for the first year), its mission was to reduce violent crime through preventive, public health approaches, including by partnering in various local projects (Hassan, 2020). But behind the narrative of 'public health' as a Scottish crime reduction success story, there are significant contradictions and tensions, and critiques of how 'public health' and 'violence' are understood.

2.3.1 *Public health and violence prevention: support, enforcement, surveillance*

Various forms of support offered by SVRU projects to individuals or groups involved, or considered at risk of being involved, in violence might be considered examples of secondary or tertiary prevention. These have tended towards social rather than situational measures, implicitly at odds with the traditional reactive and enforcement-oriented character of mainstream police culture. The Navigators programme (initially launched in partnership with SVRU and now run by Medics Against Violence) places staff in A&E departments to support patients and direct them away from further harm – the idea being that violent injury constitutes a 'teachable [or 'reachable'] moment' when people who might not otherwise be amenable can be reached – for instance, an injured person can be directed away from taking revenge and towards seeking support. More recently, the You Decide Team performs a similar service to direct people with various needs (whether or not related to crime) to sources of support.

Other SVRU projects seek to promote desistance (see Section 6.3.4) by employing people with convictions; there is also an emphasis on involving people with 'lived experience' of crime and justice. This is partly in recognition of the well-documented challenges faced by people with convictions in gaining employment. But these people may also offer life experiences not often found among employees of justice agencies, giving them a particular authenticity and relatability in their conversations with people still in the justice system.

Some SVRU projects appear to have little direct connection to criminal justice, but advocates of a multistranded 'social crime prevention' approach would argue that crime prevention requires addressing the wider social issues implicated in crime. Members of SVRU have also been active in promoting the 'ACE-Aware' movement in Scotland (see Section 9.3.5).

However, while it did include perspectives from beyond the police, the SVRU did not pursue public health *instead of* traditional criminal justice approaches. In fact, its early years were characterised by an intensification of enforcement-oriented policing. This was focused on known knife carriers, who (in public health terms) might be considered likely 'transmitters' of violence – so targeted enforcement against them is understood as stopping or slowing the spread. Much of this centred on the Gangs Task Force within Strathclyde Police (then responsible for greater Glasgow).

The approach described here (particularly the involvement of local government alongside policing) chimed with the wider antisocial behaviour agenda – as did the establishment of an 'exclusion zone' that banned known knife carriers from the centre of Glasgow (SVRU, 2010). The SVRU lobbied successfully for more prosecution and for increased sentences for knife carrying; the intensification of police stop-and-search practices contributed to the stop-and-search controversy of the 2010s (see Chapter 3).

The 'carrot and stick' combination of support with enforcement was most overt in Community Initiatives to Reduce Violence (CIRV). Modelled on a similar initiative in Cincinnati, Ohio, CIRV combined targeted enforcement against gang members with support and mentoring for those seeking to escape. CIRV began with a 'call-in' – a meeting at Glasgow Sheriff Court in October 2008, in which groups of young men from rival gangs were confronted by members of the community, who explained the consequences of violence with tragic stories and gruesome images of knife injuries – as well as threats of severe enforcement by police. Alongside this came stories of redemption and offers of support for those young people willing to contact SVRU for support exiting the gang (Donnelly and Tombs, 2008). This support included interventions from social work and local charities, but was conditional – it would be withdrawn if a young person on the programme was found to have engaged in further offending or gang-related activity.

CIRV ended in 2011, and subsequent discussions of SVRU have emphasised support and care over enforcement. However, both these approaches are underpinned by a reliance on various forms of surveillance. A public health programme requires data, and the SVRU has always embraced a range of surveillance methods, including traditional police intelligence and public health-inspired approaches. This included 'injury surveillance' – gathering data on the extent and impact of violence, beyond the limited picture provided by police-recorded crime, since many victims choose not to report

(Carnochan and McCluskey, 2010). As well as liaising with medical staff, SVRU placed police officers in A&E departments.

On the police intelligence side, a CIRV database was used to store the details of hundreds of young people, linked with other data held by Glasgow City Council and national police intelligence data, and used to target those thought to pose the most risk (CIRV, 2009). Recent SVRU strategy emphasises more data sharing with social media sites and partner agencies, but critical perspectives might highlight the implications for human rights and civil liberties of yet more surveillance.

Contemporary political discourse has arguably downplayed the SVRU's early emphasis on enforcement. Its history reflects the changing character of Scottish policing (Chapter 3) and the shifting politics of criminal justice policy in Scotland. Here, as in other justice institutions, care goes along with control and surveillance (Cohen, 1985). One might, however, argue that this doesn't matter, as long as this approach 'works' to reduce crime and violence.

Box 2.2 Cops on campus?

Scotland began placing police officers in some schools in 2002 (around the same time as similar developments in England and Wales). The programme was expanded in 2005 and was for a time affiliated with the SVRU (Black et al., 2010). A recent Freedom of Information request showed there were the equivalent of 88 officers assigned full-time to Scottish schools, while data from the Scottish teachers' trade union (Educational Institute of Scotland, 2019) suggest that eight local authorities have police officers in most or all secondary schools. It is difficult to get a clear sense of numbers since there is variation between local authorities; there may be officers who perform the role part- or full-time without the official job title, and officers may serve multiple schools.

Campus Officers (also 'School Liaison Officers', 'School Link Officers' or 'Youth Engagement Officers') are meant to reduce offending, antisocial behaviour, and truancy; improve behaviour; provide advice; and improve relations between young people and the police. The Scottish Government's (Black et al., 2010) evaluation suggests ambiguity about their role and limited evidence for any effect on crime, though the relationships between children and officers were generally seen positively.

The police presence notably appears to be concentrated in poorer areas; Glasgow has a PC in nearly every secondary school (Stewart, 2019). There is also variation in how the posts are funded. Most money comes from Police Scotland, but some posts are funded partly from education budgets – including a fund that was meant to be used to reduce the gap in educational outcomes between poorer and wealthier areas (an enduring problem in Scottish education).

There has been very little study of Scottish 'campus cops', but evidence from similar schemes in England and Wales highlights significant concerns; this has been in the context of a much higher-profile debate over police discrimination against young people from minoritised ethnic backgrounds. The recent scandal surrounding the strip-search of a 15-year-old Black girl by police (not school-based officers) in London and the 'No Police in Schools' campaign in Greater Manchester have drawn renewed attention to these issues, particularly institutional discrimination (see Box 3.1).

Some have argued that rising youth violence and concerns about disorder in schools following the COVID-19 lockdowns justify the expansion of this approach, and it may be hard to foster a culture of learning when drugs are being sold in school corridors. Yet, there is a reasonable concern that placing police officers in some schools stigmatises those schools – which are often struggling for educational resources – as 'criminal', and may do the same for particular pupils. Related to this, bringing police officers into schools can lead to the criminalisation of youthful misbehaviour: issues which might once have been dealt with informally by teachers (and, in more privileged settings, still are) come to be drawn into the purview of criminal justice. There is a risk that the school becomes a source of police intelligence and thus a locus of further surveillance of (some groups of) young people. While concerns about racism are less prominent in Scotland, the disproportionate effect on children from disadvantaged backgrounds and areas is extremely relevant, particularly in light of the overuse of stop and search against working-class young people (see Box 3.2).

Questions to consider

- Do you think police officers should be stationed in Scottish schools? What do you think their responsibilities should be?
- Did/does your school have a campus police officer/s? What do you think about them? Did/does it affect your school experience, and if so, how?

2.3.2 *Evaluating the 'Glasgow miracle'*

Since the establishment of the SVRU, violent crime in Scotland has fallen by 25%. Incidents of offensive weapon carrying fell by 69% in the decade following the foundation of the SVRU (Deuchar et al., 2021). Murders across Scotland have fallen by nearly two-thirds since the early 2000s. The story of the SVRU's success forms a redemption narrative – a 'Glasgow miracle', echoing New York's 'miracle' crime decline of the 1990s (Fraser and Gillon, 2024). Notions of rebirth tapped into a longer-standing myth of Scotland as exceptional and egalitarian, fitting well with SNP agendas.

This 'redemption' narrative was prominent in the 2014 Commonwealth Games, which happened to coincide with Scotland's independence referendum. Like other events of this sort (e.g. the 1984 LA Olympics), the Games were positioned as a consumerist vision of 'urban renewal' (Paton et al., 2012) *and* as justification for more surveillance. The use of CCTV for crime prevention was well-established, but intensified during the lead-up to the Games. Glasgow built an 'Operations Centre' where private security, local government and police monitor hundreds of CCTV cameras and coordinate activity across crime prevention, policing and traffic management. (A coda to the discussion of social housing above: Glasgow City Council originally planned to demolish five high-rise housing towers as part of the opening ceremony, but dropped this for reasons of safety and taste).

The apparent success of the SVRU and concern about rising violence in England led to the establishment of 18 local VRUs in England and Wales; the Mayor of London, Sadiq Khan, is a vocal proponent of the model. More generally, 'public health' approaches to crime problems have become popular across much of the West (Murray et al., 2021). In this 'policy transfer' narrative of the SVRU, a forward-thinking Scotland teaches England how to solve its knife crime problem.

The accepted narrative credits the SVRU and the public health approach with reducing violence in Scotland, especially Glasgow (Younge and Barr, 2017). This is certainly what the statistics suggest, but correlation does not equal causation – there is not necessarily evidence to establish that the reduction in violence can be credited to the public health approach. For much of the time the SVRU was operating, violent crime was falling elsewhere in the UK (long before the English VRUs) and other countries (in the context of a long-term decline in most recorded crime). The causes of this are likely entwined with many social, economic and cultural factors; the homicide decline may for instance be partly attributable to a wider trend of social life becoming increasingly private (Skott, 2019).

Neither the SVRU nor the public health approach has been systematically evaluated. One challenge is that in the nearly two decades since it was first established, a huge range of activities have been affiliated with the SVRU 'brand'. Only some have been evaluated, and even for these, the evidence has been mixed (e.g. Williams et al., 2014; Pagani et al., 2023). Much evidence cited in support of interventions like these is either essentially anecdotal or relies heavily on measures of how many people engaged with a service, rather than what effect that service might have had. The twist in the 'policy transfer' narrative is that English VRUs are in fact far more intensively evaluated and data-driven than Scotland's ever was (see Home Office, 2022).

As with the questions of how 'community safety' has been understood, a social harm critique might question the focus of the SVRU and related projects on specific forms of interpersonal violence (see Box 2.1). Many of these measures – while well-intentioned and sometimes genuinely supportive – have centred on individual change over addressing structural factors. This approach frames violence as an individual problem, abstracting it from social and economic factors (Riemann, 2019) which could themselves be understood as forms of violence. Furthermore, we should question the disproportionate surveillant gaze of 'preventive' interventions on working-class urban communities characterised in political discourse as already inherently problematic.

Whether or not attributable to the SVRU, the 'headline' decline in *recorded* violent crime is not necessarily the whole story. Some interpersonal violence between young people may have changed modes and/or moved online; while one-off violent victimisation has declined significantly, the number of people frequently victimised by violence (who are already affected by other forms of harm and marginalisation) has remained similar (Batchelor and Gormley, 2023).

Conclusion

This chapter has provided an overview of the development of crime prevention and community safety measures in Scotland, beginning with the early rise of preventive policing in Scotland. We have also seen how the Scottish approach to community safety, while largely tracking similar developments in England and Wales, has employed a slightly more holistic conception of safety and harm – although one in which crime and antisocial behaviour remain prominent. Yet the complex problems of the future, especially the climate crisis, might require not only the engagement of a wide range of partners beyond the police but also the decentring of police in the development of 'safety' for communities (Malik and Berg, forthcoming).

We have also discussed the development of crime prevention in two areas linked to public health – alcohol policy and the prevention of violence. Prevention has become a familiar buzzword in Scottish policy but raises questions not only about whether it 'works' but also about what exactly is being prevented and how it is possible to tell. This is particularly relevant in criminal justice, where stigmatising and punitive institutions may be mobilised in the service of 'prevention' (Cohen, 1985). Furthermore, there is a tendency to emphasise individual over social and structural factors. All these issues are highlighted in the example of the SVRU – a popular narrative of policy success which we have sought here to qualify. As we write, there is growing concern again about youth violence in Scotland, which may prove a challenge for public health approaches.

Many of these are wider issues affecting much of criminal justice, which we will encounter repeatedly throughout this book as we move through the stages of the criminal justice system proper – beginning with the police.

Critical questions

- Thinking about your everyday life and what you have been doing today/this week:
  - What measures do/did you take to avoid becoming a victim of crime?
  - What crime prevention measures did you notice in the places you went? (e.g. home, university, workplace, shops, etc.)
  - Are these measures situational or social in their focus? Primary, secondary or tertiary?
  - Do you think they are useful? Do you think there is something they might miss?

- What community/ies do you see yourself belonging to? What do you think would make it/them safer?
- Thinking about recent advertising/awareness-based crime prevention campaigns, do you think campaigns like this are useful for preventing crime?
- Do you think that alcohol consumption should be restricted further? What are the implications of this? Could there be other ways of reducing the harms associated with alcohol?
- Do you agree with the idea of characterising crime and violence as 'public health' problems? Could there be problems with this idea?
- Recent discussion of the SVRU has tended to downplay the enforcement-oriented and punitive aspects of its work, particularly in its early years. What political factors do you think might explain this?
- What developments do you think might take place in Scottish community safety after this book is published?

Key resources

Carnochan, J. and McCluskey, K. (2010) Policing, culture and society. In Donnelly, D. and Scott, K. (eds) *Policing Scotland*, 2nd ed. Routledge. 399–424.

The history of the SVRU as told by its founders.

Fraser, A. and Gillon, F. (2024) The Glasgow miracle? Storytelling, violence reduction and public policy. *Theoretical Criminology* 28(3): 328–345.

A useful overview of the 'story' of the SVRU and how the SVRU experience exemplifies the role of stories in justice policy.

Henry, A. (2012) Situating community safety: Emergent professional identities in communities of practice. *Criminology and Criminal Justice* 12(4): 413–431.

A key theoretical source drawing on one of the only empirical studies of CSPs in Scotland.

Hughes, G. (2007) *The Politics of Crime and Community*. Palgrave Macmillan.

Although focused on England, this is a vital critical overview of the development of the crime prevention multiagency partnership agenda.

Scottish Community Safety Network. https://www.safercommunitiesscotland.org/

References

Bannister, J., Croudace, R., Pickering, J. and Lightowler, C. (2011) Building safer communities: Knowledge mobilisation and community safety in Scotland. *Crime Prevention and Community Safety* 13: 232–245.

Batchelor, S. and Gormley, C. (2023) *Repeat Violence in Scotland: A Qualitative Approach*. Scottish Government. https://www.gov.scot/publications/repeat-violence-scotland-qualitative-approach/documents/

Black, C., Homes, A., Diffley, M., Sewel, K. and Chamberlain, V. (2010) *Evaluation of Campus Police Officers in Scottish Schools*. Scottish Government.

Brantingham, P.J., and Faust, F.L. (1976) A conceptual model of crime prevention. *Crime & Delinquency* 22(3): 284–296.

Brooks-Hay, O. and Lombard, N. (2018) 'Home game': Domestic abuse and football. *Journal of Gender-Based Violence* 2(1): 93–108.

Carnochan, J. and McCluskey, K. (2010) Policing, culture and society. In Donnelly, D. and Scott, K. (eds) *Policing Scotland*. Second edition. Routledge. 399–424.

Cohen, S. (1985) *Visions of Social Control: Crime, Punishment and Classification*. Polity.

Coleman, A. (1985) *Utopia on Trial: Vision and Reality in Planned Housing*. Hiliary Shipman.

Commission on the Future Delivery of Public Services (Christie Commission) (2011) *Commission on the Future Delivery of Public Services Final Report*. Scottish Government.

Community Initiative to Reduce Violence (CIRV) (2009) *CIRV Year 1 Report*. CIRV/Strathclyde Police/SVRU. Archived at https://www.svru.co.uk/wp-content/uploads/2020/02/CIRV-year1-report.pdf

Deuchar, R., McLean, R. and Holligan, C. (2021) *Gangs, Drugs and Youth Adversity: Continuity and Change*. Policy Press.

Donnelly, P.D. and Tombs, J. (2008) An unusual day in court. *British Medical Journal* 337: 2959.

Donoghue, J. (2010) *Anti-Social Behaviour Orders: A Culture of Control?* Palgrave.

Dundee City Council (2015) *Whitfield Planning Framework 2015*. Dundee City Council. https://www.dundeecity.gov.uk/sites/default/files/publications/CD_Whitfield_Planning_FrameworkAug15.pdf

Educational Institute of Scotland (2019) *Policy Papers Relating to Minutes of Council 2018–19*. EIS. https://www.eis.org.uk/Content/images/AGM/2019/Documents/Policy%20Papers.pdf

Ekblom, P. (1994) Proximal circumstances: A mechanism-based classification of crime prevention. *Crime Prevention Studies* 2: 185–232.

Fraser, A. and Gillon, F. (2024) The Glasgow miracle? Storytelling, violence reduction and public policy. *Theoretical Criminology* 28(3): 328–345.

Fyfe, N. (2010) Policing crime and disorder in Scotland. In Donnelly, D. and Scott, K. (eds) *Policing Scotland*. Second edition. Routledge. 175–200.

Hassan, G. (2020) *Violence is Preventable, Not Inevitable*. Scottish Violence Reduction Unit. https://www.svru.co.uk/wp-content/uploads/2020/02/VRU_Report_Digital_Extra_Lightweight.pdf

Henry, A. (2009) The development of community safety in Scotland: A different path? In Crawford, A. (ed) *Crime Prevention Policies in Comparative Perspective*. Willan. 86–110.

Henry, A. (2012) Situating community safety: Emergent professional identities in communities of practice. *Criminology and Criminal Justice* 12(4): 413–431.

Home Office (2022) *Violence Reduction Units, Year Ending* March 2022 *Evaluation Report*. Home Office. Available at: https://www.gov.uk/government/publications/violence-reduction-units-year-ending-march-2022-evaluation-report/violence-reduction-units-year-ending-march-2022-evaluation-report

Horgan, S., Collier, B., Stewart, J. and Thomas, D.R. (2024) Influence policing: Domestic digital influence campaigns and algorithmic strategic communications in UK law enforcement and homeland security. *British Journal of Criminology*, online ahead of print.

Hughes, G. (2007) *The Politics of Crime and Community*. Palgrave.

Johnston, L. and Shearing, C. (2002) *Governing Security: Explorations in Policing and Justice*. Routledge.

Mackenzie, S. and Henry, A. (2009) *Community Policing: A Review of the Evidence*. Scottish Government.

Malik, A. and Berg, J. (forthcoming). Polycentric governance, epistocracy and the limits of policing knowledge in preparing for the climate crisis. *Policing and Society*.

Martin, J.G., Giulianotti, R., Bandura, C., Morrow, S., Hunt, K., Bancroft, A. and Purves, R.I. (2022) Stakeholder views of current laws surrounding alcohol at UK football matches: Is it a case of using a "sledgehammer to crack a nut"? *International Journal of Drug Policy* 107: 103789.

McAra, L. (2006) Welfare in crisis? Key developments in Scottish youth justice. In Muncie, J. and Goldson, B. (eds) *Comparative Youth Justice: Critical Issues*. SAGE. 127–145.

McQueen, F. (2024) *Young Men and Violence Against Women Prevention: Exploring Reactions and Emotions*. Edinburgh Napier University.

Monaghan, B. (1997) Crime prevention in Scotland. *International Journal of the Sociology of Law* 25(1): 21–44.

Murray, J., Heyman, I., Dougall, N., Wooff, A., Aston, E. and Enang, I. (2021) Co-creation of five key research priorities across law enforcement and public health: A methodological example. *Journal of Psychiatric and Mental Health Nursing* 28(1): 3–15.

Newman, O. (1972) *Defensible Space: People and Design in the Violent City*. Architectural Press.

Pagani, S., Hunter, S.C. and Elliott, M.A. (2023) Evaluating the Mentors in Violence Prevention Program: A process examination of how implementation can affect gender-based violence outcomes. *Journal of Interpersonal Violence* 38(3–4): 4390–4415.

Paton, K., Mooney, G. and McKee, K. (2012) Class, citizenship and regeneration: Glasgow and the Commonwealth Games 2014. *Antipode* 44(4): 1470–1489.

Public Health Scotland (2024) *Evaluation of the Scottish Government Residential Rehabilitation Programme: Baseline Report*. https://publichealthscotland.scot/media/25128/v5_rr-evaluation-baseline-findings.pdf

Riemann, M. (2019) Problematizing the medicalization of violence: A critical discourse analysis of the 'Cure Violence' initiative. *Critical Public Health* 29(2): 146–155.

Scottish Community Safety Network (2020) *The Picture of Antisocial Behaviour in Scotland*. https://www.safercommunitiesscotland.org/wp-content/uploads/Analytical-exchange-The-Scottish-picture-of-ASB-final.pdf

Scottish Executive (2004) *Guide to the Antisocial Behaviour etc. (Scotland) Act* 2004. Scottish Executive.

Scottish Government (2011) *A National Strategy for Public Space CCTV in Scotland*. Scottish Government. https://www.gov.scot/publications/national-strategy-public-space-cctv-scotland/

Scottish Government (2023) *Scottish Crime and Justice Survey 2021/22: Main Findings*. Scottish Government.

Scottish Health Action on Alcohol Problems (SHAAP) (2022) *Alcohol Consumption in Scotland: The Scottish Health Survey 2022*. https://www.shaap.org.uk/alcohol-facts/what-we-drink-in-scotland.html

Scottish Violence Reduction Unit (SVRU) (2010) *VRU: Outline of Past Work and Future Projects*. SVRU. https://www.svru.co.uk/wp-content/uploads/2022/12/VRU-the-past-and-the-future.pdf

Skott, S. (2019) Disaggregating homicide: Changing trends in subtypes over time. *Criminal Justice and Behavior* 46(11): 1650–1668.

Slutkin, G. (2013) Violence is a contagious disease. In *Institute of Medicine and National Research Council, Contagion of Violence: Workshop Summary*. National Academies Press. 94–111. https://www.ncbi.nlm.nih.gov/books/NBK207245/

Smith, K. and Stewart, E. (2024) Under attack? Public accounts of health inequalities and the social determinants of health in Scotland. *Journal of Critical Public Health* 1(2): 1–74.

Stewart, C. (2019) Glasgow's campus cops 'integral' to secondary school life. *Glasgow Times* 5 June. https://www.glasgowtimes.co.uk/news/17684221.glasgows-campus-cops-integral-secondary-school-life/

Welsh, B.C. and Farrington, D.P. (2008) Effect of closed circuit television on crime. *Campbell Systematic Reviews* 4(1): 1–73.

Williams, D.J., Currie, D., Linden, W. and Donnelly, P.D. (2014) Addressing gang-related violence in Glasgow: A preliminary pragmatic quasi-experimental evaluation of the Community Initiative to Reduce Violence (CIRV). *Aggression and Violent Behaviour* 19(6): 686–691.

Younge, G. and Barr, C. (2017) How Scotland reduced knife crime deaths among young people. *The Guardian*, 3 December. https://www.theguardian.com/membership/2017/dec/03/how-scotland-reduced-knife-deaths-among-young-people

3 Policing in Scotland

Key ideas

- Since 2013, Scotland has a single national police service, the Police Service of Scotland (usually called Police Scotland).
- The creation of Police Scotland is the endpoint of a gradual shift away from many small local forces and a distancing of local government from policing.
- Police Scotland is the most prominent but far from the only agency involved in policing Scotland. Others include the British Transport Police and specialist reporting agencies.
- In its early years, Police Scotland was beset by controversies relating to its relationship with local communities, centralisation and 'Strathclydification'. These brought Scottish policing into the political spotlight where it had previously been little scrutinised.
- The process of police investigation begins with reporting and proceeds through investigation to the decision to charge the suspect; throughout this process, various rules are intended to safeguard the suspect's legal rights.
- Policing in Scotland contains a diverse range of activities each of which may pose specific challenges.

Introduction

For most people, the most visible and prominent aspect of criminal justice is policing; when a crime is dealt with formally, policing serves as the 'gateway' to the rest of the criminal justice system. This chapter starts by outlining the key agencies involved in policing in Scotland. As well as the national police service, Police Scotland, it draws attention to a wider range of regulatory bodies, organisations and actors who play a role in policing in contemporary Scotland (in what is known as the 'pluralisation' of modern policing), as well as the organisations involved in policing the police themselves. This chapter then goes on to provide a brief history of public policing in Scotland, from the foundation of the earliest police forces, through the establishment

DOI: 10.4324/9781003372882-3

of Police Scotland in 2013 and the subsequent challenges it has experienced. This chapter then takes you through the process of reporting and investigating crime in Scotland, before exploring aspects of police work in Scotland which extend beyond crime investigation: community policing, public order policing and policing mental distress. This chapter also explores the challenge of rurality in Scottish policing, along with some controversies, including the mass use of stop and search against young people, and accusations of institutional racism and misogyny.

This chapter builds on the previous chapter on community safety, and the discussion of policing here is extended in important ways by the discussion of transnational criminal justice in Chapter 11.

3.1 Key agencies

3.1.1 The public police

When people think of policing in Scotland, the first – often only – agency that comes to mind is the national police service, **Police Scotland**. Officially this is termed a 'service' (the full name is Police Service of Scotland), which is increasingly preferred over 'force'. However, even the most service-oriented police organisation is empowered to use force in a way that other parts of the state are not.

Police Scotland was established by the 2012 Police and Fire Reform (Scotland) Act. It is organised geographically into 13 local divisions grouped into three regions (East, West and North). There is a national Specialist Crime Division, which provides specialist investigative and intelligence functions, as well as regional major investigation teams for homicide and serious crime (Fyfe, 2019). An Operational Support Division handles other specialist tasks, including public order policing. Other national shared functions, such as the communications team, receive less attention, although this team's role has extended to include aspects of preventative policing (see Section 2.1.4). Police Scotland includes about 16,000 officers, 6,000 civilian staff, about 400 Special Constables (unpaid volunteers with police powers) and 1,000 Youth Volunteers.

Police Scotland is by no means the only organisation involved in policing in Scotland – or even the only police service operating in Scotland. The **British Transport Police (BTP)** provides policing functions for the UK rail network and some other transport infrastructure (including the Glasgow subway). Policy intentions and legislation (The Railway Policing (Scotland) Act 2017)) to merge the BTP's Scottish functions into Police Scotland proved controversial and no longer appear to be going ahead. Other police forces operating in Scotland include the **Civil Nuclear Constabulary** (responsible for policing nuclear power sites), the **Ministry of Defence Police** (policing UK defence sites, including the nuclear submarine base at Faslane), and the **Metropolitan Police** for royal protection. Officers from other services can also be brought in to provide assistance, known as 'mutual aid', at major incidents or events. For example, English officers supported policing of the 2021 United Nations Climate Change Conference (COP26) in Glasgow.

Much transnational crime control in Scotland involves the **National Crime Agency (NCA)**. Founded in 2013, the NCA is often described (not entirely accurately) as the 'British FBI' – it is a special, UK-wide policing organisation charged with addressing transnational and serious organised crime, using specialist investigation, coordinating and supporting other police activity, and gathering intelligence, including through undercover operations (in which role they may resemble spies more than police). The NCA are part of an Organised Crime Partnership with Police Scotland and other organisations (see Chapter 11).

Another relevant body is the **Scottish Police Federation (SPF)**, which works like a trade union for all but the most senior officers. It acts to negotiate pay and conditions and provides assistance to officers, including those who are subject to complaints or investigations. Unlike some trade unions, it does not openly support any political party but is routinely quoted in media reporting on policing and criminal justice where it often reflects the small 'c' conservatism generally associated with police culture.

In thinking about policing in Scotland, it is important to think beyond the (public) police and to consider what is known as **the 'pluralisation' of policing** (Jones and Newburn, 2002) – the idea that 'policing' is not just the business of the (public) police but also includes a diverse range of people and institutions: private security guards, bouncers, cybersecurity professionals, CCTV operators, neighbourhood watch groups, police monitoring ('Cop Watch') groups, and security agents working for state intelligence services (commonly known as 'spies').

3.1.2 Regulatory bodies and specialist reporting agencies

The Scottish policing landscape includes a number of agencies known as **'regulatory' bodies** – Scottish and UK governmental bodies which control various social and economic practices. Some breaches of these controls are criminal offences, while others – while not strictly criminal – may nevertheless result in a great deal of harm (Croall, 2016). Regulatory bodies in Scotland which investigate potential breaches of regulation and criminal offences include the **Scottish Environment Protection Agency (SEPA)**, which investigates environmental offences; and **the Health and Safety Executive**, which investigates breaches of health and safety regulation, for example, in relation to accidents in the workplace. **Trading Standards Scotland** investigates and inspects businesses to prevent illegal trading and ensure businesses are complying with legislation, working to address issues such as the illicit puppy trade and counterfeit goods. **His Majesty's Revenue and Customs (HMRC)** investigates tax fraud and **the Financial Conduct Authority** investigates financial misconduct, including money laundering.

The construction of some harmful breaches as 'not really criminal' is arguably exacerbated by placing the responsibilities for these outside the main criminal justice system (see Box 5.1). However, these agencies may investigate very serious crimes which require specialist knowledge; for example, SEPA investigate illegal waste management activities which can be the activities of serious organised crime groups, while HMRC is involved in investigating the profits from the activities of these groups.

Another set of organisations that play an important role in investigating some of these offences are **local authorities**, which have trading standards and health and safety officers located within them. They are also key players in preventative policing through community safety partnerships and activities (see Chapter 2), as well as in surveillance through CCTV and traffic cameras. Non-police agencies which investigate and report crimes for prosecution are termed **'specialist reporting agencies'**.

3.1.3 Policing the police

Policing decisions have important consequences, including both frontline decisions (e.g. whether to search someone, whether to let someone off with an informal warning) and strategic decisions about which types of crime or which geographical areas to prioritise and which resources the service needs. Much discussion of policing has therefore centred on its strategic direction (governance) and who is answerable to the public for policing decisions, especially when things go wrong (accountability). As elsewhere in the UK, policing in Scotland is underpinned by the principle of 'policing by consent' of the public. In a democratic society, accountability of the police is essential, but must be balanced against the need to ensure that police enforce the law without overt involvement in politics – and without political interference in tactical and operational decisions. These ideas are foundational in the history of UK policing, but whether they are (or can be) achieved is another question, partly because it may not be straightforward in practice to separate operational from strategic decisions. Unlike England and Wales, Scotland does not have Police and Crime Commissioners (party-political, elected figures with responsibility for police governance).

The 2012 Act set up the key Scottish police governance agency, the **Scottish Police Authority (SPA)** (Fyfe et al., 2018). The SPA appoints the Chief Constable, Deputy and Assistant Chief Constables and has the power to hold the Chief Constable to account. The SPA must prepare a strategic police plan outlining policing objectives for Scotland and has responsibility for allocating funds to Police Scotland. The Board members of the SPA are unelected, being appointed by Scottish Ministers (Henry et al., 2019). In this structure, it is the SPA which is accountable to Scottish Ministers, rather than the Chief Constable (Angiolini, 2020). The SPA also runs an Independent Custody Visitor scheme, with volunteers who visit police custody centres to ensure that people are being treated appropriately and safely (see Section 3.3.3).

His Majesty's Inspectorate of Constabulary in Scotland (HMICS) has existed since the 1857 Police (Scotland) Act; the 2012 Act extended its powers to cover the SPA as well. HMICS is charged with ensuring Police Scotland and SPA deliver the best value for money and inquiring into specific aspects of policing. The results of their investigations are published and they publicly report on progress, with thematic reports including on local policing, stop and search and call handling (Malik, 2018). While independent from Police Scotland, HMICS has generally been led by former police officers, and staff are frequently ex-officers. This may enable a better understanding of policing but raises questions about the extent to which this body is truly independent.

Complaints against the police are usually investigated by other officers and staff. Where these complaints are of a criminal nature – not just of inadequate or substandard service – they can be reported to a special division of the **Crown Office and Procurator Fiscal Service (COPFS)**, Scotland's public prosecutor (discussed in Chapter 4). Independent accountability arrived rather late in the form of an independent Police Complaints Commissioner for Scotland in 2007, replaced under the 2012 Act with the **Police Investigations and Review Commissioner (PIRC)**. The PIRC has the power to review complaint handling processes, but also investigate individual cases. Police still investigate cases themselves (under the supervision of COPFS in criminal cases) and not all cases are deemed to require an independent investigation, but if a member of the public is unhappy about how this has been conducted, they can request a review by the PIRC. In criminal cases, COPFS can also direct the PIRC to investigate, rather than the police.

We see in our discussion of the history of Scottish policing how these accountability and governance arrangements have developed alongside the policing institutions themselves.

3.2 A brief history of public policing in Scotland

This section examines the history of policing in Scotland, from the foundation of Glasgow police to the 2013 merger of multiple regional forces and the first decade or so of Police Scotland. Despite the pluralisation of policing outlined above, this history focuses on the Scottish public police.

The beginning of modern policing in Scotland is often dated back to the foundation of Glasgow's police force in 1800, although Aberdeen may have just eclipsed it by founding a police force in 1795 (Walker, 2000). These were established more than a quarter of a century before Robert Peel's Metropolitan Police, which has received far more attention in origin stories of modern British policing (although earlier experiments can also be found in England and British colonies, Moore n.d.). Barrie's (2008) history of early modern policing carefully lays out the predecessors to, introduction of, and subsequent development of policing in Scotland.

Glasgow's 1800 Police Bill established full-time, salaried officials with responsibilities for preventing and investigating crime, with a hierarchical command structure overseen by a directly elected Police Commission. Edinburgh closely followed in 1805, followed by numerous other towns (enabled by legislation in 1833 and 1839). Finally, the 1857 Police (Scotland) Act required places which did not yet have a force to establish one, thus addressing the problem of people fleeing to an area with no police force.

From the beginning, policing in Scotland (as elsewhere) was informed by capitalist and middle-class interests and concerns about the protection of private property and enterprise and the threat posed by the emerging working class (dispossessed through enclosures and clearances and increasingly reliant on wage labour) in terms of strikes, unrest and crime.

The development and proliferation of forces across Scotland was driven by Scotland's unique pattern of economic development, in which industrialisation and urbanisation happened later but more rapidly than in England. Rapid rural depopulation led to concerns, particularly among the middle class, about disorder in cities and vagrancy among those left without land or any safety net (Walker, 2000).

3.2.1 Local government and Scottish policing in the 20th century

Following an initial proliferation of local forces across Scotland, the subsequent trend was a gradual reduction in the number of forces as they merged with each other: from 89 local forces in 1859, to 64 by 1899, to 48 by 1939, and to 33 by 1959 (Davidson et al., 2016). Throughout the 20th century, policing in Scotland was a local endeavour, closely tied to the geographical boundaries of local government (Walker, 2000).

In 1975, reforms merged smaller Scottish local government units into large regional councils which funded and delivered major services (Davidson et al., 2016). This was accompanied by a further reduction in Scottish police forces to eight: Central Scotland, Dumfries and Galloway, Fife, Grampian, Lothian and Borders, Northern, Strathclyde and Tayside (Henry et al., 2019). These forces largely aligned with the geographical boundaries of the new regions; local governance and the funding and maintenance of these forces were achieved through the regional council (as the 'police authority') or – for Lothian and Borders and Northern forces, which covered more than one region – a joint 'Police Board' comprising elected members from relevant councils.

These forces varied substantially in numbers of officers, population and geographical area covered, and crimes responded to (Fyfe et al., 2018). The entire Northern Constabulary covered nearly half of Scotland's land area with fewer officers than a single division of the largest force, Strathclyde Police (Scott, 2011; see Section 3.4.4). Strathclyde Police was responsible for Glasgow and surrounding areas, but also some islands of the Inner Hebrides – covering about half the Scottish population and an even greater proportion of recorded crime. Foreshadowing debates 40 years later, this experience of regionalisation resulted in disgruntlement, as a model of policing developed for urban Glasgow was rolled out to very different areas, so that "the newly formed force was disparagingly referred to as 'Strath-Glasgow'" (Davidson et al., 2016: 109).

The Local Government (Scotland) Act 1994 again reconfigured the local government structure. It replaced the regions with 32 local authorities, breaking the alignment between local government and policing regions and making joint police boards the norm (Henry et al., 2019). Meanwhile, as in other areas of justice policy before devolution, there was a degree of neglect among Westminster politicians of the situation in Scotland (Walker, 2000). This left Scottish chief constables with wide discretion and little oversight, and the structure of police governance was arguably in disarray immediately prior to devolution (Scott, 2011). During this period, Murray and Harkin (2017) describe a 'cool' political climate in which elite actors across policing and government colluded to actively discourage scrutiny.

3.2.2 *Scottish policing post-devolution*

The early period post-devolution brought several important changes to Scottish policing. The Scottish Executive (as the Scottish Government was then known) established two centralised policing bodies (Scott, 2011). The first was the Scottish Police Services Authority (SPSA), which brought together support functions previously shared across different forces including criminal records, training and forensic science. The second, established in 2003, was the Scottish Drug Enforcement Agency, which gathered intelligence around drug crime – later renamed the Scottish Crime and Drug Enforcement Agency (SCDEA), reflecting a wider remit around organised crime. Another change was a greater emphasis on partnership working, ranging from anti-social behaviour to areas such as serious organised crime (see Sections 2.1.2 and 11.2.1).

Alongside more politicisation of justice policy, devolution brought more central oversight of policing in Scotland. While the political climate remained 'cool' in the early years of devolution (Murray and Harkin, 2017), concerns surfaced about the fissure that was seen to have emerged between police and local communities, as well as the capacity of joint police boards to hold police to account and shape policing decisions (Henry et al., 2019). Perhaps surprisingly given later events, concerns about a lost localism within Scottish policing were at the heart of political debates in the run-up to the birth of Police Scotland. In 2007 the SNP made a manifesto promise of "putting more police onto local streets with a more visible police presence" (SNP, 2007: 12), with commitments to 'visible policing' reiterated in its 2011 manifesto.

By the SNP's second term, there were growing arguments for a single national police force. Such calls date back at least to the mid-19th century (Davidson et al., 2016), but had previously been resisted by local government. Technological advancements in communication, information storage and transfer seemed to support the argument for centralisation. Another factor was the desire for "efficiency savings" in the aftermath of the 2007–08 financial crash (Fyfe et al., 2018). The counterintuitive argument was that centralisation would *preserve* local policing, by saving money on shared support services rather than cutting frontline services.

3.2.3 Police Scotland: a recent history

The Police and Fire Reform (Scotland) Act 2012 merged the eight regional police forces that had covered Scotland since 1975 (now known as the 'legacy forces') – along with the nationwide functions of SCDEA and SPSA – into one national police service. Police Scotland (officially the Police Service of Scotland) came into being on 1st April 2013, alongside the SPA and PIRC (Section 3.1.3).

The creation of Police Scotland transformed the political climate of Scottish policing. The successes and failures of the new service were seen as reflecting directly on the SNP government behind the reforms (Murray and Harkin, 2017). While the reforms were seen to have brought improvements in access to specialist services (although greater bureaucracy) (Fyfe, 2019), the years following centralisation saw a series of controversies.

Many of these centred on the connection with local communities (Fyfe, 2019), with several instances of local needs apparently being disregarded in favour of a centrally imposed 'enforcement' approach. These included a perceived overuse of stop and search powers in some areas (see Box 3.2) and repeated raids on Edinburgh saunas involved in the sex trade (which had previously been tolerated as part of a harm reduction approach). Armed officers in the relatively low-crime rural north began routinely carrying firearms on patrol (Fyfe et al., 2018; Henry et al., 2019).

In establishing the SPA – a *national* body of *unelected* members – the 2012 Act had removed the role of local authorities in providing democratic scrutiny and accountability, even though concerns about 'local policing' had been part of the rationale for the merger. Although the 2012 Act requires Police Scotland to make local policing plans and involve local authorities in policing, there were "structural disconnects" around how local democratic scrutiny could actually happen (Henry et al., 2019). When local elected officials raised concerns about these early crises, the SPA failed to intervene, seeing these as operational decisions and thus outside their remit (Malik, 2018).

These concerns related to localism but also to the approach of Police Scotland's first Chief Constable, (now Sir) Stephen House, who came to the role directly from heading Strathclyde Police (the largest of the legacy forces). Echoing the 'Strath-Glasgow' issue of the 1970s, concerns centred on the application of an approach developed for inner-city Glasgow to very different social contexts, in what was termed 'Strathclydification'. Amid a shift in working culture towards targets and statistics, Police Scotland has been beset by reports of low morale and retention issues (Souhami, 2020).

In a drive for cost savings, the restructure reduced civilian staff and began centralising police control rooms, raising concerns about a lack of local knowledge among call handlers (Terpstra et al., 2019). This issue came to a head in 2015 when Police Scotland received a 101 call reporting a car crashed off the M9. The call was logged but no patrol car was dispatched until another call three days later. By then the driver had died; the passenger later died in hospital. A subsequent HMICS (2015a) review identified implementation issues with the call-handling system, including poor (albeit improving) performance, and problems with staffing levels, training, systems and processes. This tragic event received significant political and media attention and has repeatedly returned to the headlines in subsequent years.

These controversies and criticism by bodies including HMICS and SPA led Stephen House to resign at the end of 2015. His successor, Phil Gormley, was "determined to re-establish the institutional legitimacy of the police force" (Fyfe, 2019: 202) – using the policing strategy Policing 2026*: Our 10 year strategy for policing in Scotland* (published in 2016) to reframe policing along the lines of preventive over enforcement approaches and responsiveness to local needs. This sought to align Police Scotland with a wider Scottish public policy project, which emphasised prevention (see Section 2.1.3) and community engagement, seeking to (re)present a distinctive 'Scottish' approach (as articulated in relation to the policing of protest in the early SNP years, see Section 3.4.2) – a project of myth-making related to the SNP's nation-building project.

However, controversies surrounding Police Scotland continued; Gormley was in the job less than two years before the PIRC launched a gross misconduct investigation following multiple accusations of bullying (BBC News, 2018). Subsequently, the Scottish Government invited Dame Elish Angiolini to review police complaints handling, investigations and misconduct. Angiolini's (2020) review raised concerns about the practice of police investigating most complaints, with investigations sometimes undertaken by close colleagues of the officer under complaint or even the officer themselves. Since the PIRC could not compel officers to attend for interview and could make but not enforce recommendations, it was perceived as "not [having] any teeth" (Angiolini, 2020: 73); it also tended to employ former police officers and relied on police evidence when reviewing complaints. Police officers who had witnessed or been involved in a death (in custody, or after police contact), had been allowed to confer with each other (an issue highlighted in the death of Sheku Bayoh – see Box 3.1).

The repositioning efforts evident in Policing 2026 have been sustained by subsequent Chief Constables (Iain Livingstone from August 2018 to August 2023; followed by Jo Farrell). These can be seen in an ongoing focus on vulnerability, public commitments to a distinctive – and softer – approach to drugs in Scotland, and the growing discourse of 'trauma-informed policing'. Whether these match the reality is a different question (see Fotopoulou and

Aston, 2022; Brodie et al., 2025). The new 'Vision 2030' strategy (Police Scotland, 2024) also emphasises trauma-informed approaches, but now with more emphasis on supporting victims.

Meanwhile, the 2021 abduction, rape and murder of a young woman in London, by a serving Metropolitan Police officer, has drawn attention across the UK to crime by police officers. A Freedom of Information request from 2022 found that 20 Police Scotland officers and 3 special constables were convicted of sexual offences from 2014/15, with 111 subject to allegations of on-duty sexual misconduct (Matchett, 2022). The extent to which rhetoric has succeeded in presenting Police Scotland as embodying a different, Scottish, approach to policing has been hampered by ongoing controversies, including around institutional racism (see Box 3.1).

Box 3.1 Individual and institutional racism and misogyny

The term 'institutional racism' rose to prominence in discussions of UK policing following its use in the report of the MacPherson Inquiry (1999) into the failures of the Metropolitan Police investigation into the racist murder of Stephen Lawrence. Rather than individual racist actions and beliefs, *institutional* racism refers to systemic problems in an organisation – organisational culture, policies, processes, and actions or failures to act – that produce racist outcomes. The concept is important in drawing attention to unintentional (as much as intentional) actions and omissions, and away from individual actions onto the impacts of policies and practices – though it may downplay the structural dynamics which underpin these (Souhami, 2014).

In Scotland, concerns about institutional racism in policing have been heavily influenced by high-profile incidents elsewhere, which have simultaneously raised the profile of these issues in Scotland but seemingly overshadowed concerns closer to home. Writing following George Floyd's murder in the USA in 2020 and the ensuing Black Lives Matter protests, Joseph-Salisbury et al. (2021) warned against misconstruing Floyd's death as an exceptional event and an American problem, obscuring the fact that "the UK is not innocent". In Scotland, constructions of institutional racism as an American or English problem can be linked to a broader sense that there is "no problem here" (see Chapter 1).

This narrative has been challenged by recent events, not least tireless campaigning by the family of Sheku Bayoh, a Black man who died following police restraint in Kirkcaldy in 2015. In 2022, the Sheku Bayoh Inquiry was established to examine his death, the subsequent investigation and – crucially – whether race was a factor.

There has been less discussion of the fatal police shooting of Badreddin Abdalla Adam Bosh (Sobande and Hill, 2022), an asylum seeker who had stabbed (non-fatally) six people in Glasgow. Reports suggest that Bosh was experiencing a mental health crisis at the time, while forced to reside in a hotel where substantial concerns existed about conditions (Gunna et al., 2024). In 2024, it was announced that a Fatal Accident Inquiry would be held into Bosh's death.

Evidence on the experience of ethnic minority groups with police in Scotland is limited. It paints a more positive picture of interactions between police and (at least some) communities of colour in Scotland, particularly longer-standing communities (Forrester et al., 2023), or middle-class members of the Scottish Pakistani community (Cunningham, forthcoming). Trust and satisfaction in the police seem *overall* to be slightly better among 'minority ethnic' groups (Scottish Government, 2023), and Scottish statistics do not show the same ethnic disproportionality in the deployment of stop and search as in England and Wales (see Box 3.2).

This does not mean there is no problem in Scotland. Forrester et al. (2023) found concerns about disproportionate targeting, communication and follow-up from the police, and about the ways in which some accents could be (mis)perceived by police as aggressive. They also noted fear of the police among some asylum seekers – understandably given the integration of immigration and criminal justice across the UK. Within policing, the 2020 Angiolini Review expressed concern that despite "a drive to recruit officers from the Black, Asian and minority ethnic communities" (p. 30), the culture within Police Scotland was causing some of these officers to leave.

The Angiolini Review also reported discrimination against women and LGBTI officers. Further reports found institutional and personal sexism and misogyny across Police Scotland, creating a "hostile environment for women" in the service and likely affecting policing practice (Learmonth, 2024). A high-profile employment tribunal, relating to the experiences of a female former firearms officer, accepted evidence of a sexist "boys' club" culture, also noted in criticisms of the SPF (Brooks, 2023).

Another family campaign by the mother of Emma Caldwell, who was murdered in 2005, finally led to a conviction in 2024. This long delay raised serious questions for Scottish policing since women had raised concerns at the time (which were ignored) about the man who was ultimately convicted (Brooks, 2024). As a result of these concerns, another public inquiry was announced by the Justice Secretary in March 2024.

There have been concerns about responses to victims and underreporting of hate crimes among a range of groups (HMICS, 2021). There is evidence of lower trust of the police particularly among women under 44 (SPA, 2022), and especially among people who identify as gay, transgender, non-binary or other gender. LGBTQI+ young people in Scotland interviewed by Moir et al. (2023) found distrust and visible anxiety about interactions with the police (influenced in some cases by previous interactions), with fears of homophobic and transphobic discrimination "never far from the surface" (p. 18).

There has been some recognition of these problems by Police Scotland. In May 2023, the outgoing Chief Constable Iain Livingstone said Police Scotland was "institutionally racist and discriminatory", an assessment then reaffirmed by his successor, Jo Farrell. This has been accompanied by some attempts to address these issues, including through The Police Scotland Equality, Diversity and Inclusion Strategy, 'Policing Together', now incorporated into 'Vision 2030'.

However, progress in reflecting on the culture of Police Scotland (as the Angiolini Review recommended) has been slow. To some people working within Police Scotland, public statements attesting to institutional racism appear as an attack on individual officers, rather than as a structural problem. This interpretation may have some basis, given the emphasis on individual psychology in Police Scotland training materials around diversity and inclusion (Moir et al., 2023). This echoes Souhami (2014)'s finding that English and Welsh efforts to address institutional racism tended to focus on individual behaviour and language – contrary to the Macpherson inquiry's intentions.

Questions to consider

- Is 'institutional racism' (or other forms of discrimination) a useful way of understanding problems of discrimination and policing?
- Police participation in Pride marches, including in Scotland, has been criticised from a range of political standpoints. What are some arguments for and against it?
- What might explain institutional misogyny in Scottish police organisations?

Angiolini recommended a range of reforms to strengthen police governance and accountability, with many of those requiring legislation taken forward in the Police (Ethics, Conduct and Scrutiny) (Scotland) Act 2025. When in force, this will introduce a statutory code of ethics and duty of candour (for the organization and individual officers, intended to encourage cooperation with investigations), enhance the role of the PIRC in the complaints and misconduct processes, including giving them additional powers to take over consideration of complaints at any stage, and introduce a barred list for officers who were, or would have been, dismissed due to gross misconduct.

The implications of the changes remain to be seen, but for now, it seems a more 'heated' political climate is here to stay, and Police Scotland and the Scottish Government can no longer expect policing decisions and practices to escape scrutiny.

3.3 The process of reporting and investigating crime in Scotland

One important aspect of policing is the investigation of crime. This includes interviewing suspects and witnesses and pursuing other forms of evidence such as fingerprints, DNA, CCTV, and analysis of phones and computer systems – to determine if a crime has occurred and who is responsible. At the same time, the rights of people suspected of or charged with crime must be protected.

3.3.1 Reporting and investigating

One of the main ways in which crime comes to the attention of the police is through reporting by victims or witnesses. In Scotland, this can happen over the phone (through the emergency 999 or non-emergency 101 number), in person at a police station, or anonymously via Crimestoppers.

Many victims however choose not to report. They may not see what has happened to them as a crime; even if they do, they may decide to deal with it personally. They may be deterred by previous negative experiences with the police, or believe they would not be interested or that the incident is not serious enough to report. The largest victim survey in Scotland, the Scottish Crime and Justice Survey (SCJS), suggests that from 2008/09 until 2019/20, around 40% of crime which would be identified through their survey was reported to the police, with violent crime reported more frequently than property crime (Scottish Government, 2021b). (As a victim survey, SCJS does not include 'victimless' crimes.)

Some social groups are less likely to report than others. Fohring's (2015) analysis of SCJS data found that people in deprived areas, especially young men affected by unemployment and with a history of offending, were more likely to be victimised but less likely to report. Not seeing what happened as a crime or oneself as a victim are key influences on whether someone reports to the police.

As well as reacting to reports, police proactively seek to identify crime, including through intelligence gathering or searches. While this can be another way in which crime comes to police attention, it raises ethical questions, including around privacy – it can involve surveillance or intrusion into the lives of people who may not have committed any crime.

When police are called to a crime scene, first response officers undertake initial investigations, speaking to witnesses and preserving the scene (e.g. preventing unauthorised access) to ensure forensic evidence, where present, can be secured without contamination. Forensic evidence is collected by forensic scientists provided by the SPA, who subject it to appropriate testing. Despite its prominence in popular fiction, most police investigations do not involve extensive forensic testing – SPA Forensic Services had a caseload of about 6,000 cases in 2023 (SPA, 2024). Where the victim reports a sexual assault, they may be referred to a Sexual Assault Referral Centre (SARC), an NHS service which provides healthcare and support but also collects forensic evidence. A victim may also self-refer to a SARC if they do not (yet) want to tell the police.

Pursuing forensic evidence has cost implications, so decisions need to be made about use of resources, with police having some discretion about which avenues they pursue. Police Scotland raised controversy by announcing (following the 'Proportionate Response to Crime' pilot scheme in the North-East) that they would not be investigating crimes where there were "no investigative opportunities", following an assessment of threat, harm, risk, vulnerability and available evidence. However, arguably the availability of investigative opportunities is not absolute but relative to the resources available, and some members of the public have more resources and capacity to gather useful evidence than others.

For (possible) crimes including suspicious deaths, attempted murder, serious assault, robbery, sexual crimes, abduction, firearms crimes, deaths in police custody, and sudden unexplained deaths in infancy, the **Criminal Investigation Department** is notified, which has officers based in each division. The most serious crimes fall within the remit of the **Specialist Crimes Division**, which includes a Major Investigations Team working across Scotland, as well as responsibilities for organised crime and counterterrorism.

Police lead initial investigations, but under Scots law, the ultimate responsibility for the investigation of crime falls to the Crown Office (see Chapter 4). Historically, the investigation was undertaken by the Sheriff, and subsequently the Procurator Fiscal, with police merely responsible for arresting the suspect – but over time the police took on a greater investigatory function (Carloway, 2011). Current practice is that the investigating body (Police Scotland or a specialist reporting agency) sends a report on the investigation to COPFS. In some serious cases, COPFS may instruct police in the early stages of an investigation or where further investigation is required. COPFS also investigate allegations of crimes committed by on-duty police officers.

3.3.2 *Law and rights*

Police investigatory powers and rules around evidence in criminal procedure are determined by law. In England and Wales, police powers for investigation are set out in the Police and Criminal Evidence (PACE) Act 1984, which is intended to ensure that due process is followed and suspects' rights are protected. No such single act exists in Scotland, where police investigatory powers come principally from common law, the Criminal Procedure (Scotland) Act 1995, and the Criminal Justice (Scotland) Act 2016.

Considerable changes to police powers in Scotland were introduced following the decision of the UK Supreme Court in the case of Cadder v HM Advocate, Lord Carloway's subsequent review and finally the Criminal

Justice (Scotland) Act 2016. The decision in the Cadder case related to the compatibility of Scottish law and practice with obligations under the European Convention of Human Rights, specifically the implied right of access to a lawyer. Before the Cadder judgment, a suspect could be detained for up to six hours without access to a lawyer – a practice previously upheld by the High Court of Justiciary, which had considered other safeguards in Scottish rules of evidence and criminal procedure sufficient to ensure fairness. The case also raised the troubling prospect of Scottish justice being subordinated to an English court (albeit through an interpretation of European law).

For criminal justice, the Cadder case was "a serious shock to the system" (Carloway, 2011: p2), resulting in hundreds of prosecutions being abandoned. Emergency legislation was passed to require access to a lawyer in detention (making the necessary changes to legal aid to fund this) and extend the period of detention from 6 to 12 hours (Carloway, 2011).

The subsequent review by Lord Carloway proposed a range of restrictions of pre-charge detention and more safeguards for suspects. Many of these were made law in the Criminal Justice (Scotland) Act 2016. The Act specified time limits (usually 12 hours) for holding a suspect (now called a 'Not Officially Accused' person) in custody pre-charge (see Section 3.3.3) and allows for the person to be freed pending further investigation (for up to 28 days) and later re-arrested. The Act also allowed certain circumstances in which police, with court approval, could interview people post-charge ('Officially Accused') in relation to new evidence.

The Act requires police to take precautions to avoid unnecessarily holding someone in police custody and explicitly protects the right to remain silent. All suspects must now be advised of their right to legal advice at any stage of the interview, and all investigative interviews of suspects must take place at a police station. The Act afforded greater protections for children; when deciding whether to arrest a child, it introduced a duty to safeguard and promote the wellbeing of the child as a primary consideration. Under-16s, or people over 16 who are unable to understand what is happening or communicate effectively due to a mental disorder, cannot consent to an interview without a solicitor and during the interview should be supported by an 'appropriate adult' to facilitate understanding and communication.

If the police believe they have sufficient evidence to prove a crime has been committed and that the suspect is responsible, the suspect may be **charged** – referred to COPFS who decide whether to prosecute (Section 4.3.1). The person may then be released or kept in police custody until their first court appearance (which must be the next working day, under the 2016 Act). Alternatively, rather than charging the person, the police can dispose of the case themselves, by issuing a **Recorded Police Warning** (often known informally as a 'caution') or **Fixed Penalty Notice**, a type of on-the-spot fine (Chapter 5). These measures avoid a criminal conviction (although some information can still appear on criminal records disclosure) and going to court, but also arguably circumvent some due process rights, with police acting as judge and jury.

Box 3.2 Stop and search

Stop and search is a hot topic in policing. This tactic involves stopping members of the public and asking or requiring them to submit to a search. Police have argued it is an important tool to detect and deter crime, especially drug or weapon possession, although there is little evidence for any deterrent effect.

Elsewhere in the UK (and beyond), the debate about stop and search has centred on its substantial overuse against people of colour, in relation to institutional racism. After the Macpherson report (Box 3.1), stop and search was reformed in England and Wales but not in Scotland – because Scottish analyses had not found evidence of ethnic disproportionality in its use (Lennon and Murray, 2018).

Scotland retained 'non-statutory' stop and search, which England had banned in 2003. This allowed officers to ask people to 'voluntarily' submit to a search – in contrast to a 'statutory' search, which required suspicion that the person was doing or carrying something they shouldn't. Non-statutory stop and search was problematic partly because of its ambiguous legal status and because officers did not have to inform people of their right to refuse. Particularly problematic was its deployment against people too young to meaningfully consent – a feature of Strathclyde Police's response to knife crime from the 1990s onwards (see Section 2.3).

Just after the formation of Police Scotland, stop and search went from a "non-issue" to a national scandal (Murray and Harkin, 2017). In 2014, a report by Kath Murray (2014) on the use of stop and search among the 'legacy' forces raised concerns about the disproportionate targeting of specific groups and the resulting impact on trust and confidence in the police. Unlike in England and Wales, these centred on age and class rather than ethnicity (Murray, 2015a, 2015b).

Murray (2014) found that the use of stop and search had increased dramatically in Scotland from 2005 to 2010; far from being an English (or London) issue, Scotland's rate of stop and search per capita (i.e. accounting for different population sizes) was nearly four times higher than in England and Wales; the legacy Strathclyde force used it at double the rate of the Metropolitan Police. The rise was driven by non-statutory searches and disproportionately targeted young people (with 500 searches of children under ten). This disproportionality exceeded any differences in the probability of offending among age groups, with a lower rate of detection (finding a prohibited item) in searches of younger age groups.

Following the creation of Police Scotland, stop and search numbers fell overall by 6% in 2013/14, but increased in most divisions

(Murray, 2015a). Stop and search remained disproportionately focused on young people – in 2013/14, there were more searches recorded on 16-year-old boys than there *were* 16-year-old boys in Scotland.

There are important questions about *which* young people were stopped and searched. Murray's (2015b: 214) research describes a policy of targeting (supposedly) preventative stop and search based on the profiling of people involved in knife crime, and practice based on the "premise of conditioning suspect populations via routine intensive policing" – described explicitly using the classist term 'neds' by one senior legacy Strathclyde officer interviewed by Murray.

In terms of ethnicity, both Murray (2015b) and more recent statistics (Scottish Government, 2023) highlight a slight *under*-representation of people of colour among those stopped and searched. However, overall national statistics may hide considerable disproportionality within and between local areas. Furthermore, while police in England and Wales have long been required to publish data on race and criminal justice, including rates of stop and search, no such practice (nor *any* publication of stop and search data) existed in Scotland until the scandal (Lennon and Murray, 2018).

Murray's concerns were largely echoed by critical reports from the SPA (2014) and HMICS (2015b). The Scottish Government and Police Scotland initially coordinated efforts to downplay the issue and shore up public support for stop and search, but the creation of Police Scotland had produced a newly politically 'hot' climate around policing; policing tactics were now subject to intense media and political scrutiny (Murray and Harkin, 2017).

The result was substantial reforms to reduce the over-policing of young people and protect their rights (O'Neill and Aston, 2018). The 2016 Criminal Justice (Scotland) Act abolished non-statutory stop and search, such that (with limited public order exceptions) a search requires reasonable grounds for suspicion (Clayton, 2024); from this point, stop and search numbers declined dramatically. Alongside this, a new Code of Practice was developed to regulate stop and search, which McVie's (2018) evaluation found led to increases in detection and a reduced (albeit continuing) disproportionality in its deployment against young people.

Policymakers made much of improved 'engagement' with young people and the quality of police-young person interactions. However, Clayton's (2024) ethnographic research on the reforms argues that along the way, engagement came to be understood by officers not as a mechanism for positive interactions with young people but as a tool for *investigation*, which might ultimately lead to a search if the person was deemed not to have responded appropriately.

In place of (non-statutory) stop and search with little oversight, a widespread practice of 'stop and *engage*' had emerged. As a 'voluntary' intervention, this relied on young people's lack of awareness of their right not to engage or their belief that they could not enforce such rights in practice. There remains more to do to address the disproportionate police targeting of young people in Scotland.

Questions to consider

- What are some possible implications of mass stop and search for legitimacy of and trust in the police?
- Using the Police Scotland statistical dashboard (https://scotland.shinyapps.io/ps-stop-search/), look up your local area/police division. Looking at rates and numbers of stop and search, is there anything that surprises you?
- In what ways is 'stop and engage' an improvement on previous practices of 'stop and search'? In what ways is it more of the same? How might a young person experience these practices?
- What do you view as appropriate grounds for reasonable suspicion for a search?

3.3.3 Police custody as a setting of confinement

When the police arrest someone they can be kept in '**police custody**' while they are investigated. This is different to being 'remanded in custody' (a decision made by a court to imprison someone ahead of trial or sentence).

Police custody usually lasts no more than 12 hours but can be extended to 24 hours (and up to 14 days in terrorism cases). Reforms, including under the 2016 Act, have roughly halved the number of people in custody in the decade up to 2023 and reduced the average time spent there. Current police strategy may reduce these further. People in police custody are kept in cells in any of 77 'custody centres' across Scotland, ranging from large purpose-built facilities to single cells in local stations, and run by officers alongside civilian staff. People can be held in custody in a hospital if they require medical treatment, and recent youth justice reforms (see Section 9.2.4) will require police to consider alternatives to custody cells when holding young people. A person in custody may be questioned (but retains the right to silence), photographed, fingerprinted, DNA tested and searched (including intimately). They may also have possessions (including clothing) taken from them, as evidence or to prevent them harming themselves. They have the right to legal advice (from their own lawyer or an on-call 'duty solicitor'), and for a friend or family member to be informed where they are. There are special conditions for young people and vulnerable adults.

The police have a duty to keep detainees safe. Particularly important is the role of the Custody Sergeant, a police officer (working under within the national Criminal Justice Services Division), who decides whether holding someone in police custody is legal, proportionate, necessary and required to carry out further investigations. An assessment is conducted of the risk the detained person may pose to themselves or others, including because of mental ill-health, intoxication or internal concealment of substances; the highest-risk detainees should be kept under constant observation, with examples of tragic outcomes where there have been failures in procedures (Armstrong et al., 2025). In addition to the distressing features of confinement generally (such as a lack of autonomy), people detained in police custody are especially vulnerable since there is significant uncertainty about what might happen to them, and (unlike in prison) they are subject to investigative as well as punitive procedures (Skinns and Wooff, 2021).

Despite this, officers and civilian staff working in custody may have had only limited training about mental health and managing risk. Concerns remain about long waits for medical treatment and the degraded state of many cells (SPA, 2023), and there are further challenges for *rural* police custody (Wooff, 2024). A recent report (Armstrong et al., 2025) on deaths in custody found that 29 people had died in police custody in Scotland between 2015 and 2024.

This section has laid out the process by which a crime comes to the attention of the police and is investigated. While these activities are key to how we think about policing, it is important to highlight that what the police actually *do* includes a much broader range of activities than outlined by this process.

3.4 Policing beyond crime investigation

Much policing scholarship highlights that most police time is spent in 'service' or 'social work' calls. Around three-quarters of incidents attended by Police Scotland do not involve a crime being recorded (HMICS, 2022). This brief overview gives a sense of the variation and complexities in Scottish policing.

3.4.1 Community policing

In theory, **community policing** means an approach which prioritises building relationships with (geographical and to a certain extent identity-based) communities and responding to their concerns – rather than a narrow focus on responding to individual crimes. This gained popularity following a deterioration in community–police relationships and high-profile crises for policing in the 1980s and 1990s, which threatened the legitimacy and trust of the police among (especially) Black American and Black British communities – alongside a more general crisis resulting from a rise in crime (Henry and Mackenzie, 2009).

Henry and Mackenzie (2009) suggest that tactics associated with community policing include foot patrol, public meetings, youth work, local substations, coordinating neighbourhood watch activities, and survey research to evaluate public satisfaction with police.

A critical perspective might contend that community policing is more rhetoric than reality; a way of extending surveillance and social control under the guise of community engagement. Other concerns relate to the potential stigmatisation of communities through visible police presence and "a risk that [community policing] can become a vehicle for the practical implementation of punitive attitudes against marginalized or minority groups" (Henry and Mackenzie, 2009: 6). Community policing therefore raises questions about which communities are being *served* and which are being *policed* (Box 2.1).

It has been argued, given some of the early community safety approaches discussed in Chapter 2, that Scotland was an early leader in community policing. However, a national coordinated approach to community policing was late in coming (Henry and Mackenzie, 2009). In 2009 the *Scottish Community Policing Engagement Principles* (Scottish Government, 2009) outlined the following aspects:

- Visible police presence;
- Communication and consultation with the community;
- Responsiveness to community needs;
- Responsiveness to individual needs and to those who may be particularly vulnerable;
- Accountability to the community;
- Partnership working with public and private agencies;
- A commitment to local problem-solving (Henry and Mackenzie, 2009).

The 2012 Act made local policing – and the development of local police plans – a statutory requirement. There were however concerns that the move to one national police service, motivated in large part by cost-saving arguments, would damage community policing. Many would argue these fears came to pass, with changes to traditional working patterns and local beat areas, as well as to the roles, resources and workloads of local policing personnel, and with the "closure of police stations, reduction in opening hours, scale enlargement, centralisation of specialist units and a stronger reliance on IT" (Terpstra et al., 2019: 351; Figure 3.1).

Alongside these organisational changes, there were changes in the philosophy of how policing should be done – with a shift immediately after the Act to an enforcement-led policing style and an emphasis on 'intelligence-led' policing (focused on data analysis rather than community knowledge). Terpstra et al. (2019) have described these changes as a move towards 'Abstract Policing', with more distant relationships between frontline police and management, as well as between police and communities. They emphasise that this does not necessarily mean police are not "oriented to local problems and partners, but increasingly this is being realised in more abstract or

Figure 3.1 Leith police station, awaiting closure in January 2025.

decontextualised ways, less dependent on local knowledge and personal and informal relations" (p. 343). The ten-year policing strategy Policing 2026 (Police Scotland and SPA, 2017) contained continued commitments to prevention, community engagement ("listening more and responding to [communities'] diverse needs") and partnership working.

The '2030 vision' (Police Scotland, 2024), launched in October 2024, is more emphatic, promising an expansion of community policing, with "identifiable local officers" in all parts of Scotland. This however is to occur alongside increased efficiency, enabled by further uptake of technological optimisations to back-office functions – so the issues discussed here may yet remain unresolved.

3.4.2 *Public order and political policing*

As the history of policing showed, concerns about civil unrest and public order were early motivations for a professionalised police force. Police play a role in order maintenance and arguably in ensuring safety, including at large events such as football matches and political demonstrations. Such events can be challenging for police, with large crowds, road traffic or security concerns. This aspect of policing can be a source of considerable contention, with implications for police legitimacy.

The European Convention of Human Rights includes the right to freedom of peaceful assembly and association with others but allows for 'proportionate' restrictions, for example, to protect national security and public safety, prevent disorder or crime, or protect the rights and freedoms of others. Scotland is not subject to the raft of anti-protest legislation passed in England and Wales in the 2020s. Nevertheless, many common nonviolent protest tactics can be criminalised, through offences such as criminal damage, trespass and breach of the peace, and there have been repeated historic and recent examples of arrests and prosecution of nonviolent protesters in Scotland. Research has suggested that during the 1984–85 strikes, miners in Scotland were twice as likely to get arrested than those down South, and on low-level charges such as breach of the peace or obstructing the police – with many ultimately pardoned by The Miners' Strike (Pardons) (Scotland) Act 2022 (Phillips, 2023). While police feel an obligation to prevent disruption to the lives of ordinary citizens and businesses, protesters often draw attention to moral questions about a balance of harm (the harm protesters cause versus the harm they are seeking to prevent).

In the early devolutionary years, police narratives described a distinct 'Scottish approach' in relation to the policing of public protest (such as at the 2005 G8 summit in Gleneagles), emphasizing policing by consent (Gorringe and Rosie, 2010). The Metropolitan Police response to the G20 protests in London in 2009 raised concerns about tactics such as containment of protesters in a controlled area, sometimes for hours ("kettling") and use of force – including unlawful force which caused the death of a passerby, Ian Tomlinson. Following this, the Lothian and Borders Police response to protests surrounding the 2009 NATO Parliamentary Assembly in Edinburgh placed greater emphasis on police liaison with protesters, ostensibly to facilitate dialogue but raising concerns about surveillance (Gorringe et al., 2012).

Police Scotland emphasises their role in "facilitating" peaceful protest, framing their role within a human rights perspective and articulating a desire to avoid aggressive tactics. This rhetoric has resulted in some changes, but other practices have continued. 'Containment' – arguably a euphemism for 'kettling' – is still deployed against some groups, such as Celtic fans at anti-racist protests in Glasgow in 2020 and 2024 (Atkinson, 2022; Figure 3.2), as well as members of the Youth Communist League at a climate march in Glasgow coinciding with the COP26 climate conference in 2021. This tactic can escalate crowd tensions and anti-police sentiment (Gorringe et al., 2024). Conversely, the facilitation of anti-monarchy protests appeared to work smoothly at the National Service of Thanksgiving for King Charles and Queen Camilla in Edinburgh in 2023, with police facilitating a prime position for protesters (Gorringe and Rosie, 2023).

Figure 3.2 Police containment at a protest in Glasgow.

Many of these events occurred under intense international media attention. Smaller, local protests have raised questions about police commitment to facilitation of peaceful protest and about police tactics. At a series of protests at Thales' factory in Glasgow, against the sale of arms to Israel in the context of the assault on Gaza, police were accused of heavy-handed and violent tactics and threatened to arrest a journalist covering the protest (McKay, 2024).

Police strategies now differentiate between different groups within a crowd, for example, distinguishing between 'community groups and occasional protesters' and 'anti-capitalist' and 'anarchist' groups assumed to be more intent on violence and disorder (Gorringe et al., 2024). While potentially useful tactically, such categorisations may make police intervention against specific groups more likely, restricting some people's right to protest (Atkinson, 2022). This also suggests that police actions are affected by moral judgements about protesters' politics, and the extent to which these are seen as challenging the system which police reinforce.

Another area of controversy is the deployment of surveillance techniques (sometimes the same tactics used against serious organised crime) against citizens not involved in any criminal activity – a practice with a long history in British (including Scottish) policing (Malloch, 2023). Police in Scotland have deployed plain-clothes officers ('spotters') within football crowds to gather intelligence and even approached fans to act as informants on other supporters, resulting in a "disruptive and unsettling effect" on these fans and contributing to wider breakdowns in trust (Atkinson et al., 2021: 864).

The use of 'subterfuge' within relationships, including sexual relationships, has been highlighted in the 'spycops' scandal (Malloch, 2023). This centred on activities of undercover police units based in England, but Scotland has not escaped involvement. A strategic review by HMICS (2017) purportedly found no evidence that Police Scotland officers had infiltrated activist groups, suggesting undercover policing was not widespread in Scotland – but confirmed *English* undercover officers had been deployed in Scotland. Activists have described increased police interest and harassment following contact with the undercover officer Mark Kennedy (Lubbers, 2019), who travelled to Scotland at least 17 times (HMICS, 2017).

The period covered by the review was largely limited to 2000 onwards, and limitations in its scope have been identified by campaigners (Lubbers, 2019). The public inquiry established in England did not extend to Scotland (including the activities of English officers in Scotland), and the Scottish Government – relying on the HMICS review – rejected calls to establish its own inquiry. Despite the more heated political climate, the issue passed with limited scrutiny.

3.4.3 *Policing and mental distress*

Although a criminal justice agency, the police play a broader role in responding to people experiencing mental health crisis. While many of those involved in criminal incidents experience mental health problems, the police role extends beyond this to include responding to people in distress or whose behaviour in public is causing concern. Police may need to return someone who has absconded from hospital or undertake welfare checks on people at home. Under sections 297 and 298 of the Mental Health (Care and Treatment) (Scotland) Act 2003,[1] if the police encounter someone in public who appears to have a mental disorder, they may remove them to a 'place of safety' for their protection or to protect public safety.

The role of police in responding to mental distress and vulnerability has been contentious. Both police officers and people with experience of mental distress have expressed concerns that police are not health professionals and are being expected to substitute for shortfalls in other services. While these shortfalls are themselves cause for concern, some of these arguments reflect differing philosophies about the police role and what constitutes 'real' police work. Police officers are concerned about the considerable time demands associated with, for example, accompanying people to hospital, where they may need to wait for several hours (HMICS, 2023).

Although officers may respond compassionately, their involvement can be detrimental to the person's wellbeing and increase the criminalisation of people in distress (HMICS, 2023). It may not be immediately apparent whether the officer should use mental health or justice powers – behaviour that indicates mental distress, such as shouting in the streets, may be considered threatening or fall within the broad definition of 'breach of the peace' (Thomson et al., 2022). Even where well-intentioned, officers may rely on criminal justice powers to resolve challenging situations or avoid immediate harm. Thomson et al. (2022) have critiqued the continued use of criminal sanctions as a response to suicidality in the UK, evidenced by prosecutions in both Scotland and England. PIRC (2023) data revealed that 45% of deaths in police custody or after police contact in Scotland in 2022–23 were related to someone with a background of mental ill-health.

More can be done to support police in Scotland to better fulfil this aspect of their role – although many would agree with Chief Constable Jo Farrell that "policing is not the best agency to provide people living with poor mental health with all the care and support they need and deserve" (Police Scotland, 2023). There have been innovative pilot projects in Scotland to improve responses to people experiencing mental distress, as well as partnership working between police and health services (see McGeough and Foster, 2018). HMICS (2023)' *Thematic Review of Policing Mental Health in Scotland* nevertheless called for better national coordination and oversight of initiatives and a whole system review of responses to mental health in Scotland across all services. The Scottish Government's (2025) subsequently published their *Multi-Agency Partnership Approach to Distress* framework, setting out that Police Scotland should only be deployed in mental health incidents where "appropriate and necessary" but that sometimes their presence is "vital" (p. 21). HM Chief Inspector of Constabulary in Scotland Craig Naylor concluded that Police Scotland "will always have a key role in supporting those experiencing poor mental health" (p.5).

More radical perspectives would challenge police involvement in responses to mental distress altogether, alongside other carceral responses to mental ill-health, such as secure hospital care. We encourage you to engage with these in your broader reading (see for example Klukoff et al., 2021), but they fall beyond the scope of this book.

3.4.4 *Rural policing*

A large proportion of Scotland is rural, with some rural areas extremely sparsely populated and far from the nearest town or city (Figure 3.3). Although rural areas report lower crime rates, the smaller numbers of (and fewer specialist) staff mean officers must deal with a wider range of crime than in urban areas (Fenwick, 2015). Police officers may need to undertake tasks or (back)fill roles for which they are not trained or make decisions usually undertaken by more senior or specialist staff (e.g. around rural police custody, Wooff, 2024).

This has been exacerbated by cuts in police officer numbers and station closures, changes not unique to rural areas but with particularly acute impacts there. Individual officers may cover very large policing beats without

Figure 3.3 A rural police station in the Highlands.

being able to rely on timely backup in case of problems (Fenwick, 2015; Souhami, 2020).

These can be exacerbated by environmental challenges – for instance, the reliance on boat travel in island communities – and geographic isolation, combined with lengthier and deeper darkness (in winter), may lead rural areas to feel particularly hostile or disorientating (Souhami, 2020, 2023). Rural officers are more likely to live and work in the same community (Wooff, 2017); this results in a blurring of boundaries between being on and off duty and a feeling of being constantly surveilled and judged by neighbours (Fenwick, 2015; Souhami, 2020).

Together, these factors arguably necessitate a different approach to policing in rural areas, sometimes described as a 'soft' approach involving greater use of discretion and less use of enforcement (Wooff, 2017). In small or rural communities, it is less appealing to use arrest (still less force) to resolve a problem when the officer is alone, likely to cross paths soon with the person at a local shop or social event, and where arresting someone will require taking an officer off shift to oversee custody (Fenwick, 2015; Souhami, 2020; Wooff, 2024). Instead, a greater focus is given to 'peace-keeping', de-escalating and resolving problems without enforcement, and to 'policing by consent', recognising and responding within the norms and expectations of particular communities. As a result, Souhami (2020) has argued that 'rural policing' is in fact much closer than urban policing to the idealised traditional model of British policing, such that it is the peculiarities of *urban* – rather than rural – policing that require explanation.

It is however important to recognise that "there is not one but many ruralities" (Fenwick, 2015: 240). Approaches to policing may differ according to particular rural contexts, such as proximity to a town, area deprivation and police officers' own perceptions of local problems (Wooff, 2017).

The ability of the police to respond to rural crime effectively – and to tailor their approach – is affected by strategic decisions around organisational structure, tactics and resources. Given the distinctive aspects of rural policing, the creation of a single police service covering all of Scotland has probably had important consequences. Historically, rural officers were from and embedded long term within the communities they policed (Smith, 2010), enabling a depth of knowledge about specific rural offences (e.g. poaching) and locally specific approaches that engendered a degree of professional pride (Fenwick, 2015). Following the merger into Police Scotland, police officers in Shetland are now frequently transferred from other areas without knowledge of the local context, creating unease for the community upon their arrival (Souhami, 2020). These officers may ultimately find the challenges of rural policing overwhelming in the long term.

As we have already seen, one prominent early crisis in the history of Police Scotland centred on enforcement approaches developed for Glasgow, such as armed patrols, being inappropriately applied in rural settings. Given that much of the research referenced above (except Souhami, 2020, 2023; Wooff, 2024) was undertaken before the creation of Police Scotland, the extent to which a distinct approach to rural policing will be preserved remains to be seen.

Issues outlined in this section extend from everyday operational decisions to strategy and policy; in Scotland as elsewhere, policing is shaped by its social context and hence inescapably political. Some other police activities are covered elsewhere in this book: community safety and crime prevention (Chapter 2), imposing Fixed Penalty Notices (Chapter 5), administering criminal records and surveilling people on licence (Chapter 10), and cybercrime and transnational policing (Chapter 11).

Conclusion

This chapter has given an overview of policing in Scotland, the agencies involved and the history of the public police from formation up through the creation of the national service. This chapter has also taken you through the process by which a crime investigation progresses from a crime report until a report is sent to COPFS. We continue this process through prosecution and the courts in Chapter 4.

In providing this overview we have attempted to grapple with the issue of whether Scottish policing is distinct. There certainly seems to be evidence that policing and government actors have used the rhetoric of a distinctively "Scottish" approach to policing – more consultative, consent-based and softer – contrasting itself to policing, and high-profile scandals, south of the border (particularly involving the Metropolitan Police). The extent to which this rhetoric reflects substantive differences in policing practice has been contested (Fyfe, 2019), and, as political and media scrutiny of policing has increased in Scotland, policing actors have had to contend with a range of scandals which challenge this self-presentation of a consultative, consent-based and softer policing style, devoid of the problems seen south of the border. Despite this, it is certainly important to attend to local particularities, such as the political context which left mass stop and search unchecked for years; and how the geography of rural Scotland changes the nature and experience of policing within those areas.

Critical questions

- Some major scandals involving Scottish policing have not been discussed here. Using news media and/or academic materials, research any of these and discuss how they might relate to themes discussed in this chapter:
  - 'Fettesgate' (Lothian and Borders Police, 1990s);
  - Shirley McKie (Strathclyde Police and SCRO, 1997–2011).
- What should democratic accountability for policing look like, at local and national level?
- Protesters sometimes chant 'Who do you protect? Who do you serve?' at police. Thinking about the history of policing in Scotland and what you have read and experienced of current policing, how would you answer this question?
- What role should the police have in responding to people experiencing mental distress? How should police act when they encounter people in this situation?
- Can you think of examples from your own life of 'policing' that did not involve the police? For example, in your workplace, school, university or hometown?
- What has happened in Scottish policing of relevance to the themes in this chapter, since this book has been published?

Key resources

HMICS website. https://www.hmics.scot/
SPA website. https://www.spa.police.uk/
These websites contain numerous reports on Scottish policing.
Murray, K. and Harkin, D. (2017) Policing in cool and hot climates: Legitimacy, power and the rise and fall of mass stop and search in Scotland. *The British Journal of Criminology* 57(4): 885–905.

An overview of political developments around Scottish policing and stop and search.

Scottish Institute for Policing Research (SIPR). https://www.sipr.ac.uk/

A collaboration between Police Scotland, the SPA and Scottish universities, SIPR publishes reports ranging from applied practice evaluations to more critical academic work.

Terpstra, J., Fyfe, N. R., and Salet, R. (2019). The abstract police: A conceptual exploration of unintended changes of police organisations. *The Police Journal* 92(4): 339–359.

A comparison of police centralisation in Scotland and the Netherlands.

Note

1 The broadly equivalent power in England and Wales is s136 of the Mental Health Act 1983; the more extensive literature on this may be helpful for further reading.

References

Angiolini, E. (2020) *Independent Review of Complaints Handling, Investigations and Misconduct Issues in Relation to Policing: Final Report*. Scottish Government.

Armstrong, S., Barkas, B., Allan, L., Allan, S. and Cairns, D. (2025) *Nothing to See Here? Deaths in Custody and their Investigation in Scotland in 2024*. SCCJR. https://www.sccjr.ac.uk/wp-content/uploads/2025/04/Nothing-to-See-Here-2024-FINAL-DRAFT.pdf

Atkinson, C. (2022) 'Football fans are not thugs': Communication and the future of fan engagement in the policing of Scottish football. *Policing and Society* 32(4): 472–488.

Atkinson, C., McBride, M. and Moore, A. (2021) Pitched! Informants and the covert policing of football fans in Scotland. *Policing and Society* 31(7): 863–877.

Barrie, D.G. (2008) *Police in the Age of Improvement*. Willan.

BBC News (2018) Police Scotland chief constable quits. 7 February. https://www.bbc.co.uk/news/uk-scotland-42977072

Brodie, Z.P., Gillespie-Smith, K., Goodall, K., Deacon, K., and Collins, K. (2025) The impact of trauma-awareness session on police officers' trauma-informed attitudes in Scotland. *Psychology, Crime & Law*, 31(1), 26–40.

Brooks, L. (2023) Scottish Police Federation accused of failing women. *Guardian*, 4 June. https://www.theguardian.com/uk-news/2023/jun/04/scottish-police-federation-accused-failing-women

Brooks, L. (2024) Police face scrutiny after man found guilty of 2005 Emma Caldwell murder. *Guardian*, 28 February. https://www.theguardian.com/uk-news/2024/feb/28/emma-caldwell-murder-police-scotland-faces-scrutiny-man-found-guilty

Clayton, E. (2024) Mechanisms of the social control of children and young people: From 'stop and search' to 'stop and engage' in Police Scotland. *Criminology & Criminal Justice*, online ahead of print.

Croall, H. (2016) Crimes of the powerful in Scotland. In Croall, H., Mooney, G. and Munro, M. (eds) *Crime, Justice and Society in Scotland*. Routledge. 131–148.

Cunningham, A. (forthcoming) *Encountering Policing: a dialogic exploration of Scottish Pakistanis' experiences of 'policing'*. PhD thesis, Edinburgh Napier University.

Davidson, N., Jackson, L. and Smale, D. (2016) Police amalgamation and reform in Scotland: The long twentieth century. *Scottish Historical Review* 95(1): 88–111.

Fenwick, T. (2015) Learning policing in rural spaces: 'Covering 12 foot rooms with 8 foot carpets'. *Policing: A Journal of Policy and Practice* 9(3): 234–241.
Fohring, S. (2015) An integrated model of victimization as an explanation of non-involvement with the criminal justice system. *International Review of Victimology* 21(1): 45–70.
Forrester, K., Mendel, J. and McArdle, K. (2023) *Inquiring Together: Collaborative Research with BAME Communities and Serving Officers*. Scottish Institute for Policing Research.
Fotopoulou, M. and Aston, E. (2022) Policing of drugs in Scotland: Moving beyond the stalemate to redesigning the chess board. In Bacon, M. and Spicer, J. (eds) *Drug Law Enforcement, Policing and Harm Reduction: Ending the Stalemate*. Routledge. 151–173.
Fyfe, N.R. (2019) The challenges of change: Exploring the dynamics of police reform in Scotland. *International Journal of Police Science & Management* 21(4): 196–205.
Fyfe, N.R., Anderson, S., Bland, N., Goulding, A., Mitchell, J., and Reid, S. (2018) Experiencing organizational change during an era of reform: Police Scotland, narratives of localism, and perceptions from the 'frontline'. *Policing: A Journal of Policy and Practice* 15(1): 263–276.
Gorringe, H. and Rosie, M. (2023) Research note: Protest, liaison and legitimacy. *Scottish Affairs* 32(4): 467–476.
Gorringe, H., Rosie, M., Portice, J., Tekin, S., Reicher, S., and Hamilton, M. (2024). First they came for the Young Communists: police facilitation and control at COP26, Glasgow. *Policing and Society* 34(8): 781–796.
Gorringe, H. and Rosie, M. (2010) The 'Scottish' approach? The discursive construction of a national police force. *The Sociological Review* 58(1): 65–83.
Gorringe, H., Rosie, M., Waddington, D. and Kominou, M. (2012) Facilitating ineffective protest? The policing of the 2009 Edinburgh NATO protests. *Policing and Society* 22(2): 115–132.
Guma, T., Blake, Y., Maclean, G., MacLeod, K., Makutsa, R. and Sharapov, K. (2024) "Are we criminals?" – Everyday racialisation in temporary asylum accommodation. *Ethnic and Racial Studies* 47(4): 742–762.
Henry, A. and Mackenzie, S. (2009) *Community Policing: A Review of the Evidence*. Scottish Government.
Henry, A., Malik, A. and Aydın-Aitchison, A. (2019) Local governance in the new Police Scotland: Renegotiating power, recognition and responsiveness. *European Journal of Criminology* 16(5): 573–591. https://doi.org/10.1177/1477370819856528
His Majesty's Inspectorate of Constabulary in Scotland (HMICS) (2015a) *Independent Assurance Review Police Scotland – Call Handling Final Report*. HMICS.
HMICS (2015b) *Audit and Assurance Review of Stop and Search: Phase 1*. HMICS. Archived at https://web.archive.org/web/20220121062205/https://www.hmics.scot/sites/default/files/publications/HMICS%20-%20Audit%20and%20Assurance%20Review%20of%20Stop%20and%20Search%20-%20Phase%201_0.pdf
HMICS (2017) *Strategic Review of Undercover Policing in Scotland*. HMICS. https://www.hmics.scot/media/pa1e5sko/hmics20180207pub.pdf
HMICS (2021) *Thematic Inspection of Hate Crime*. HMICS. https://www.hmics.scot/media/jbyb11aw/hmics20210603pub-thematic-inspection-of-hate-crime.pdf
HMICS (2022) *Annual Report 2021–22*. HMICS. https://www.hmics.scot/media/hp1pgxkc/hmics20220630pub.pdf

HMICS (2023) *HMICS Thematic Review of Policing Mental Health in Scotland*. HMICS.

Jones, T. and Newburn, T. (2002) The transformation of policing? Understanding current trends in policing systems. *British Journal of Criminology* 42(1): 129–146.

Joseph-Salisbury, R., Connelly, L. and Wangari-Jones, P. (2021) "The UK is not innocent": Black Lives Matter, policing and abolition in the UK. *Equality, Diversity and Inclusion* 40(1): 21–28.

Klukoff, H., Kanani, H., Gaglione, C. and Alexander, A. (2021) Toward an abolitionist practice of psychology: Reimagining psychology's relationship with the criminal justice system. *Journal of Humanistic Psychology* 61(4): 451–469.

Learmonth, A. (2024) Sexism and misogyny in Police Scotland: Review exposes discrimination. *Herald*, 12 September. https://www.heraldscotland.com/news/24579033.sexism-misogyny-police-scotland-review-exposes-discrimination/

Lennon, G. and Murray, K. (2018) Under-regulated and unaccountable? Explaining variation in stop and search rates in Scotland, England and Wales. *Policing and Society* 28(2): 157–174.

Lord Carloway (2011) *The Carloway Review: Report and Recommendations*. Available at https://lx.iriss.org.uk/sites/default/files/resources/0122808.pdf

Lubbers, E. (2019) *Political Undercover Policing in Scotland: The Facts about Spycops in Scotland & the Questions that Remain Unanswered*. Scottish Campaign Opposing Police Surveillance.

Macpherson, W. (1999) *The Stephen Lawrence Inquiry: Report of an Inquiry by Sir William Macpherson of Cluny*. Command paper 4262-1. HMSO.

Malik, A. (2018) Police governance and accountability in Scotland following reform: Revisiting the policy rationale for the creation of the Scottish Police Authority. *Scottish Affairs* 27(4): 438–464.

Malloch, M.S. (2023) Policing controversies: Undercover policing. In Corteen, K., Steele, R., Cross, N. and McManus, M. (eds) *Forensic Psychology, Crime and Policing*. Policy Press. 263–268.

Matchett, C. (2022) 20 Police Scotland officers convicted of sexual offence crimes since 2014. *Scotsman*, 20th February. https://www.scotsman.com/news/politics/20-police-scotland-officers-convicted-of-sexual-offence-crimes-since-2014-3575398

McGeough, E. and Foster, R. (2018) *What Works? Collaborative Police and Health Interventions for Mental Health Distress*. Scottish Government. https://www.gov.scot/publications/works-collaborative-police-health-interventions-mental-health-distress/

McKay, G. (2024) Police Scotland 'astonishing and shocking' to journalist at protest. *The Herald*, 16 May. https://www.heraldscotland.com/news/24323694.police-scotland-astonishing-shocking-journalist-protest/

McVie, S. (2018) *Six Month Review of the Code of Practice for Stop and Search in Scotland*. Scottish Government.

Moir, J., Jola, C., Scott, D. and Law, J. (2023) *The Role of Empathy in Police Contact with Young People from Disadvantaged Backgrounds: (Policing Young Care-Experienced and LGBTQI+ People)*. SIPR.

Moore, J. (n.d.) *A brief history of the British police (Part 1 – Up to 1800)*. https://abolitionistfutures.com/latest-news/a-brief-history-of-british-policing-part-one-up-to-1800

Murray, K. (2014) *Stop and Search in Scotland: An Evaluation of Police Practice*. SCCJR. https://www.sccjr.ac.uk/wp-content/uploads/2014/01/Stop_and_Search_in_Scotland1.pdf

Murray, K. (2015a) *Stop and Search in Scotland: A Post Reform Overview – Scrutiny and Accountability*. SCCJR.
Murray, K. (2015b) *The Proactive Turn: Stop and Search in Scotland (A Study in Elite Power)*. PhD thesis, University of Edinburgh.
Murray, K. and Harkin, D. (2017) Policing in cool and hot climates: Legitimacy, power and the rise and fall of mass stop and search in Scotland. *British Journal of Criminology* 57(4): 885–905.
O'Neill, M. and Aston, E. (2018) Changing stop and search in Scotland. *European Journal of Policing Studies* 5(4): 129–154.
Phillips, J. (2023). Strategic injustice and the 1984–85 miners' strike in Scotland. Industrial Law Journal, 52(2): 283–311.
Police Investigations and Review Commissioner (PIRC) (2023) *Annual Report & Accounts 2022/23*. PIRC.
Police Scotland (2023) *New Chief Sets Out Her Vision for Policing*. Police Scotland. Available at: https://www.scotland.police.uk/what-s-happening/news/2023/november/new-chief-sets-out-her-vision-for-policing/
Police Scotland (2024) *Three-Year Business Plan 2024–27*. Police Scotland.
Police Scotland and Scottish Police Authority (2017) *Policing 2026: Our 10 Year Strategy for Policing in Scotland*. Police Scotland and SPA.
Scott, K.B. (2011) Politics and the police in Scotland: the impact of devolution. *Crime, Law and Social Change* 55(2–3): 121–132.
Scottish Government (2009) *The Scottish Community Policing Engagement Principles*. The Scottish Government.
Scottish Government (2021) Scottish *Crime and Justice Survey 2019/20: Main Findings*. Scottish Government.
Scottish Government (2023) *Ethnicity in the Justice System*. Scottish Government.
Scottish Government (2025) *Multi-Agency Partnership Approach to Distress: Framework for Collaboration*. Scottish Government.
Scottish National Party (SNP) (2007) *Manifesto 2007*. SNP.
Scottish Police Authority (SPA) (2014) *Scrutiny Review – Police Scotland's Stop and Search Policy and Practice. Final Report and Recommendations* – May 2014. SPA. Archived via https://web.archive.org/web/20160307044501/https://www.spa.police.uk/assets/126884/230479/scrutinytaskgroupreport
Skinns, L. and Wooff, A. (2021) Pain in police detention: A critical point in the 'penal painscape'? *Policing and Society* 31(3): 245–262.
Smith, R. (2010) Policing the changing landscape of rural crime: A case study from Scotland. *International Journal of Police Science & Management* 12(3): 373–387.
Sobande, F. and Hill, L.-R. (2022) *Black Oot Here: Black Lives in Scotland*. Bloomsbury.
Souhami, A. (2014) Institutional racism and police reform: an empirical critique. *Policing and Society* 24(1): 1–21.
Souhami, A. (2020) Understanding Police Work in the Remote Northern isles of Scotland: The Extraordinary Ordinariness of Island Policing (August 13, 2020). Edinburgh School of Law Research Paper No. 2020/17, Available at https://dx.doi.org/10.2139/ssrn.3673425
Souhami, A. (2023) Weather, light and darkness in remote island policing: Expanding the horizons of the criminological imagination. *British Journal of Criminology* 63(3): 634–650.

SPA (2022) *Fact Sheet 8: Public Confidence in Policing*. SPA. https://www.spa.police.uk/spa-media/m0pdt4dp/public-confidence-survey-factsheet-11-july-2022.pdf

SPA (2023) *Independent Custody Visiting Scheme Scotland: Annual Report 2022–23*. SPA. https://www.spa.police.uk/spa-media/fdxjt5nj/icvs-annual-report-2022-23-final-v3.pdf

SPA (2024) *Forensic Services Performance Report,* Q3 2023/4. SPA. https://www.spa.police.uk/spa-media/xwhftisi/item-3-2-ppt20240108-forensic-services-performance-report-merged-final.pdf

Terpstra, J., Fyfe, N.R. and Salet, R. (2019) The abstract police: A conceptual exploration of unintended changes of police organisations. *The Police Journal* 92(4): 339–359.

Thomson, A.B., Eales, S., McAllister, E. and Molodynski, A. (2022) Criminal sanctions for suicidality in the 21st Century UK. *The British Journal of Psychiatry* 221(5): 653–654.

Walker, N. (2000) *Policing in a Changing Constitutional Order*. Sweet & Maxwell.

Wooff, A. (2017) 'Soft' policing in rural Scotland. *Policing: A Journal of Policy and Practice* 11(2): 123–131.

Wooff, A. (2024) Police custody in rural Scotland: Negotiating boundaries, risk and organisational change. *Policing: An International Journal* 47(3): 407–419.

4 Courts, prosecution and sentencing in Scotland

Key ideas

- Scots law (including criminal law) is separate from that of other UK jurisdictions. The Scottish system is largely adversarial and based on common law, but with some elements of European-style civil law systems.
- Unlike in England and Wales, trained legal professionals (not lay magistrates) hear all but the most minor cases.
- Scotland has its own independent public prosecutor (the Crown Office and Procurator Fiscal Service), with considerable discretion in prosecuting crime.
- In recent years, prosecutors have increasingly imposed alternative sanctions on accused people, to resolve the case quickly without going to trial.
- Concerns about low conviction rates for sexual offences have led to significant controversy about two distinctive features of Scottish criminal trials: the rule of corroboration and the 'not proven' verdict.

Introduction

This chapter focuses on the role of the courts in the criminal justice system. However, before we begin it is worth pointing out that criminal trials are only part of the business of courts – much of their activity is taken up with civil litigation, which covers disputes between private individuals (e.g. divorce proceedings, part of family law). This chapter starts with some background to the historical development of Scots criminal law, which continues to influence the practices and procedures taking place in Scottish criminal courts today. It then outlines the current court structure within Scotland, introducing the different court types and judicial roles, and discussing arrangements for appeals and types of specialist courts. This chapter then moves step by step through the court process, picking up where Chapter 3 left off, when the case first comes before prosecutors, and taking you through to sentencing and appeals. Along the way, it will introduce you to key players in this process and their roles, along with important debates and developments affecting Scottish courts. Criminal courts have important roles across the

DOI: 10.4324/9781003372882-4

justice system – specific sentences are covered in Chapters 5–8, and Chapter 10 discusses the role of the court in setting licence conditions.

4.1 A brief history of Scots criminal law

Reflecting their distinct national histories, Scots law has evolved separately from English law. Following the Treaty of Union in 1707, the English "**common law**" system played a much greater influence on Scots law, but Scotland has retained more **continental** influence, and is often described as a **"mixed" legal system** (see Clark and Keegan, 2012 for more on Scots law's distinct historical development). Scottish criminal law today is still largely a common law system (as in other English-speaking countries, due to its spread through colonisation).

In such systems, most offences are not defined in written legislation enacted by parliament ('**statute**'). Instead, they are established by "**common law**" – the law of the land, as determined by previous court judgments and recorded in prior cases. Many crimes such as theft, assault and murder are common law crimes. Reliance on past court decisions can support consistency, but feminist legal writers have highlighted how this can also support the continuity of a 'status quo' carried over from past times with different social attitudes and where certain segments of society's views and interests (thinking intersectionally about gender, race, class and cis/hetero-normativity) have dominated legal decision-making (these ideas are explored in the Feminist Legal Judgments Project – Cowan et al., 2019).

Constitutional changes have had important consequences for Scots law and the Scottish courts. Following the Treaty of Union, Scottish courts retained their autonomy. With the UK Parliament more focused on English affairs, the Scottish judiciary were left with greater discretion, playing a more active and creative role in determining the evolution of the law and blurring the lines between law-interpreter and law-maker (Cowan et al., 2019). Following devolution in 1999, the Scottish Parliament took (back) responsibility for many areas of legislation in Scotland, including most criminal law and justice, although not – increasingly controversially (see Box 1.1) – legislation around 'the misuse of drugs'. In preparation for devolution, the 1995 Criminal Procedure (Scotland) Act was passed, consolidating much of the criminal procedure developed over the previous decades into a single large and complex Act that continues to underpin much of Scottish criminal justice.

While many crimes in Scotland remain 'common law' crimes, since devolution there has been substantial growth in legislation ('statute'), introducing a wide range of 'statutory offences' to respond to new problems or capture actions previously covered in common law. The legislative role of the Scottish Parliament has also reduced the requirement for judicial involvement in creatively interpreting the law (Cowan et al., 2019). As with other areas discussed in this book, the post-devolution politicisation of crime and justice has arguably furthered a process of 'detartanisation' through closer alignment with policies pursued internationally in response to a public clamour for law and order (Tata, 2010). Furthermore, since the Human Rights Act 1998, Scottish courts must consider judgments made in the European Court of Human Rights (Section 11.1.3). As Cowan et al. argue (2019), "The potential consequence of [all] this is that the distinctiveness of Scots law might, somewhat ironically, be increasingly diluted post-devolution" (p. 23).

Having discussed the development of Scottish criminal law, we turn now to the institutions and procedures involved in implementing it, beginning with the criminal courts.

4.2 Key agencies

4.2.1 Overview of courts in Scotland

Table 4.1 Overview of criminal courts in Scotland

Court (procedure)	*Presiding official*	*Jury?*	*Types of case*	*Sentencing powers*
High Court of Justiciary (Solemn)	Lord Justice General, Lord Commissioners of the Judiciary	Yes	Murder, rape, treason, other serious crimes; (1% of trials in Scotland) Appeals from Sheriff (solemn) and High Court	Unlimited fine, any community sentence, up to life imprisonment
Sheriff Appeal Court	Appeal Sheriffs	No	Appeals from Sheriff/JP courts (summary)	n/a
Sheriff (Solemn)	Sheriff	Yes	More serious crimes except murder, rape and treason (about 6% of trials)	Unlimited fine, any community sentence, up to 5 years' imprisonment
Sheriff (summary)	Sheriff/Summary Sheriff	No	Less serious criminal offences (about 70% of trials)	Fine up to £10,000, any community sentence, up to 1 year's imprisonment
Justice of the Peace (summary)	Justice of the Peace	No	Driving offences, shoplifting, breach of the peace (about 20% of trials)	Fine up to £2,500, limited community sentences, up to 60 days' imprisonment

There are three main types of criminal court in Scotland: the High Court, Sheriff Courts and Justice of the Peace Courts. **The High Court (of Justiciary)** deals with the most serious cases. It sits in several locations across Scotland, with permanent bases in Edinburgh, Glasgow and Aberdeen. It is presided over by the Lord Justice General and the Lord Justice Clerk, with other full-time judges known as Lord Commissioners of the Judiciary.

Most criminal cases are heard at the **Sheriff Courts**, presided over by a Sheriff (usually assigned to a specific court) who acts as judge in a wide range of civil and criminal cases (Figure 4.1). Scotland is divided into six Sheriffdoms for the administration of justice (Courts Reform (Scotland) Act 2014), each headed by a Sheriff Principal.

Overwhelmingly, criminal cases are dealt with under what is known as '**summary**' procedure, in which the Sheriff decides the verdict alone. Summary cases can also be heard by Summary Sheriffs, who have more limited powers. Sheriff Courts can also hear cases under **solemn** procedure, in which a jury is charged with determining the verdict (see Section 4.3.6). Unlike in England and Wales, the accused cannot choose a trial by jury – this is the prosecutor's decision. Sheriff Courts deal with cases approximately equivalent to the Crown Court and top end of the magistrates' courts of England and Wales.

Both Sheriffs and Summary Sheriffs have formal legal training and are at least ten years post-legal qualification. This is in marked contrast to England

Figure 4.1 Edinburgh Sheriff Court and Justice of the Peace Court.

and Wales – where most cases are heard by volunteer 'lay magistrates'. In line with Northern Ireland and increasingly elsewhere in the commonwealth, Scotland's judiciary is now almost entirely professionalised.

The only courts remaining within Scotland presided over by volunteer 'lay' members of the judiciary are the lowest tier court, **Justice of the Peace (JP) courts** – although JPs may still have a legal background or other relevant experience.

Appeals are discussed in Section 4.3.8. Unlike other UK jurisdictions, the Scottish High Court's decisions in criminal cases are not generally subject to review by the UK Supreme Court. Exceptions are where cases raise 'devolution issues' – i.e. whether the Scottish Parliament had the power to make relevant laws – or where there are human rights concerns (as with Cadder v HMA, discussed in Section 3.3.2).

There are also specialist courts in Scotland, focused on particular problems or types of offending and generally sitting within Sheriff Courts. Domestic abuse courts, focused on supporting complainers, have been piloted in Edinburgh and Livingston. Other specialist courts employ a 'problem-solving' approach originating in the USA, in which offending is understood as resulting from a specific problem which can be addressed through interdisciplinary monitoring and partnership working under the court's direction (Tata, 2013). These include the Glasgow Drug Court which opened in 2001 and uses the Drug Treatment and Testing Order (DTTO, Section 6.1.3) alongside a personalised approach to supervise the treatment of people with dependent drug use.

Research on specialist and problem-solving courts suggests some evidence of positive benefits, in terms of process, satisfaction and outcomes, although more research is needed (Eunson et al., 2018). Potential issues include their limited geographical scope risking a "postcode lottery". If people in different parts of Scotland get different criminal justice responses, this is at odds with supposed liberal ideas of 'blind justice' and equality of outcomes. More fundamental critiques of the model relate to the way in which narratives of health and therapy are deployed to justify coercion by the criminal justice system (Tiger, 2012; see Section 2.3).

4.2.2 Other key players, stakeholders and bodies

There are several other important stakeholders and bodies in criminal trials.

Perhaps most important is the **Crown Office and Procurator Fiscal Service (COPFS** – often known as 'the Crown Office'), Scotland's public prosecution service. It is roughly equivalent to the English/Welsh Crown Prosecution Service (CPS) founded in 1986, but Scotland has a much longer history of independent public prosecution. A Scottish prosecutor is known as a **Procurator Fiscal** (sometimes abbreviated 'fiscal' or 'PF'), who oversees a group of Depute Procurators Fiscal. COPFS is headed by the Lord Advocate, who has overall responsibility for the system and sets prosecution policy (Wolffe,

2017), assisted by the Solicitor General; both are senior legal professionals who are also appointed as Ministers of the Scottish Government. As with other ministers, they are held to account through the Scottish Parliament and scrutiny mechanisms such as the Justice Committee, but the activities of COPFS, and the Lord Advocate as its head, are also scrutinised through **HM Inspectorate of Prosecution in Scotland (IPS)**.

People accused of a crime have the right to a legal defence (including legal advice while in custody – see Chapter 3). This is provided by private solicitors' firms (sometimes called '**defence agents**'). They advise the accused and aim to ensure their legal rights are protected. In the pretrial and trial stages, defence solicitors present the accused's plea, present evidence for the accused and challenge the Crown's evidence (including by cross-examining witnesses). While some people can afford to pay for their own defence, most use **legal aid** – public funds that cover much (but not always all) of the cost. Legal aid in Scotland is run by the **Scottish Legal Aid Board (SLAB)** (see Section 4.3.4).

The **Scottish Courts and Tribunals Service** provides administrative support to the courts and judiciary; another important body, the Scottish Sentencing Council, is discussed below.

4.3 Process and procedure

We now follow the criminal justice process through the courts, starting with the pre-court stage, through the prosecution process, to sentencing and appeal (Figure 4.2).

4.3.1 *Charging decisions, entering a plea and plea bargaining*

When the police charge someone (Section 3.3), they refer the case to COPFS, who decide whether to prosecute them. This begins with '**Initial Case Processing**' (often called '**marking**') in which the prosecutor decides whether and how the case should proceed (Gormley, 2022). They decide whether there is sufficient evidence to take further action, assessing its credibility, reliability, and admissibility in court (Wolffe, 2017). They may sometimes instruct further investigation before deciding (a **"pre-petition investigation"**). They also decide whether prosecution is in the public interest.

Prosecutors make other important decisions, such as which initial charges should be brought against the person. For example, for a particular incident, the prosecutor might decide whether a person should be charged with assault, assault to injury, severe injury or to danger of life, or even attempted murder. This decision is not wholly objective, involving both consideration and interpretation of the evidence. Decisions regarding which and how many charges to bring can have significant consequences for the accused – affecting the type of criminal procedure (summary or solemn) and the eventual sentence. The prosecutor may also influence the court's decision about the

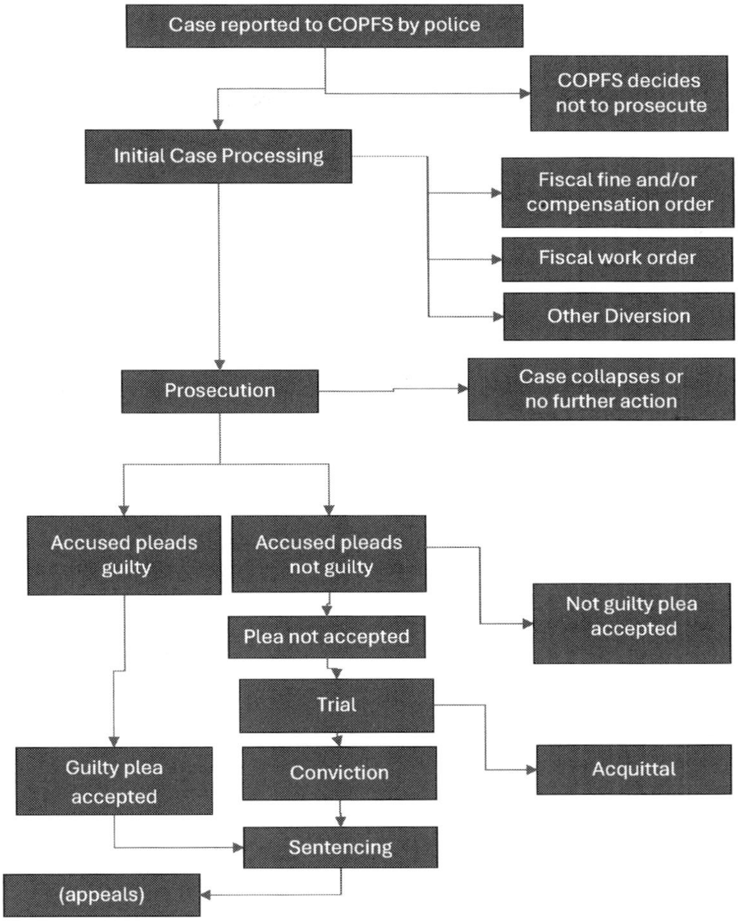

Figure 4.2 A diagram of the prosecution and court process.

person's liberty while they await trial, for example by requesting that the person should be remanded into custody (see Chapter 8). In making these decisions, the prosecutor uses guidelines but is believed to have considerable discretion. Remarkably little is known about prosecutorial decision-making, with researchers highlighting a surprising and alarming lack of transparency from COPFS (Gormley, 2022).

The issue of prosecutorial discretion was brought to public attention in the decisions not to prosecute the driver in the fatal 2014 Glasgow bin lorry accident, or the police officers involved in the death of Sheku Bayoh (see Chapter 3), alongside concerns about low prosecution rates for sexual offences.

The Victims and Witnesses (Scotland) Act 2014 introduced **the Victims' Right to Review (VRR)** of a decision not to prosecute, in force since 2015.

This can only be requested where COPFS has not accepted a plea or used an alternative to prosecution. Another prosecutor (independent from the original decision but within COPFS) carries out the review. The VRR can lead to decisions being overturned if incorrect factors were considered, or the decision was unreasonable – but the bar is high, requiring that "the decision was so unreasonable that no reasonable prosecutor would have made it" (HM Inspectorate of Prosecution in Scotland, 2018: 10). Sheku Bayoh's family requested a VRR which upheld the original decision (Inquest, 2019 and see Box 3.1). The VRR decision is final, with no right of appeal – and although Sheku Bayoh's death is the subject of an independent Inquiry, its terms of reference exclude the decision not to prosecute and the VRR.

4.3.2 *Alternatives to prosecution*

If prosecutors decide that prosecution is not in the public interest, they may simply stop proceedings ('No Action' accounts for about a quarter of 'non-court disposals' in 2023–24, COPFS, 2024) or offer what is known as a 'direct measure' (distinct from those used by the police – Section 5.1.1). This isn't a conviction, but still entails a penalty – most commonly financial: **the fiscal fine** (see Chapter 5).

Alternatives to prosecution were expanded significantly by reforms under the 2007 Criminal Proceedings etc. (Reform) (Scotland) Act, known as 'Summary Justice Reform' (SJR). These were intended to speed up the progress of cases through the system, particularly those tried under summary procedure. SJR created JP Courts to replace the old District Courts, as well as **the fiscal work order**, another direct measure allowing prosecutors to impose 10–50 hours of unpaid work.

SJR was designed to reduce costs by dealing with more cases early on through financial penalties, expanding the use of financial out-of-court disposals (see Section 5.1.2). The emphasis was not on justice but efficiency – the smooth processing of cases by and through the system (McCallum, 2009). As with other managerialist justice reforms, these raise concerns about the appropriate balance between efficiency and due process.

Diversion can also occur into a range of alternative interventions, intended to provide a swift, person-centred response to prevent reoffending (Wolffe, 2017). Purported benefits include support to address issues while avoiding unnecessary criminal justice contact and the stigma of a conviction and criminal record – and saving the system the cost of a prosecution and trial. The person may be provided with tailored interventions, including advice, support, offence-focused work, mediation, restorative approaches and referral to other agencies. Engagement with the intervention is ostensibly 'voluntary', but the alternative is frequently prosecution; however, the person doesn't have to accept guilt to take part. The decision to prosecute is usually deferred (i.e. put on hold) to establish whether the person successfully completes the intervention (usually within three months). The person could in theory still participate – even successfully – and be prosecuted anyway.

Diversion from prosecution has grown significantly with little scrutiny or public awareness. People subject to diversion are in a sense still punished, without the legal rights (including legal aid) entailed in a court trial (Padfield and Tata, 2023). Between 2019 and 2024, the number of diversion cases commenced by social work has risen, with 3,400 cases commenced in 2023–24 (Scottish Government, 2024), predominantly with younger people (16- and 17-year-olds, and to a lesser extent 18- to 20-year-olds).

There are however concerns that such interventions remain underused in some instances. Despite calls for a non-criminalising public health response for people with drug use problems (see Box 1.1), for this group, the practice termed "diversion" in Scotland is frequently a misnomer since interventions often occur *alongside* (not instead of) prosecution, for example through community sentences (see Chapter 6) (Price et al., 2021).

It is important to bear in mind the number of cases that leave the system at every stage. Even where prosecutors *do* decide to prosecute, it is common for them to drop cases (or 'No Further Action'), when (for instance) an important witness, or the accused, can no longer be found. We turn now however to the next stage of the prosecution process.

4.3.3 *Prosecution in court*

The accused must plead 'guilty' or 'not guilty' to each charge. Many cases do not go to trial, but are resolved through a guilty plea, or if the judge/Sheriff or prosecution decide not to proceed. As elsewhere in the UK, a high volume of cases has led to explicit attempts by policymakers to encourage guilty pleas and avoid long and costly processes, especially jury trials: requiring prosecution evidence to be disclosed to the defence in advance of the trial (to demonstrate the likelihood of conviction if the case went to trial); promoting the *expectation* of a discount (i.e. reduction) in sentence for early guilty pleas (Gormley and Tata, 2024); and changes to how defence lawyers are paid, intended to encourage them to encourage their clients to plead guilty, or at least plead guilty earlier than they otherwise would (Tata, 2007).

Most accused people plead guilty. However, this may not necessarily be because they are – particularly given the anxiety of the process, power differentials between accused people and legal professionals (including the defence), and the self-fulfilling expectation of guilty pleas by efficiency-driven court processes (Padfield and Tata, 2023).

This raises serious questions about the consequences for justice and for the presumption of innocence supposedly at the heart of the system. There is little research on prosecutorial decision-making, but Gormley (2022) suggests that accused people and defence lawyers perceive that COPFS routinely add extra charges with a view to dropping them, as part of negotiations to obtain a guilty plea ('charge bargaining', a form of plea bargaining). Rather than increasing efficiency, this may create *new* inefficiencies, as defence lawyers and accused people, who might otherwise have pleaded guilty promptly, feel obliged to negotiate, introducing costly delays (Gormley, 2022).

Unlike in some other jurisdictions, there is no explicit bargaining between the accused and the prosecutor over the sentence *length*, and accused people are not informed in advance of the maximum sentence they will get if they plead guilty (Gormley, 2022). Nevertheless, alongside charge bargaining, 'implicit sentence bargaining' (Tata, 2010: 202) exists, in that people can expect (although may not always get) a discount for a guilty plea, with an early guilty plea resulting in a discount of up to one-third (Gormley, 2022).

It can take many months for the case to go to trial, during which the judge/Sheriff may decide that the person should be held in prison ('remanded in custody'), released into the community with conditions ('bailed'), or without conditions ('ordained' to appear at a later date). The probability of remand is much greater under solemn than under summary procedure, and where someone has previously breached bail conditions (Scottish Government, 2022a). In recent years there has been controversy over high numbers of people on remand, exacerbated by court delays associated with the COVID-19 pandemic. In May 2024, the remand population reached a new record high of 2,360 people (28% of the prison population, previously reaching 30% in May 2023), the vast majority of them untried (JAS, 2023; 2024). This is even more egregious given the high proportion of those remanded who do not then receive a custodial sentence (57% in summary proceedings, 29% in solemn), calling into question whether they should have been remanded at all (Justice Committee, 2018). The Bail and Release from Custody (Scotland) Act 2023 was passed with the intention of addressing this issue; among other things, it will reframe the test in deciding bail to give the accused (in most cases) the right to bail unless there is good reason for refusal; and require courts to record reasons for denying bail (its impact remains to be seen). However, it leaves room for discretion which may limit its impact. Remand is discussed further in Chapter 8.

4.3.4 *The adversarial model and going to trial*

Scotland is generally regarded as having an '**adversarial**' (sometimes called '**accusatorial**') legal system. Such systems attempt to secure justice by making the trial a battle between two opposing parties: the prosecution (acting on behalf of the state, not the victim), and the defence (on behalf of the accused). This differs from 'inquisitorial' systems seen within continental models, where the emphasis is on discovering the truth (see Nicolson, 2019). The adversarial approach is reflected in the convention of naming Scottish criminal cases as HMA (for His/Her Majesty's Advocate) v. the accused. During the trial, each party selects the evidence that best supports their case, calling witnesses to testify under oath. The opposing party can cross-examine each witness.

The accused's right to hear evidence against them, and their access to legal representation in criminal proceedings, have a long history in Scots law. This has been further safeguarded through Article 6 of the European Convention on Human Rights (ECHR), the right to a fair trial. Among other things, this makes clear that the accused should receive free legal assistance for their defence (if unable to pay for this) "when the interests of justice so require". In Scotland, this is funded through a system of 'legal aid', administered by the Scottish Legal Aid Board, but there is longstanding concern from defence lawyers that legal aid is inadequate and that this threatens the right to an adequate defence and hence a fair trial (Law Society of Scotland, 2022). Changes to *how* legal aid is paid (block payments rather than hourly rates) may reduce contact between defence lawyers and their clients without necessarily speeding up cases (Tata, 2007; Gormley and Tata, 2024).

To prove its case, the prosecution must prove the person's guilt 'beyond reasonable doubt' – known as the '**standard of proof**'. Importantly, the 'burden of proof' is on the prosecution – the defence does *not* need to prove the person's innocence, just show that the prosecution's evidence does not meet the standard of proof. Sometimes, the defence may not need to present evidence at all, if the prosecution evidence is so poor that the court considers there is 'no case to answer'. However, the prosecution has advantages of their own, not least greater resources for investigation and greater credibility with the judge/jury – despite the official presumption of innocence (Nicolson, 2019). The legal aid funding crisis also means prosecution lawyers are paid comparatively at higher rates than defence lawyers. These inequalities raise important questions about access to justice.

It is worth briefly noting the arrangements in place for what are known as 'mentally disordered offenders'. It is not uncommon for people involved in the criminal justice system to experience mental health problems or mental distress. For a small number of people, their state of mind will prevent them from participating effectively in a trial. In such cases, an 'Examination of Facts' is used instead of a trial (with different disposals available to the court) to determine whether the person committed the offence.

Even where someone *is* deemed fit to stand trial, their state of mind at the time of the offence may mean they can plead – and be found – not guilty, due to "a lack of criminal responsibility due to a mental disorder" (formerly called the "insanity defence"). This 'special defence' applies if, at the time of the incident, the person was unable "to appreciate the nature or wrongfulness of the conduct". For murder cases, where the impact of the mental disorder is considerable but insufficient for the mental disorder defence, the defence can make a plea in mitigation of 'diminished responsibility'. If successful, this reduces the conviction from murder to culpable homicide (similar to 'manslaughter' elsewhere). Initially introduced in Scotland and then later imported to England, diminished responsibility can be used "if the person's ability to determine or control conduct" was – at the time – "substantially impaired by reason of abnormality of mind". In this case, the person is not acquitted – diminished responsibility is only a 'partial defence' – but the downgrading of the offence opens the way to different sentences and mental health disposals.

These defences are reserved for those whose poor mental health is seen as directly contributing to their conduct and are only rarely used successfully, despite the relatively high levels of mental health problems among those in the criminal justice system (see Forrester and Hopkin 2019).

4.3.5 *Victims and witnesses in the court process*

A key driver of recent criminal procedure reform in Scotland has been political pressure and the will to improve the experience and outcomes for victims (known in legal procedure as 'complainers') and vulnerable witnesses. The Vulnerable Witnesses (Scotland) Act 2004 widened the legal definition of a 'vulnerable witness' and outlined an expanded range of special measures that could be implemented to support them to give evidence. These provisions have been expanded through the Victims and Witnesses (Scotland) Act 2014, which created new rights for victims and witnesses such as the right to information about their case, communicated in forms they understand, and the right to give evidence in a closed court (HM Inspectorate of Prosecution in Scotland, 2017). It also specifically defined victims of sexual offences, domestic abuse, trafficking and stalking as vulnerable, automatically entitling them to some special measures. Subsequent research found that although these measures were broadly welcomed by victim-survivors, they were not always well-explained or understood, despite them having to make important decisions on this information (IPS, 2017; Brooks-Hay et al., 2019). The Vulnerable Witnesses (Criminal Evidence) (Scotland) Act 2019 was intended to significantly increase the use of pre-recorded evidence.

A related driver of change to criminal justice procedure has been concern about the response to incidents of sexual violence (Burman and Brindley, 2021), which – unlike wider recorded crime trends – have been increasing in number. Not only is the conviction rate for such cases problematically low (compared to other crimes) but the court process has also been repeatedly described by victim-survivors as adding to their distress. Brooks-Hay et al. (2019) report that even where their case resulted in a conviction, victim-survivors rarely believed 'justice' had been achieved, with issues reported throughout the process including delays, being subject to hostile cross-examination and poor communication (HM Inspectorate of Prosecution Scotland, 2017). Perhaps unsurprisingly, victims frequently withdraw from the process before its conclusion.

Following Lord Justice Clerk Lady Dorrian's 2021 review into the management of sexual offence cases, the latest proposed addition to the raft of Scottish legislation on victims and witnesses – the Victims, Witnesses and Justice Reform Bill – would introduce the right to anonymity for complainers in sexual offence cases (as in England), some access to legal support, require the court to be 'trauma-informed' (minimising re-traumatisation) and create a national specialist sexual offences court with trained personnel and expanded pre-recording of complainants' evidence. A controversial proposal to pilot judge-only trials for rape in Scotland was ultimately dropped due to a lack of cross-party support.

The desire to improve conviction outcomes for sexual violence victim-survivors, among other groups, fuelled high-profile debates in the lead-up to the Bill around two unique features of Scottish criminal procedure – 'the rule of corroboration' (see Box 4.1) and the 'not proven' verdict (Section 4.3.6).

Box 4.1 Corroboration and sexual offences

The rule of **corroboration** is complex, but: "[t]he basic principle [...] is that an accused cannot be convicted of a crime, unless the essential facts of the crime are able to be established by evidence from at least two independent sources" (Scottish Government, 2021: 28). The aim of this is to safeguard against wrongful convictions.

This means that one witness's testimony – however credible – is never enough to convict. This presents obvious problems for crimes like sexual assault or domestic abuse, which usually occur in private. Appeal Court judgments have resulted in changes to how the corroboration rule should be interpreted, which have gone some small way to lessen its effects. Notably, these judgments have removed an effective time limit on which evidence of signs of distress from the victim about the incident can act as corroboration (previously limited to the immediate aftermath of the event). Additionally, the Moorov doctrine means that witnesses to different but sufficiently similar events (e.g. two victims of similar assaults) can corroborate each other, obviating the need for two witnesses to one event. Nevertheless, corroboration remains a "significant hurdle for the prosecution to overcome" (IPS, 2017: 4), and contributes to victim-survivor perceptions that the system is not designed in their interests (Brooks-Hay et al., 2019).

These concerns led Lord Carloway's 2011 review to recommend abolishing the rule. This proposal was taken forward by the Scottish Government in the Criminal Justice (Scotland) Bill 2013 (later the 2016 Act), but dropped following strong opposition from the legal profession (Maclennan, 2016), who highlighted its role as a safeguard against wrongful conviction. The corroboration rule was once again subject to consultation in 2021, and despite recommendations to reform or remove the rule from academics and advocacy groups (Brooks-Hay et al., 2019; Burman and Brindley, 2021), this unique feature of Scots criminal law has once again survived.

Questions for discussion

- What do you think would be the implications of abolishing corroboration: for victims, the accused, the system itself?
- What do you think should happen to the rule of corroboration?

4.3.6 *The jury and the verdicts*

Scottish juries are used in a tiny minority of trials but have been at the centre of several legal and policy debates. They are large, by international standards – 15 rather than 12 people. Unusually, they have historically had three possible verdicts available to them: **Not Guilty, Not Proven** and **Guilty** (see Chalmers and Leverick, 2017). The first two verdicts result in acquittal, while the third is a finding of guilt.

Repeated government consultation (most recently in December 2021) has considered abolishing 'not proven', bringing Scotland in line with other English-speaking jurisdictions. The verdict's precise meaning is unclear, and its distinction from 'Not Guilty' is hard, if not impossible, to articulate. Controversy has centred less on its legal meaning than on how it is understood by those involved in the trial, especially juries.

Groups advocating for both victims and accused argue that the verdict gives juries an opportunity to 'hedge their bets', producing an outcome which pleases no one. For victims, it offers little in the way of justice, being functionally indistinguishable from 'not guilty'. 65% of respondents to the 2021 consultation agreed that the "not proven verdict can cause particular trauma to victims of crime and their families" (Scottish Government, 2022b). 'Not proven' is disproportionately reached by juries in rape cases (Burman and Brindley, 2021), possibly because they wish to convict, but see the evidence as insufficient (see Box 4.1). 'Not proven' arguably also leaves the accused in limbo – acquitted, but with a shadow over their name which they have no legal means of clearing (Scottish Government, 2022b).

A second unusual aspect of Scottish criminal procedure is the requirement of only a **simple majority** of the 15 jurors for conviction (i.e. 8 of 15). This in theory makes conviction more likely than a unanimous decision or '**qualified majority**' (i.e. a specified higher proportion of the jury being required to vote for conviction). Given this relatively low threshold, some legal professionals argue that the 'not proven' verdict should be retained as a safeguard against wrongful conviction (Curley et al., 2021); however, most consultation respondents supported some form of 'qualified majority' instead.

The Not Proven verdict appears to have met the end of the road. Following a concerted campaign by organisations including Rape Crisis Scotland and political support, the Victims, Witnesses, and Justice Reform (Scotland) Bill included abolishing this verdict and replacing the simple majority with a qualified majority (likely to be two-thirds required for conviction). If and when this Bill passes, a number of distinct features of the Scottish system may therefore be removed and a long-running debate relegated to history.

These debates reflect important concerns about how to balance the interests of victims with the accused's rights, and avoid the very severe consequences posed by wrongful convictions. We will return to these issues later, after discussing sentencing.

4.3.7 Sentencing

Around 90% of criminal trials result in a conviction; this most commonly follows a guilty plea rather than a fully contested trial. Excluding any appeal, the final stage of the court process is sentencing, which happens at a hearing called the 'sentencing diet'. The sentence received by the person is determined by the type of court and procedure (see Table 4.1), and a range of processes and practices undertaken by various professionals – some of which inform or limit the sentencer's (Sheriff's, judge's or JP's) decision, while others affect how that sentence is carried out (such as when someone is released from prison) (Tata, 2020).

Velasquez Valenzuela's (2018) research describes Sheriffs using a two-stage process for sentencing. The first stage is to review the facts of the case as outlined in the papers and narrow down the range of possible outcomes, by considering the relative seriousness of the offence type and the law surrounding sentencing of this type of offence. In the Sheriff Court, relevant legislation might include mandatory maximums for certain statutory offences, the 'Presumption Against Short Sentences' (see Box 4.2), as well as limits based on court and procedure (see Table 4.1). The second stage is the 'individualisation' of punishment, in which the Sheriff considers the details of the particular case (both the offence and the person being sentenced). This stage starts with a review of the papers, alongside a report by the Justice Social Worker. This report is perceived as extensive, but in many cases, a less extensive but faster 'same day report' (orally or in writing) might be provided instead (Tata, 2020: 75–117). The second stage continues into the sentencing diet, as the Sheriff listens to the fiscal's presentation of the facts of the case and possibly a 'plea in mitigation' in which the defence can lay out any mitigating circumstances (reasons for applying a less severe sentence).

It is important to recognise sentencing as a social practice, as much as a legal decision (Hutton, 2006; Tata, 2020). The decision has been described as holistic and intuitive, so that, at least in routine cases, sentencers sense intuitively the 'right' decision and work *backwards* to the justification.

In trying to maintain an 'independent' 'objective' stance, sentencers attempt to take account of victims without being overly influenced by them (Millie et al., 2007), and to minimise the impact of their own emotions on decision-making (Jamieson, 2021). Unlike in some continental systems, where being a judge is a professional career path in its own right, in Scotland, people become judges/Sheriffs following years as a practising lawyer. This may help give them a sense of what decisions are appropriate (Hutton, 2006; Velasquez Valenzuela, 2018) and act as a brake on discretion. However, it is another factor in maintaining a status quo, inherently influenced by the predominantly white, cis male and middle-class perspective which still dominates the profession (Cowan et al., 2019).

As well as an (early) guilty plea, other important factors in determining the sentencing outcome include case seriousness, the criminal history of the person being sentenced, their past compliance with sentences (multiple breaches of community penalties can increase the likelihood of a prison sentence) and – at least in cases on the 'borderline' between a community and custodial sentence – the personal circumstances of the person being sentenced (Millie et al., 2007). Research suggests that in making their decision, some Sheriffs prioritise the circumstances of the *offence*, while others prioritise the circumstances of *the person being sentenced* (Velasquez Valenzuela, 2018). Sheriffs in small or rural areas may also be influenced by how far behaviours are viewed as troublesome for local communities (Velasquez Valenzuela, 2018).

Box 4.2 The Presumption Against Short Sentences

The 2010 Criminal Justice and Licensing (Scotland) Act enacted various reforms intended to reduce imprisonment. As well as streamlining community penalties and creating the Scottish Sentencing Council (Section 4.3.7), it introduced a presumption against prison sentences of three months or less (the **Presumption Against Short Sentences**, or **PASS**). The law does not ban short prison sentences but requires sentencers to impose them only if no other sentence would do, and to give their reasons.

PASS was conceived in light of evidence showing that short sentences damage prisoners' links to families and communities, but without sufficient time for prison-based programmes (e.g. education or drug treatment). It was also thought that the offences which attracted these sentences could be appropriately (and more efficiently) dealt with by a community sentence.

Although PASS brought a sharp fall in sentences of 0–3 months, this was accompanied by a rise in sentences of 3–6 months, suggesting its initial effect was simply to make some prison sentences longer, not reduce imprisonment. Since then, there has been a slight fall in short prison sentences but this is probably attributable partly to changes in prosecution practices. Despite limited evidence of positive impact (Roberts and Tipple, 2019), PASS was extended in 2019 to sentences of less than 12 months. Its effect has been less than hoped for; as we write, Scotland's prisons are once again in an overcrowding crisis (Section 8.3.1).

Even before PASS, the 1995 Criminal Procedure (Scotland) Act (s.204) had already set out that prison was only to be used where "no other method of dealing with [the person] is appropriate". Evidence suggests that when sentencers impose short prison sentences, it is for repeated low-level offending and where there have already been multiple previous breaches of community sentences (Velasquez Valenzuela, 2018).

PASS cannot in itself address this. Arguably, this approach to reducing imprisonment also misses more significant drivers of the prison population, particularly remand and life sentences – and falls prey to systemic issues around community penalties (Section 6.2.4).

Questions for discussion

- What approach should be taken to people who repeatedly breach community penalties, but whose offences are not serious enough to attract a longer prison sentence?

The **Scottish Sentencing Council (SSC)** was established in 2015 (despite controversy around its implications for judicial independence) by the Criminal Justice and Licensing (Scotland) Act 2010 to promote consistency in sentencing practice, assist sentencing policy development and improve awareness of sentencing policy and practice. The SSC prepare guidelines for sentencing. These are presented for approval by the High Court of Justiciary, who can accept, reject or modify them. The first guideline, approved in October 2018, set out 'The Principles and Purposes of Sentencing' in Scotland (see Box 4.3).

Sentencing councils which produce guidelines exist in other jurisdictions. Unlike England and Wales where guidelines are binding, Scottish courts must only 'have regard to' guidelines and outline the reasons if these are not followed. The SSC is developing a series of guidelines on specific offences and groups, including a guideline on sentencing young people (approved November 2021). This guideline proved controversial in 2023 when a judge imposed a community sentence on a 21-year-old (17 at the time of the offence) for a rape against a 13-year-old. COPFS decided to appeal the sentence as 'unduly lenient' (although the conviction was ultimately overturned altogether due to misdirection from the judge to the jury on the issue of corroboration, see Box 4.1).

Box 4.3 The Principles and Purposes of Sentencing

What are we as a society – and the court on our behalf – trying to achieve by sentencing someone? In its guideline 'The Principles and Purposes of Sentencing', the Scottish Sentencing Council (2018) set out the following 'purposes':

- **Protection** of the public – prevention (**incapacitation**) and **deterrence**.
- **Punishment** – infliction of loss (not necessarily through prison) (i.e. **retribution**).

- **Rehabilitation** – reducing risk of offending and providing opportunity to change.
- Making amends – **reparation** of harm caused to victims and communities.
- Expressing society's disapproval (i.e. **denunciation**).

The different purposes are linked to philosophical (and sociological) debates regarding how punishment can be justified in a liberal democratic society, given that it involves the infliction of 'loss' or 'pain' on a person by the state. Although not explicit within the guideline, the second of these purposes – 'punishment' – is linked to the idea that the infliction of loss/pain can be justified, in **retribution** for the loss/pain inflicted on others through the offence to (somehow) balance pain/loss with further pain/loss (sometimes captured by the phrase 'eye for an eye'). The fourth of these purposes 'making amends' focuses on the harm caused by the offence, but prioritises trying to repair this harm rather than infliction of loss/pain on the person being punished (although this may happen as a side-effect of the reparation). The link from punishment back to crime is also contained within the principle of 'proportionality'.

Conversely, the first and third of these purposes are concerned less with proportionality than with reducing further harm in the future – they are **reductivist**. These link to utilitarian philosophical ideas which argue that society should seek the greatest good for the greatest number of people and that this justifies the pain of punishment. There is a paucity of evidence for, even counterevidence to, many reductivist claims (e.g. high reoffending rates). The final purpose of sentencing – expressing society's disapproval – is linked more to sociological theories of punishment, particularly the work of Durkheim (1893) who interpreted punishment as communicative, a means by which society can convey its values to others and to its members, setting out the kind of society it is and what it will tolerate. For an extended discussion on the justifications for punishment and challenges to these, see Cavadino and Dignan (2013).

Sociologists have challenged the idea that we can understand the purposes of punishment in society in purely philosophical terms. Instead, those seeking to understand punishment have been encouraged to think about punishment beyond particular cases, thinking instead about its wider social functions (as Durkheim has), the history of punishment, and how punishment contributes to maintaining the social order (including racial and class hierarchies) (Garland, 1990). When we look at the inequalities in who actually gets punished (disproportionately young working-class men, and people of colour) then perhaps we should question the narrow terms on which the debate is framed and ask is this really a fair system at all? (Fassin, 2018).

Questions for discussion

- Can you think of situations where these sentencing purposes might come into conflict with each other?
- In your view, how (if at all) can punishment be justified and what purposes (if any) are the most important?
- Which factors could explain the fact that some social groups in society experience a lot more punishment than other groups?

Conversely, the experience in England and Wales indicates that caution is needed to ensure guidelines do not inadvertently *increase* the punitiveness of sentencing. Some Magistrates in England and Wales have argued that the introduction of their guidelines had an inflationary effect on sentencing, increasing the numbers of people sent to prison and the length of sentences (Millie et al., 2007). However, increases in life sentence minimum tariffs have occurred in Scotland even without rigid guidelines (see Section 8.3.2).

4.3.8 Appeals and miscarriages of justice

In many cases, the convicted person might be unhappy with the verdict, and in some cases, they can appeal. They might think they should not have been found guilty, or think the sentence was too harsh. The prosecutor can also appeal the sentence if they think it was too lenient, but cannot usually appeal an acquittal. The victim has no right to appeal (SSC, n.d.)

The convicted person (through their lawyer) must apply to the court for permission to appeal. The relevant appeal court depends on where the case was originally heard, and the procedure used (see Table 4.1). It decides whether there are 'arguable grounds' for an appeal. Most appeals are against sentences, and these are more likely to be 'sustained' (SCTS, 2024) – meaning the court agrees with at least some grounds of the appeal. Following a successful appeal, the verdict might be overturned, another trial ordered, or the sentence changed. In 2023/24, there were 923 appeals registered, 18% of which were sustained (SCTS, 2024). Of these, only 8% involved an appeal against conviction, amounting to approximately 13 people who successfully appealed against conviction that year.

Despite features of the Scottish system (and adversarial systems generally) which are intended to prevent wrongful conviction, miscarriages of justice can and do occur. Innocent people are convicted of crimes in Scotland and are subject to state-sanctioned punishment, including sometimes lengthy periods of imprisonment. A notable example is that, by February 2025, at least

64 Scottish people had been exonerated after the Horizon Post Office IT scandal (BBC News, 2025). The central role of the Crown Office in Scottish justice arguably should have prevented this (in contrast to England, where the Post Office could prosecute privately).

For those whose appeal is unsuccessful, the only remaining option is to apply for a review of the case by the **Scottish Criminal Cases Review Commission (SCCRC)**. The SCCRC can refer a case to the High Court where they believe a 'miscarriage of justice' may have occurred, and it is in the interests of justice to refer the case. In 2006, Billy Allison and Steven Johnston had their murder conviction quashed, with the High Court finding that Fife police "suppressed and altered evidence", for which the Detective Inspector leading the investigation was ultimately imprisoned (Billy Allison & Steven Johnston v. HMA).

However, SCCRC referrals to the High Court are rare. Out of 177 applications received by the SCCRC in 2023/4, only 32 were accepted for review, and only four were referred to the High Court (SCCRC, 2024). Even then, only some subsequent appeals succeed. Even where the Appeal court views the verdict as unsatisfactory, it is not their role to substitute the jury's view of the evidence with their own, unless new evidence has come to light or the verdict is one which no reasonable jury, properly directed, could have reached (Sinclair, 2005). From the establishment of the SCCRC in 1999, up until the end of March 2024, only 161 cases were referred to the High Court, and of the 159 where an outcome had been determined, the conviction was quashed or the sentence reduced in only 96 cases (SCCRC, 2024). Some wrongful convictions may never be overturned.

There are profound consequences for those who are wrongfully convicted, including imprisonment and associated pains, problems re-adjusting back into the community, and impacts on the person's personality, mental health, relationships, finances and employment prospects, persisting even after exoneration (Brooks and Greenberg, 2021). Despite this, only some people are eligible for compensation after wrongful conviction and/or imprisonment. A response by the Scottish Government to a Freedom of Information request reported that from 2000 to the end of March 2019, only 19 people had been paid compensation for a miscarriage of justice (amounting to £12 million in total), 17 of whom had spent time in prison as a result (on average just over 8 years) (Scottish Government, 2019).

Conclusion

Scots law and criminal procedure have a unique and long history; although closer alignment with the English system occurred after the Treaty of Union, Scots criminal law remained distinct. However, as with other areas of criminal justice, Scottish criminal procedure has arguably undergone 'detartanisation' in the years since devolution, with distinct features being lost or, at least, diluted, though there may be an element of nostalgia in this (Tata, 2010).

Supposed detartanisation has been attributed to the politicisation of criminal justice following its devolution to the Scottish Parliament, bringing Scotland in line with international punitive trends.

Looking forward, there are a number of recent and planned changes affecting distinctively Scottish features of the system. Some have been the subject of particular and interrelated controversy: proposed reforms to the simple majority and abolition of the 'not proven' verdict – as well as ongoing debate about the rule of corroboration. Proposed reforms have been driven by political pressure to improve the process for victims and witnesses, especially in sexual and domestic violence cases. In sentencing, there are also some relatively new introductions, notably the Presumption Against Short Sentences reforms. It is important to be attuned to the particular procedures, practices and legislation that apply in Scottish courts, despite an apparent shift towards alignment with other common law jurisdictions.

We have also touched on the pressures for efficiency in criminal trials and their implications for justice. These pressures were heightened by the COVID-19 pandemic and lockdown, which created a backlog of cases (peaking at over 40,000 trials), taking several years to clear (Audit Scotland, 2023).

The criminal justice process needs to carefully balance the rights of the accused and the victim, and avoid perpetrating further harm to either. The serious enduring consequences of wrongful conviction highlight what's at stake in this difficult but critical challenge. Creating a very high evidential threshold for conviction (e.g. through corroboration and demonstrating the case 'beyond reasonable doubt') has been deemed necessary to avoid punishing innocent people – but as we have seen, even with this supposedly high evidential threshold, miscarriages of justice can and do occur.

This chapter has not explored the critical issue of potential ethnic, gender and class disparities in the process and outcomes. Research from other jurisdictions (Lammy, 2017) suggests disparities may exist, but understanding these dynamics in Scotland is hampered by a woeful lack of data. With regard to ethnicity for example, the limited data there is, has been collected for operational and not research purposes, and analyses of differences in outcomes between groups have not accounted for well-known factors such as age, seriousness of offence, or offence history, making them of very limited use (Scottish Government, 2023). Improving the quality of data and the research in this area is vital for scrutiny of the system and for questions of social – as well as criminal – justice.

Ensuring the process facilitates a just outcome is clearly harder within a society where power and resources are not equally distributed (determining access to the most expensive defence lawyers/experts, whose testimony is given the greatest weight, and the ability to influence the formation of criminal laws in the first place) and where groups are subject to different cultural expectations regarding their behaviour and different choices in the first place. Additionally, the approach of the court is to consider a criminal case as a decontextualised incidence of harm: they look at what happened in this event and try to crystallise a complex set of human actions and interactions down into a verdict: guilty, not guilty or (until removed by legislation) not proven. In labelling the person as guilty, this complexity can be erased – and little consideration is given to the harms they have experienced over the course of their life (which may be far greater). The adversarial process also contributes to the social construction of crime by placing victims opposite the accused (or 'offender'). It is however important to bear in mind the very large overlap between the two groups; the reality of offending is often less clear-cut than it may seem.

For these reasons and more, some groups have suggested that criminal courts are always going to be limited in the extent to which they can really facilitate meaningful justice. This has encouraged some people to look for new ways of responding to harm, which eschews traditional criminal justice procedures, for example, restorative and, more radically, transformative justice processes. These are beyond the scope of this book, but now that you have a better understanding of the criminal justice process, we hope you will explore these in your future studies (see for example Kim, 2021). Subsequent chapters will discuss the different sentences that the court could impose, starting with financial penalties.

Critical questions

- Most trials in Scotland can be viewed by the public, so we suggest you attend a trial or sentencing at your local Sheriff Court. (Make sure you check the rules for attending before you go). Afterwards, think about your experience – was there anything you found interesting or surprising?
- Courts have been described as a site in which crime and justice are socially constructed – can you suggest any examples of how this happens?
- Many of the reforms discussed here aim to make trials more efficient, by diverting cases away from trial and by encouraging people to plead guilty. Can you identify the implications of this for justice, both for complainers/victims-survivors and the accused?
- What are the advantages and disadvantages of alternatives to prosecution, for the parties in the case and for the justice system itself?
- Do you think that increasing rates of prosecution and conviction is necessarily the best way to achieve justice for victim-survivors of sexual offences?

Key resources

Brooks-Hay, O., Burman, M. and Bradley, L. (2019) Justice Journeys: Informing policy and practice through lived experience of victim-survivors of rape and serious sexual assault. SCCJR. https://www.sccjr.ac.uk/wp-content/uploads/2019/08/Justice-Journeys-Report_Aug-2019_FINAL.pdf

This research gives insights into the criminal justice process, including through courts, for victim-survivors of sexual assaults.

Gormley, J. (2022) The inefficiency of plea bargaining. *Journal of Law and Society* 49(2): 277–293.

A useful critical overview of the impact of 'efficiency' pressures on prosecutorial decision-making.

Legislation.gov.uk. https://www.legislation.gov.uk/

An essential website for looking up legislation across the UK, although not always quickly updated.

Nicolson, D. (2019) *Evidence and Proof in Scotland: Context and Critique.* Edinburgh University Press – especially Chapter 4 'The sociological context: Truth, justice and institutional practices'. Pp.127–177.

This book considers how evidence and proof in court processes are not just legal issues, but must be understood in the context of learning from sociology, philosophy and psychology.

Scottish Courts and Tribunals Service website. https://www.scotcourts.gov.uk/

An overview of the work of SCTS, including the various courts and their roles.

Scottish Government. *Criminal Proceedings in Scotland.* https://www.gov.scot/collections/criminal-proceedings-in-scotland/

Reports of the annual Criminal Proceedings in Scotland series, which provide a useful overview of sentencing and other criminal procedure statistics.

Scottish Sentencing Council. https://www.scottishsentencingcouncil.org.uk/

Full of useful resources to help you understand sentencing in Scotland.

Tata, C. (2020) *Sentencing: A Social Process: Re-thinking Research and Policy.* Palgrave Macmillan.

Jamieson, F. (2021). Judicial independence: The master narrative in sentencing practice. *Criminology & Criminal Justice* 21(2): 133–150.

Velásquez-Valenzuela, J. (2024) Sentencing individuals on cusp-cases: The use of offenders' backgrounds by Scottish Sheriffs. *The Howard Journal of Crime and Justice* 63: 304–320.

Three important contributions on sentencing in Scotland.

References

Audit Scotland (2023) *Criminal Courts Backlog.* Audit Scotland. https://www.audit-scotland.gov.uk/publications/criminal-courts-backlog

Billy Allison and Steven Johnston v. Her Majesty's Advocate. [2006] HCJAC 30.

BBC News (2025) We're giving Horizon compensation claims kick up the backside, 2 April 2025. https://www.bbc.co.uk/news/articles/c3r8xq10jqpo

Brooks, S.K. and Greenberg, N. (2021) Psychological impact of being wrongfully accused of criminal offences: A systematic literature review. *Medicine, Science and the Law* 61(1): 44–54.

Brooks-Hay, O., Burman, M. and Bradley, L. (2019) *Justice Journeys: Informing Policy and Practice through Lived Experience of Victim-Survivors of Rape and Serious Sexual Assault – Final Report.* Scottish Centre for Crime and Justice Research.

Burman, M. and Brindley, S. (2021) Challenges in the investigation and prosecution of rape and serious sexual offences in Scotland. In Killean, R., Dowds, E. and McAlinden, A.- M. (eds) *Sexual Violence on Trial: Local and Comparative Perspectives.* Routledge. 199–211

Cavadino, M. and Dignan, J. (2013) The Penal System: An Introduction. Sage.
Chalmers, J. and Leverick, F. (2017) No, 'not proven' did not come first. *Scottish Legal.* https://www.scottishlegal.com/articles/blog-no-not-proven-did-not-come-first
Clark, B. and Keegan, G. (2012) *Scottish Legal System Essentials.* Third edition. Edinburgh University Press.
Cowan, S. (2019) Sense and sensibilities: A feminist critique of legal interventions against sexual violence. *Edinburgh Law Review* 23(1): 22–51.
Cowan, S., Kennedy, C. and Munro, V.E. (eds) (2019) *Scottish Feminist Judgments: (Re)creating Law from the Outside in.* Bloomsbury Publishing Plc.
Crown Office and Procurator Fiscal Service (COPFS) (2024) *COPFS Statistics on Case Processing in the Last 5 Years (2019–24).* COPFS. https://www.copfs.gov.uk/publications/case-processing-statistics-2019-to-2024/html/
Curley, L.J., Munro, J., Frumkin, L.A. and Turner, J. (2021) Informing reform: The views of legal professionals on the unique aspects of Scottish Law. *Medicine, Science and the Law* 61(4): 256–265.
Durkheim, E. (1893) *The Division of Labour in Society.* Macmillan.
Eunson, J., Murray, L., Graham, H., Malloch, M. and McIvor, G. (2018) *Review of the Aberdeen Problem-Solving Approach.* Scottish Government.
Fassin, D. (ed) (2018) *The Will to Punish.* Oxford University Press.
Forrester, A. and Hopkin, G. (2019) Mental health in the criminal justice system: A pathways approach to service and research design. *Criminal Behaviour and Mental Health* 29(4): 207–217.
Garland, D. (1990) *Punishment and Modern Society: A Study in Social Theory.* OUP.
Gormley, J. (2022) The inefficiency of plea bargaining. *Journal of Law and Society* 49(2): 277–293.
Gormley, J. and Tata, C. (2024) Guilty pleas, sentencing and sentence 'discounting': who is 'sentence discounting' really for? In Langer, M., McConville, M. and Marsh, L. (eds) *Research Handbook on Plea Bargaining and Criminal Justice.* Edward Elgar. 264–277.
HM Inspectorate of Prosecution in Scotland (IPS) (2017) *Thematic Review of the Investigation and Prosecution of Sexual Crimes.* Inspectorate of Prosecution in Scotland.
HM Inspectorate of Prosecution in Scotland (2018) *Victims' Right to Review: Report, Complaints Handling and Feedback: Follow-Up.* Inspectorate of Prosecution in Scotland.
Hutton, N. (2006) Sentencing as a social practice. In Armstrong, S. and McAra, L. (eds) *Perspectives on Punishment: The Contours of Control.* Oxford University Press. 155–174.
Inquest (2019) *Lord Advocate Confirms Decision Not to Bring Charges against Police Scotland Officers Involved [in] Death of Sheku Bayoh.* https://www.inquest.org.uk/sheku-bayoh-crown-review
Jamieson, F. (2021). Judicial independence: The master narrative in sentencing practice. *Criminology & Criminal Justice* 21(2): 133–150.
Scottish Government Justice Analytical Services (JAS) (2023) *Justice Analytical Services (JAS) Safer Communities and Justice Statistics Monthly Data Report.* June 2023 Edition. Scottish Government.
Scottish Government Justice Analytical Services (JAS) (2024) *Justice Analytical Services (JAS) Safer Communities and Justice Statistics Monthly Data Report.* June 2024 Edition. Scottish Government.

Justice Committee (2018) *An Inquiry into the Use of Remand in Scotland*. SP Paper 363. Scottish Parliament. https://bprcdn.parliament.scot/published/J/2018/6/24/An-Inquiry-into-the-Use-of-Remand-in-Scotland/JS052018R07.pdf

Kim, M.E. (2021) Transformative justice and restorative justice: Gender-based violence and alternative visions of justice in the United States. *International Review of Victimology* 27(2): 162–172.

Lammy, D. (2017) *The Lammy Review an Independent Review into the Treatment of, and Outcomes for, Black, Asian and Minority Ethnic Individuals in the Criminal Justice System*. Ministry of Justice.

Law Society of Scotland (2022) *Law Society Backs Call for Urgent Reform to Legal Aid System*. https://www.lawscot.org.uk/news-and-events/law-society-news/law-society-backs-call-for-urgent-reform-to-legal-aid-system/

Maclennan, S. (2016) Safer and stronger? The decline of managerial competence and liberal welfarism in ustice policy. *Scottish Affairs* 25(1): 62–82.

McCallum, F. (2009) *SPICe Briefing: Summary Criminal Justice Reform*. https://archive2021.parliament.scot/Research%20briefings%20and%20fact%20sheets/SB09-84.pdf

Millie, A., Tombs, J. and Hough, M. (2007) Borderline sentencing: A comparison of sentencers' decision making in England and Wales, and Scotland. *Criminology and Criminal Justice* 7(3): 243–267.

Nicolson, D. (2019) *Evidence and Proof in Scotland: Context and Critique*. Edinburgh University Press.

Padfield, N. and Tata, C. (2023) Understanding penal decision-making: courts, sentencing, and parole. In Liebling, A., Maruna, S. and McNeill, F. (eds) *The Oxford Handbook of Criminology* 7th edition. Oxford University Press. 676–697.

Price, T., Parkes, T. and Malloch, M. (2021) 'Discursive struggles' between criminal justice sanctions and health interventions for people who use drugs: A qualitative exploration of diversion policy and practice in Scotland. *Drugs: Education, Prevention and Policy* 28(2): 118–126.

Roberts, M. and Tipple, C. (2019) *What could England and Wales Learn from Scotland's Approach to Justice? A Study of the Impact of a Presumption Against Custodial Sentences of Three Months or Less in Scotland*. Crest Advisory.

Scottish Courts and Tribunals Service (SCTS) (2024) *Courts Data Scotland: Criminal (Edition 24) Annual Bulletin*. SCTS.

Scottish Criminal Cases Review Commission (SCCRC) (2024) *Annual Report*. https://irp.cdn-website.com/8f56052e/files/uploaded/2023_SCCRC_annual_report_6_%28FINAL%29_web.pdf

Scottish Government (2019) *Wrongly convicted awarded compensation payments: FOI release*. FOI/201900000824. https://www.gov.scot/publications/foi-201900000824/

Scottish Government (2021) *The Not Proven Verdict and Related Reforms: Consultation*. Scottish Government.

Scottish Government (2022a) *Occasional Paper: Remand and Bail Outcomes at First Bail Decision Points in Sheriff Courts*. Scottish Government.

Scottish Government (2022b) *The Not Proven Verdict and Related Reforms: Analysis of Responses to Consultation*. Scottish Government.

Scottish Government (2023) *Occasional Paper: Analysis of the Ethnicity of Individuals Subject to Hearings in Scottish courts*. Scottish Government. https://www.gov.

scot/publications/analysis-ethnicity-individuals-subject-hearings-scottish-courts/documents/

Scottish Government (2024) *Justice Social Work Statistics in Scotland: 2023–24 – Part 1*. Scottish Government. https://www.gov.scot/publications/justice-social-work-statistics-scotland-2023-24-part-1/.

Scottish Sentencing Council (SSC) (n.d.). *Disposals and Appeals*. Scottish Sentencing Council. https://www.scottishsentencingcouncil.org.uk/sentencing-information/disposals-and-appeals

Scottish Sentencing Council (SSC) (2018) *Principles and Purposes of Sentencing: Sentencing Guideline*. Scottish Sentencing Council. https://www.scottishsentencingcouncil.org.uk/media/1964/guideline-principles-and-purposes-of-sentencing.pdf?wrap=true&view=plain

Sinclair, G. (2005) Miscarriages of justice. *Journal of the Law Society of Scotland* 50(8). https://www.lawscot.org.uk/members/journal/issues/vol-50-issue-08/miscarriages-of-justice/

Tata, C. (2007) In the interests of clients or commerce? Legal aid, supply, demand, and 'ethical indeterminacy' in criminal defence work. *Journal of Law and Society* 34(4): 411–659.

Tata, C. (2010) Sentencing and penal decision-making: Is Scotland losing its distinctive character? In Croall, H., Mooney, G. and Munro, M. (eds) *Criminal Justice in Scotland*. Willan. 195–215

Tata, C. (2013) Beyond the revolving court door: Is it time for problem-solving courts in Scotland? *Scottish Justice Matters* 1(1): 17–18.

Tata, C. (2020) *Sentencing: A Social Process: Re-Thinking Research and Policy*. Palgrave Macmillan.

Tiger, R. (2012) *Judging Addicts: Drug Courts and Coercion in the Justice System*. NYU Press.

Velasquez Valenzuela, J. (2018) *Doing Justice: Sentencing Practices in Scottish Sheriff Courts*. PhD thesis, University of Glasgow.

Wolffe, J. (2017) *Prosecution in the Public Interest. Apex Scotland Annual Lecture*, 5 September 2017. https://www.apexscotland.org.uk/wp-content/uploads/2014/07/apex_annual_lecture_2017.pdf

5 Fines and financial penalties in Scotland

Key ideas

- Financial penalties are the most common sentence in Scotland as in many other jurisdictions, but are little discussed even by criminologists.
- Scotland makes especially extensive use of these penalties at various stages of the criminal justice process: by the police, by prosecution and at sentence.
- Financial punishment is inherently problematic given high economic inequality and what is known about the impacts of criminal justice on the poorest members of society.
- For much of the 20th century, Scotland was characterised by a very high rate of imprisonment for fine default. While this is now rare, it has been replaced by an increasing interconnection of fine enforcement with agencies of the welfare state, notably through deductions from benefits.

Introduction

We sometimes refer to punishment as people 'paying the price' for their offence, and the majority of offending is punished by financial means. This chapter focuses on financial penalties – requiring a person or business to pay a sum of money as a penalty for an offence. Properly speaking, the fine is only one of a complex range of financial penalties, but the term 'fines' is often used informally to apply to all such penalties.

Compared to imprisonment and community penalties (Chapters 6 and 8), financial penalties have an extremely long history. They appear in some of the earliest legal texts (Einat, 2014) and may be nearly as old as corporal and capital punishment. In medieval Scotland, 'assythment' was a payment for causing death, payable to the victim's family; 'spuilzie' (pronounced 'spooly') was compensation for property crimes. These were effectively civil remedies, in an era before civil and criminal litigation were generally understood as separate (Munro, 2016).

Financial penalties levied by criminal justice continue to sit alongside the widespread use of court-imposed payments in **civil law** cases (e.g. damages for defamation). Our focus is on the former, but the boundary is sometimes

DOI: 10.4324/9781003372882-5

blurred – and some of the most harmful acts tend to attract civil as opposed to criminal penalties.

Financial penalties have been described as an 'ideal' classical or neoclassical penalty – allowing the punishment to be tailored to the crime and the circumstances of the person being punished, and optimally suited to a capitalist society in which the movement of money is central to social life (O'Malley, 2009). The harm done in any miscarriage of justice is easier to repair – a wrongfully imposed fine can be repaid (although not the experience of financial hardship), unlike years of freedom lost to wrongful imprisonment. However, financial penalties are problematic in a society characterised by high economic inequality and an ongoing cost-of-living crisis.

This chapter outlines the various ways in which the criminal justice system can levy financial punishments – as **Fixed Penalty Notices** (FPNs) usually issued by police, **alternatives to prosecution** issued by the Crown Office, and as sentences passed down by courts, as well as the use of civil measures to confiscate money in organised crime cases. We discuss critical issues for financial penalties – their disproportionate impact on those with the least ability to pay and their intersection with other criminal justice and welfare agencies. Despite their widespread use, fines remain relatively under-studied compared to other penalties.

5.1 Financial penalties in the criminal justice system

Widespread use of the term 'fine' to refer to all financial penalties hides the fact that there are various types of financial penalty, which can be imposed by police, prosecutors and courts; we discuss each of these here.

5.1.1 Policing and fixed penalty notices

FPNs are a range of 'on the spot' financial penalties usually imposed by the police. Timely payment avoids prosecution and a probable conviction and criminal record. Failure to pay quickly leads to the fine being increased and, potentially, prosecution (see Section 4.3). The intention is to offer a quick deterrent against minor offending, which avoids the expense and difficulty of a trial, conviction and criminal record (though FPNs may be recorded by police). The effect is that those with resources to pay quickly can escape criminalisation and harsher punishment.

Someone issued with an FPN can reject it (effectively 'pleading not guilty') but this may require going to court and could result in the FPN being re-imposed plus court costs. The police may also withdraw the FPN e.g. if information is found to be incorrect. Both scenarios are very rare. In about a quarter of cases, the person pays the FPN promptly.

Police FPNs were initially developed for driving offences, especially speeding. As part of the wider 'antisocial behaviour' agenda (Chapter 2), the 2004 Antisocial Behaviour Act created the **Anti-Social Behaviour Fixed Penalty Notice (ASBFPN)** (Murray et al., 2024). ASBFPNs are currently set at £50 and usually imposed for breach of the peace and public drinking. As the antisocial behaviour agenda declined, the number of ASBFPNs decreased from a peak of 56,000 in 2013/14 to approximately 5,000 in 2021–22 (Scottish Government, 2023a). Other influences on this decline include the introduction of Recorded Police Warnings and wider controversies around Scottish policing (Chapter 3; Murray et al., 2024).

During the COVID-19 pandemic, the UK government and those of the devolved nations used a new regime of FPNs to enforce lockdown restrictions, resulting in considerable controversy. **COVID FPNs** were intended as a last resort following attempts at securing voluntary compliance. In Scotland, they were imposed in a relatively small proportion (12%) of COVID-related interactions, but once the respective *populations* are considered, Scottish police were apparently more willing to use FPNs than their English counterparts (McVie et al., 2023), especially in and around Glasgow (Gorton et al., 2022). There was concern about discriminatory impacts against certain groups (see Section 5.2.1); as with other financial punishments, the impact of FPNs was inevitably unequal given people's differing ability to pay. When senior UK politicians were issued FPNs for holding parties that breached their own restrictions ('Partygate'), they paid the same flat fee as the poorest citizens (Murray et al., 2024). Another controversy was the increasing level of the fine in England, although in Scotland it was reduced.

Figure 5.1 A sign warning dog owners about FPNs.

FPNs can also be issued for littering and dog fouling (set at £80, increasing to £100 if not paid quickly, Figure 5.1), payable to local authorities and enforced by community safety staff (see Chapter 2) and police. FPNs for fly-tipping (dumping rubbish) are higher, set at £500. However, Freedom of Information requests to local authorities suggest these FPNs are rarely issued and even more rarely enforced (Tibbitt, 2019). Finally, some **specialist reporting agencies** such as the Scottish Environment Protection Agency (SEPA) and Trading Standards have their own regimes of fixed penalties, with the potential for prosecution if unpaid. These exemplify the pervasiveness of financial punishment – and its complex roles in criminal justice.

5.1.2 Prosecution, summary justice and out-of-court disposals

Financial penalties can also be issued after arrest but before going to court, as an out-of-court disposal, almost always in cases subject to summary procedure (see Section 4.2.1).

Most prominent of these are '**fiscal fines**' – fixed fines issued by prosecutors. These were expanded significantly following Summary Justice Reform (Section 4.3.2), which switched them from an opt-in to an opt-out model – so a person offered a fiscal fine, who does not explicitly reject it, is assumed to have accepted it. The reforms also introduced a new financial out-of-court penalty, the **compensation offer** – similar to a fiscal fine, except that the payment goes to the victim (in fact, the *alleged* victim, since the offer is made without going to court). Compensation imposed at this stage works on the same scale as fines imposed at conviction (see below), so can go up to £5,000. Fiscals can also make a 'combined offer' of both fiscal fine and compensation offer.

Fiscal fines were previously fixed at £300. Legislation during the COVID pandemic replaced this with a scale from £50 to £500, to ease pressure on courts by allowing prosecutors to divert a wider range of cases. This increase has been extended and in late 2024, consideration was given to making it permanent. Summary justice reform and fiscal fines raise issues for due process, since (as with other alternatives to prosecution – see Section 4.3.2), people who may be innocent are incentivised to accept the fine and avoid a trial. It is also unclear how (or whether) these out-of-court disposals are calibrated to be proportional to the person's income (Padfield and Tata, 2023).

The Crown Office may also issue **Crown Office Fixed Penalties (COFPs or Fiscal Fixed Penalties)** for driving offences, most commonly speeding. These are distinct from other out-of-court disposals and from police FPNs, although with similar consequences– a fine and/or points on the driver's licence. Through direct measures at the police and prosecution stage, most road traffic offences do not come to court, although those which do usually result in conviction (speeding has the highest conviction rate in Scotland, at 98%).

5.1.3 *In court: fines and compensation orders*

At conviction, financial penalties are the most common sentence, accounting for about 45% of cases (26,705 convictions) in 2021–22 (Scottish Government, 2023a). They are typically imposed for less serious offending such as road traffic offences, theft or minor acts of violence, but can be imposed in a very wide range of cases. The court can sentence someone to a **fine** (paid to the court) and/or a **compensation order** (which goes to the victim). Compensation orders are distinct from the rarely used compensation requirement in Community Payback Orders (CPOs – see Chapter 6); although infrequently used as a main penalty, they may be imposed alongside a fine (the limited available statistics give no sense of how often this happens).

Fines for statutory offences – those defined in legislation – and tried under summary procedure (see Chapter 4), are set on a scale of 'tiers' from £200 (Level 1) to £5,000 (Level 5) (1995 Criminal Procedure (Scotland) Act, Section 225). The maximum for Justice of the Peace courts is £2,500 (Level 4). The law provides for these to be adjusted for inflation. For **common-law** offences, the maximum fine at summary conviction by a Sheriff Court is £10,000 (known as the 'prescribed sum' in the Act). Under solemn procedure, the Sheriff or High Court can impose unlimited fines. Compensation orders operate on the same system of tiers and limits. The median fine in 2021–22 was £280, while the median compensation order was £300.

The 2014 Victims and Witnesses (Scotland) Act created the '**victim surcharge**'; since 2019 this is added on top of any fine (but not other sentences). The surcharge runs from £10 (for fines up to £200) to 7.5% of the fine (for fines over £5,000). This money is not paid to the victim but into the Victim Surcharge Fund, which is run by the Scottish Government to fund organisations to provide services for victims.

Although financial penalties still account for the largest 'share' of sentences, this has declined drastically – from over half of sentences in 2013–14 and over 80% in the 1980s (McIvor et al., 2013). This decrease is likely due partly to increased use of out-of-court disposals like fiscal fines; another potential factor is that efforts to encourage sentencers to impose more community sentences have led to these being imposed in cases that would previously have attracted fines, rather than (as intended) in cases that would previously have attracted prison sentences (an example of 'up-tariffing').

Box 5.1 Fines of the powerful

As well as being the most common sentence for individuals, fines are one of the main sentences imposed when companies are convicted of crimes. This is distinct from (but may be accompanied by) the punishment of individual employees and the more common use of civil damages or settlements to punish corporate misconduct.

Use of criminal fines against companies is rare. A notable case involved Iraq, then under the authoritarian government of Saddam Hussein. After its invasion of Kuwait (defeated by a US-led coalition in 1991), Iraq was subject to economic sanctions. Although intended to punish the regime and provide reparation to Kuwait, in practice the sanctions inflicted famine and illness on ordinary Iraqis. To mitigate this, the UN established the 'Oil for Food' programme. This allowed Iraq, under UN supervision, to export oil and import food and other humanitarian necessities (but not military equipment) but created significant opportunities for corruption. Companies were expected to pay 'kickbacks' (bribes) to the regime to secure contracts; among these was Scotland's biggest engineering company, Weir Group. Weir Group paid over £3 million in bribes to the Iraqi government between 2000 and 2002; facilitated by an agent who was paid an additional £1.4m, this enabled Weir to secure £35m worth of contracts.

After internal and UK government investigations and significant changes in its corporate structure, the company admitted wrongdoing, pleading guilty at the High Court in 2010. The fine was set at £3m – reduced from £4.5m to reflect the guilty plea and the company's efforts to address the wrongdoing through corporate restructuring. A further £13.9m, thought to account for profits made through bribery, was subject to a confiscation order under proceeds of crime legislation; some went to projects to rebuild Iraq.

The extent and impact of corporate harms is huge, yet criminal penalties like this are extremely rare. As Croall (2016) notes, these harms have an ambiguous criminal status, partly because the powerful can affect whether an activity is criminalised and how cases are dealt with. It may also be difficult to attribute responsibility, either to individuals or to the organisation as a whole. Crimes of the powerful may be investigated not by police, but by specialist reporting agencies (see Chapter 3) with the power, but rarely the resources, to bring criminal prosecutions.

Such cases are often dealt with under civil procedure or by settling out of court. Pragmatically, this enables some measure of recompense and justice while avoiding some of the costs of complex investigations and prosecution. However, the outcome rarely stops the company operating – indeed, fines and damages may be *negotiated* to maintain normal operations. This is particularly relevant for the biggest corporations, whose power and importance mean severe financial penalties against them could have a knock-on effect on wider society (as with banks following the 2008 financial crisis). The Weir Group remains one of Scotland's most successful companies, with a profit after tax of £229m in 2023 (Weir Group, 2023).

This contrasts sharply with the use of financial penalties against individual people, even though the impact of 'conventional' crime is likely far smaller than that of corporate harms (Croall, 2016). These might include not only corruption and complicity in authoritarian regimes but also pollution, deaths in unsafe workplaces, involvement in war (legally and otherwise), (legal) tax avoidance and (illegal) tax evasion.

Questions to consider

- Do you think fines are appropriate for dealing with this sort of case?
- If so, do you think the penalties in this case were appropriate?
- If not, how else could harms like this be dealt with?
- Does the distinction between civil and criminal fines matter in a case like this?

5.1.4 Proceeds of crime

Scottish criminal courts are empowered by the Proceeds of Crime Act 2002 (applying across the UK) to seize the 'proceeds' of crime, where it is established that a convicted person has made considerable financial gains from their offending. The Crown can seek a **confiscation order**, requiring the convicted person to pay a certain amount to the court. This is not exactly a financial penalty, but can be enforced the same way.

Controversially among legal practitioners, there is no requirement that confiscated assets be proven as proceeds of crime. Reversing the usual presumption of innocence, the onus is generally on the convicted person to prove that money is *not* the proceeds of crime. In cases of group or corporate offending, individuals may be charged far more than the crime benefited them personally; the Act also applies a civil standard of proof (balance of probabilities, not beyond reasonable doubt) to otherwise criminal proceedings (Ulph, 2010). Failure to pay a confiscation order can lead to imprisonment, even if the original offence did not. In Scotland, confiscation orders are imposed quite rarely; they tend to be used only in large-scale fraud, trafficking or tax evasion cases. Separately, the Scottish Government may use purely civil measures to recover suspected proceeds of crime – despite the dramatic language of 'seizure', this money is generally paid after a process of legal negotiation.

Advocates of this approach argue that it can support criminal investigation and enable 'disruption' of complex organised crime networks, which may be skilled at hiding or laundering their illegally gained assets (Collins and King, 2013; see Chapter 11). However, that this action can be taken without the usual standards around criminal cases raises questions about due process.

Unlike in England and Wales,[1] money seized as proceeds of crime cannot be used to fund criminal justice activities. However, the 'Cashback for Communities' scheme has operated in Scotland since 2008, distributing £130m of seized money to various community-oriented projects, largely run by charities (but including police-run schemes for young people).

The complex procedural detail largely relates to civil, not criminal law, but demonstrates how financial punishments can blur lines between the two. Now, we return to ordinary criminal fines and how they are enforced.

5.2 Enforcing fines: critical issues

Following Summary Justice Reform in the 2000s (McIvor et al., 2013), the Scottish Courts and Tribunals Service's (SCTS) Fines Enforcement Team is responsible for enforcing all financial penalties in Scotland – FPNs, fiscal fines, fines and compensation orders.

Fines are typically paid in instalments and payment plans can be negotiated with the court. Collection rate data (SCTS, 2024) suggest that most people who are fined cannot pay it off at once, so they must experience financial punishment over a period of months or years. If a person fails to pay, they can have their benefits deducted, their bank account or earnings frozen (known as an 'arrestment order'), or their car seized and sold. SCTS (2024) statistics generally show bank arrestments and benefit deductions each accounting for just under half of enforcement action, with earnings arrestment accounting for most of the remainder. Very rarely, the payment plan may be revised or a Community Payback Order (Chapter 6) issued in place of the fine. Collection rates have been rising slowly but steadily, with the 'three-year collection rate' sitting above 80% for most financial penalties and as high as 90% for Sheriff Court fines (SCTS, 2024); SCTS credits this to expanded use of tracing facilities and the shift to automatic benefits deduction (Section 5.2.3).

5.2.1 Fines, poverty and discrimination

One critical issue of financial punishment is people's (differing) ability to pay. Courts are expected to have regard to the person's financial situation in deciding whether and at what level to impose a financial penalty; measures like 'time to pay' and instalment plans are intended to ensure people can pay without, for instance, losing their tenancy or going without food. However, it is not clear that these measures are sufficient, and consideration has previously been given to a 'unit fine' system (see Box 5.2).

Box 5.2 Unit fines, proportionality and fairness

In some countries, especially in Europe, criminal fines are calibrated to the income of the person being fined. These are known as 'unit fines' or sometimes as 'day fines' (since one way of calibrating them is to fine the person a certain number of days' worth of income). This approach occasionally makes headlines when rich people receive huge fines for minor offences, as in the case of the Finnish businessman Anders Wiklöf, who was fined €121,000 (£104,000) – half his income over 14 days – for speeding (Henley, 2023). Attention here is directed to the disproportionality of the fine, ignoring the income inequality which led to it.

Unit fines supposedly avoid the problems associated with socioeconomic inequalities and financial punishment; rather than the court merely 'having regard to' the person's financial circumstances, the fine could be calibrated exactly to these circumstances and to the offence. However, despite being set proportionally the same, the loss of one day's income is likely to inflict greater financial hardship on someone with a lower income (similar to arguments against a flat tax rate).

In the 1980s, Scotland considered introducing unit fines in response to the high levels of imprisonment for fine default. However, it was noted at that time that "the courts were reluctant to set fines at realistically low levels for offenders on low incomes since this would not have the desired denunciatory effect" (McIvor, 1994: 437–438). The proposal did not attract sufficient political support and the Supervised Attendance Order was developed to deal with fine default instead. The Sentencing Commission for Scotland considered the idea again in 2006 but rejected it, highlighting the issue of disproportionally large fines for minor offences and practical difficulties implementing this (requiring knowledge of the person's financial status) (Warner, 2012). Reductions in imprisonment for fine default have rendered the issue of day fines largely moot.

Questions to consider

- Do you think using unit fines is fair? Why/why not?
- Do you think a system like this should be introduced in Scotland?
- If such a system were introduced, what might the implications be for criminal justice?

International research (e.g. Harris, 2016) suggests that, as with other punishments, fines fall disproportionately on members of marginalised and minoritised social groups. Research conducted during the COVID-19 pandemic offers rare UK insights into this under-studied area. Across England, Wales and Scotland, COVID FPNs were more often issued to younger people, especially men, with significant ethnic disproportionality (McVie et al., 2023). The limited evidence on ethnicity in Scotland's justice system suggests that monetary penalties account for a larger share of sentences among minoritised ethnic groups than white Scottish/British people (Scottish Government, 2023b). However, differences between ethnic groups in sentencing outcomes are not straightforward to interpret, especially with so little evidence (see Chapter 4). While men make up the majority (being far more likely to be arrested, prosecuted and convicted), women make up a larger percentage (17% in 2021–22) of people sentenced to financial penalties, compared to community and custodial sentences (15% and 6%, respectively). This is partly explained by differing patterns of offending; women are far less often convicted of serious or violent offences (Scottish Government, 2023a).

The impact of fines differs across different groups in society. Even if the fine is set at a higher level, those with adequate (or plentiful) resources to pay will be impacted less than those without. Since it is legal to pay a fine on someone's behalf (but not to serve their prison sentence for them; Young, 1999) relationships can become strained as people become indebted to family and friends. Poverty in the UK is increasingly 'feminised', i.e. disproportionately affecting women, so the impact of fines *may* be experienced in different, gendered, ways: for instance, women are more likely to have caring responsibilities and associated financial commitments (e.g. feeding children for whom they are the sole caregiver) which may make them less able to pay fines.

People who come through the criminal justice system are more likely to be experiencing various forms of social and economic deprivation. The consequences of non-payment of fines are serious – but faced with the 'choice' to pay a fine instalment *or* feed one's family, not paying may appear the only option and the 'price' of the original offence may become disproportionate. If a person is driven (further) into poverty by fine payments (particularly if automatically deducted from benefits or earnings), then fines could contribute to *causing* further offending (Barr, 2019: 86–87). This is particularly relevant in the current context of a 'cost-of-living crisis' linked to rapid rises in inflation, increased prices, wage stagnation, precarity and long-term cuts to public services. While penologists highlight the criminal justice system's contribution to the relentless punishment of the poor under capitalism, zemiologists and researchers of corporate crime contrast this with inadequate responses to social harms at the corporate/institutional level (see Box 5.1).

5.2.2 *Fines and criminal justice*

Failure to pay fines, known as **'fine default'**, can lead to higher costs and more punishment. Imprisonment for fine default – in which a (usually) short prison term is substituted for part or all of an unpaid fine – was a serious concern for much of the 20th century in Scotland (Young, 1999), when fine defaulters comprised over half of prison arrivals (though a small proportion of the prison population, since the prison term was usually only a few days). This was problematic since those unable to pay were punished more harshly – with fine defaulters overrepresented among women prisoners – and the cost of imprisoning defaulters was generally many times the original fine amount.

The situation led to the creation of a new community penalty, Supervised Attendance Orders (SAOs), introduced in 1990 and rolled out nationally in 1998. These were described as a 'fine on time' rather than money (McIvor et al., 2013). Imprisonment for fine default decreased, but remained a significant problem until SAOs were made mandatory for most fine default in 2007, restricting courts' ability to use imprisonment. SAOs were later merged into Community Payback Orders (CPOs), but CPOs as a fine default measure have now been almost entirely superseded.

Box 5.3 A Blether with ... Amy Cullen, PhD candidate, University of Glasgow

Can you tell us a bit about your research?

"My thesis title is *Enforcement, Extension and Entanglement: Punishing Non-Payment of Financial Penalties in Scotland*. My project aims to offer a critical account of fines and fines enforcement in contemporary Scotland [...] I'm quite keen to argue that we start understanding it as a *process* rather than a thing, and that we can then have more detailed conversations about how fines can potentially affect and be experienced differently in different contexts.

It's probably no surprise that there's a cyclical element to some of the fines enforcement processes – where a fine's imposed, fines enforcement action follows, and then another fine is imposed, and then more fines enforce enforcement action follows. So in some cases, this really extends the length of time that people are in contact with the criminal legal system. And fundamentally, these methods don't engage with situations where people cannot at baseline afford to pay their fine".

Can you say a bit about how fines might impact on different groups of people differently and how they might be implicated in patterns of inequalities in the UK?

"We don't have that much of a tradition of that kind of [research] work at all. A good example, of course, is women – as it stands, we don't really know if there are gender-specific experiences, outcomes or elements to fining, but in 2021–22, 47% of women sentenced received a financial punishment, so it's far and away the most common. It's striking to me that we know that economic marginalization is a key motivator of women's offending, and we also know that fines and financial penalties are primarily used to respond to types of offences that high numbers of women are typically convicted of, and in many cases these offences are directly linked to forms of economic marginalization.

As we know, shoplifting has been in the news recently for massive increases in shoplifting during the cost-of-living crisis. One of the reasons why fines and financial penalties are so common and prevalent is because fundamentally most offending is not hugely violent or a huge affront to the social order. It's often things like acquisitive crimes, crimes that are linked to addiction or substance misuse. This all sort of shines a light on questions of structural inequality for sure, because we seem very comfortable with the fundamental inequality of fines".

So why do you think it is that fines and other forms of financial penalty are still so under-studied and under-discussed?

"I think there are still a set of assumptions about what it means to get a fine. [...] There seems to be something very taken for granted about fines and financial punishment. Maybe this is a controversial thing to say, but I think some of the taken-for-grantedness has to do with criminology [...] So much theory is dominated by models of punishment that are heavily influenced by imprisonment. I think that if there was perhaps slightly less siloing, we would have a really good chance of creating much more holistic and in some cases accurate accounts of contemporary punishment and potentially coming up with new and sort of radical findings about how the model and the structure works all together".

Listen to the full podcast at https://www.sccjr.ac.uk/project/criminal-justice-in-scotland/ in which Amy talks about her research and gives advice for those thinking about doing a PhD. Amy's SCCJR profile is at *https://www.sccjr.ac.uk/person/amy-cullen/*.

Thanks to restrictions on imprisoning defaulters and the expansion of fiscal fines and measures to collect fines directly, imprisonment for fine default is now extremely rare – but can still occur. Scottish Prison Service statistics refer to 13 fine defaulters released from prison in 2022/23 (see Cullen and Telling, 2021). Additionally, a person with a warrant for unpaid fines may still spend a period in police custody before coming to court, which may be disruptive and punitive out of proportion to the original offence (Amy Cullen, personal communication).

5.2.3 Fines and the welfare state

Despite a somewhat slow start (Clark, 1998), deductions from benefits and directly from bank accounts are now the most common fines enforcement measures. Benefit deductions pose a problem; successive UK governments have shifted away from the comparatively generous and universal benefits of postwar social democracy to a far more limited and conditional provision.

The benefits system is not part of the criminal justice system, but if used to enforce fines, it becomes a(nother) vector by which people are punished – and this system has become increasingly inclined, on its own account, to punish people for things that are *not* crimes.

Most people who claim benefits receive too little to afford even essentials and failure to meet a strict set of conditions (e.g. missing Jobcentre appointments) leads to punitive deductions from benefits (often called 'sanctions') (Adler, 2018). While no evidence exists specifically on the impact of *criminal fine*-related deductions, research on benefit sanctions (Wright and Dwyer, 2022) identified overwhelmingly negative effects including negative impacts on mental and physical wellbeing, financial hardship, debt and rent arrears and fear of eviction.

Some critical voices see these developments as exemplifying a 'shadow carceral state' (Beckett and Murakawa, 2012) or as part of a wider 'criminalisation of social policy' (Kiely and Swirak, 2022). In this analysis, the problem is not just that criminal justice and other agencies are working more closely together, but also that logics of punishment have diffused out from criminal justice and into other areas of the public sector and social life, with people who claim benefits increasingly stigmatised and constructed as suspect. (We note similar arguments about the increasingly criminalised character of immigration in Chapter 11.) Recent developments in Scotland have partly bucked this trend (Kiely and Swirak, 2022: 34–55), but this has been within tight limits resulting from the limited power of the Scottish Government over social security and benefits.

Young's (1999) account of men imprisoned for fine default shows them largely choosing to trade a period of freedom for an amount of money. While harsh relative to the original offence, these terms of imprisonment were usually short. Imprisonment for fine default has been replaced by a range of less apparently punitive but longer-lasting measures, in which the wider public sector (beyond criminal justice) is enlisted in punishing through a complex range of deduction orders and other penalties which can affect people's lives for a great deal longer. The use of benefit deductions to enforce fines may therefore sit uneasily with rhetoric about the progressive and welfare-oriented character of Scotland.

Conclusion

This chapter has discussed the use of financial penalties in Scotland's criminal justice system. As well as being the sentence most commonly imposed by the courts, financial penalties can be issued at all stages of the criminal justice process.

A question not yet touched on in this chapter is whether fines could be said to 'work'. Although reconviction rates fluctuate significantly, the rates for fines are *consistently* lower than for other sentences – around 20%, compared to about 25% for community and around 40% for custodial sentences. Repeat rates of non-court disposals (FPNs and fiscal fines) are lower still, at under 20% (Scottish Government, 2023c). This may however be accounted for by a range of factors other than the fine itself, including the nature of the initial offence.

Fines are generally understood as the least severe form of punishment. Although they may not be experienced as intensively as community penalties or imprisonment, they nonetheless raise questions about due process and about the justice of demanding payments from people who are disproportionately likely to be in conditions of severe deprivation. The next chapter considers the second of the three main types of sentence – community penalties.

Critical questions

- If a person can pay a fine on another person's behalf, what are the potential implications for justice? Would it be possible to ensure that the person being fined is the one who actually pays?
- Thinking about the rationales for punishment (retribution, deterrence, rehabilitation, denunciation, reparation and incapacitation – Box 4.3), which of these can fines fulfil?
- At several points, this chapter refers to financial penalties as muddling the distinction between civil and criminal law and process. How does this happen? Why might it be problematic?
- Do you think it is possible to devise a system of financial punishment which does not impact disproportionately on the poorest members of society?
- If you were carrying out criminological research on fines in Scotland, what would you try to find out? What might your study look like?

Key resources

Courts Data Scotland: Fines (Formerly Known as 'Quarterly Fines Reports'). https://www.scotcourts.gov.uk/about-us/official-statistics/courts-data-scotland-fines-cdsf/

A regular statistical bulletin on the numbers of fines, compensation orders, fiscal fines and FPNs in the Scottish justice system, including data on rates of payment and enforcement measures.

Cullen, A. (2022) *No Longer 'Little Studied': Challenging Criminological Narratives about Financial Punishment.* SCCJR. https://www.sccjr.ac.uk/publication/no-longer-little-studied-challenging-criminological-narratives-about-financial-punishment/

A brief but very recent and relevant report about Scottish financial punishment.

Murray, K., McVie, S., Matthews, B. and Gorton, V. (2024) From parking tickets to the pandemic: Fixed penalty notices, inequity and the regulation of everyday behaviours. *British Journal of Criminology* 64(6): 1310–1327.

An overview of FPNs in the UK, with an emphasis on their use to enforce COVID lockdowns.

Note

1 And parts of the USA, where 'asset forfeiture' has been criticised as discriminatory, unaccountable 'legalised theft' by police.

References

Adler, M. (2018) *Cruel, Inhuman or Degrading Treatment? Benefit Sanctions in the UK*. Palgrave Macmillan.

Barr, U. (2019) *Desisting Sisters: Gender, Power and Desistance in the Criminal (In) Justice System*. Palgrave Macmillan.

Beckett, K., and Murakawa, N. (2012) Mapping the shadow carceral state: Toward an institutionally capacious approach to punishment. *Theoretical Criminology*, 16(2): 221–244. https://doi.org/10.1177/1362480612442113

Clark, I. (1998) The use of direct deductions from benefits in Scottish courts. *Howard Journal of Criminal Justice* 37(3): 291–305.

Collins, M. and King, C. (2013) The disruption of crime in Scotland through non-conviction based asset forfeiture. *Journal of Money Laundering Control* 16(4): 379–388.

Croall, H. (2016) Crimes of the powerful in Scotland. In Croall, H., Mooney, G. and Munro, M. (eds) *Crime, Justice and Society in Scotland*. Routledge. 131–148.

Cullen, A. (2022) *No longer 'Little Studied': Challenging criminological narratives about financial punishment*. SCCJR. https://www.sccjr.ac.uk/wp-content/uploads/2022/12/Amy-Cullen_Final-Paper-2022.pdf

Cullen, A. and Telling, H. (2021) The More Things Change… *Inside Time*. https://insidetime.org/the-more-things-change/

Einat, T. (2014). History of fines. In Bruinsma, G., Weisburd, D. (eds) *Encyclopedia of Criminology and Criminal Justice*. Springer. https://doi.org/10.1007/978-1-4614-5690-2_275

Gorton, V., Matthews, B., McVie, S. and Murray, K. (2022) *Police Use of Covid-19 Fixed Penalty Notices in Scotland: Trends in Enforcement from March 2020 to May 2021*. University of Edinburgh.

Harris, A. (2016) *A Pound of Flesh: Monetary Sanctions as Punishment for the Poor*. Russell Sage Foundation.

Henley, J. (2023) Finnish businessman hit with €121,000 speeding fine. *The Guardian*, 6 June. https://www.theguardian.com/world/2023/jun/06/finnish-businessman-hit-with-121000-speeding-fine

Kiely, E. and Swirak, K. (2022) *The Criminalisation of Social Policy in Neoliberal Societies*. Bristol University Press.

McIvor, G. (1994) Social work and criminal justice in Scotland: Developments in policy and practice. *British Journal of Social Work* 24(4): 429–448.

McIvor, G., Pirnat, C. and Grafl, C. (2013) Unpaid work as an alternative to imprisonment for fine default in Austria and Scotland. *European Journal of Probation* 5(2): 3–28.

McVie, S., Murray, K., Gorton, V. and Matthews, B. (2023) *Policing the Pandemic in England and Wales: Police use of Fixed Penalty Notices from 27 March 2020 to 31 May 2021*. University of Edinburgh.

Munro, M. (2016) 'Victims' in Scotland: A review. In Croall, H., Mooney, G. and Munro, M. (eds) *Crime, Justice and Society in Scotland*. Routledge. 151–166.

Murray, K., McVie, S., Matthews, B. and Gorton, V. (2024) From parking tickets to the pandemic: Fixed penalty notices, inequity and the regulation of everyday behaviours. *British Journal of Criminology* 64(6): 1310–1327.

O'Malley, P. (2009). Theorizing fines. *Punishment & Society* 11(1): 67–83.

Padfield, N. and Tata, C. (2023) Understanding penal decision-making: Courts, sentencing, and parole. In Liebling, A., Maruna, S. and McNeill, F. (eds) *The Oxford Handbook of Criminology*. Seventh edition. OUP. 676–697.

Scottish Courts and Tribunals Service (2024) *Courts Data Scotland: Fines 2023–24 Q4*. SCTS. https://www.scotcourts.gov.uk/media/lhfckvro/courts-data-scotland-fines-edition-61.pdf

Scottish Government (2023a) *Criminal Proceedings in Scotland*, 2021–22. Scottish Government.

Scottish Government (2023b) *Occasional Paper: Analysis of the Ethnicity of Individuals Subject to Hearings in Scottish Courts*. Scottish Government.

Scottish Government (2023c) *Reconviction Rates in Scotland: 2019–20 Offender Cohort*. Scottish Government.

Tibbitt, A. (2019) Thousands of Glaswegians let of with £1.5m in litter fines. *The Ferret*, 17 January. https://theferret.scot/glasgow-litter-fine-unpaid/

Ulph, J. (2010) Confiscation orders, human rights, and penal measures. *Law Quarterly Review* 126: 251–279.

Warner, K. (2012) Equality before the law and equal impact of sanctions: Doing justice to differences in wealth and employment status. In Zedner, L. and Roberts, J. V. (eds.) *Principles and Values in Criminal Law and Criminal Justice: Essays in Honour of Andrew Ashworth*. Oxford University Press. 225–244.

Weir Group (2023) *The Weir Group PLC Annual Report and Financial Statements 2023*. Weir Group. https://www.global.weir/siteassets/pdfs/2023-annual-report/weir-group-2023-annual-report.pdf

Wright, S. and Dwyer, P. (2022) In-work Universal Credit: Claimant experiences of conditionality mismatches and counterproductive benefit sanctions. *Journal of Social Policy* 51(1): 20–38.

Young, P. (1999) The fine as an auto-punishment: Power, money and discipline. In Duff, P. and Hutton, N. (eds) *Criminal Justice in Scotland*. Ashgate. 182–197.

6 Community justice in Scotland

Key ideas

- Unlike most other European countries, Scotland does not have a probation service; instead, probation supervision is mainly the responsibility of local social work departments, often called 'Justice Social Work' (JSW).
- Scottish community justice has been repeatedly reorganised; although these reforms have sometimes been controversial, it has somewhat resisted shifts towards punitiveness witnessed elsewhere in the UK.
- Despite impressive rhetoric, attempts in Scotland to use community justice to reduce imprisonment have met with little success.
- Initially developed with a penal welfarist orientation, community justice practice in the contemporary era espouses a focus on desistance (supporting people to move away from crime) and reintegration, alongside risk management.
- Scottish community justice is as much shaped by developments in Scottish politics, including in our system of local government, as by changing ideas about rehabilitation.

Introduction

This chapter looks at community penalties in Scotland and the role of community-based justice agencies. These seek to rehabilitate people through supervision in the community meaning that, although the person is punished, they are also meant to be helped and supported in their rehabilitation. The first part of this chapter elaborates how community justice is defined, with an explanation of Scottish community sentences, particularly the Community Payback Order (CPO). **Justice Social Work (JSW)** is the main community justice institution, but this sector involves a wide range of other bodies and actors.

The second part outlines the history of community justice in Scotland, beginning with the 1968 Social Work (Scotland) Act, which established the distinctively Scottish principle of making probation part of a social work service and not a (criminal) justice agency. We then explore how our system of community penalties has been shaped by the changing Scottish political context and by efforts to use community penalties as an instrument of justice policy to address Scotland's consistently high rates of imprisonment.

DOI: 10.4324/9781003372882-6

This chapter finishes by examining how the ways in which we think about rehabilitation and desistance have shaped the practice of community justice and, in turn, the experience of being punished in the community.

6.1 Procedures and processes in community justice

6.1.1 *Defining community justice*

Most of us at least *think* we know what prison looks like, but community and non-custodial penalties are harder to 'pin down'. The term '**community justice**' is currently preferred in Scotland, defined as "the collection of agencies and services in Scotland that individually and in partnership work to manage offenders, prevent offending and reduce reoffending and the harm that it causes, to promote social inclusion, citizenship and desistance" (Scottish Government, 2014: 1). While the focus of this chapter is on JSW, 'community justice' also includes a wide range of other bodies (Section 6.1.5).

The core business, in Scotland as elsewhere, is the supervision of convicted people in the community with the intention of rehabilitating them to prevent further offending. Alongside supervision by specialist professionals, this might include various forms of training or treatment, movement restrictions (e.g. a curfew) enforced by electronic monitoring (EM) technologies (Chapter 7), or unpaid work in the community. Unpaid work is sometimes called 'community service' or 'community payback'; in Scotland, the latter term may also refer to a wider agenda around the CPO (discussed below). In common with other jurisdictions, the business of community-based justice services is not limited to ensuring community sentences are completed successfully – and community justice is not solely the responsibility of JSW or any single agency.

This complexity is reflected in a diverse terminology. 'Probation' originally referred simply to the supervision of convicted people in the community, but is commonly used in most English-speaking countries to refer generally to community penalties and relevant agencies. European scholarship sometimes uses the term 'Community Sanctions and Measures' (CSM). The term 'alternatives to imprisonment' is also sometimes used – the problems with this are discussed in Section 6.2.4.

6.1.2 *Community Payback Orders*

In terms of sentencing, community penalties are in the middle of the range of severity, sitting between fines and imprisonment. Community penalties are *not* intended to punish 'minor' offences like shoplifting or speeding – which are more likely to attract fines, admonitions or out-of-court disposals. According to *Criminal Proceedings in Scotland 2022–23* (Scottish Government, 2024), offences most commonly attracting a community sentence include assault, handling offensive weapons, supplying drugs, fire-raising, domestic abuse and many sexual offences. They are intended to punish offending that *could* result in a prison sentence, reflecting their historical role as 'alternatives' to imprisonment.

The main community sentence in Scotland is the **Community Payback Order (CPO)**. The CPO was introduced in the 2010 Criminal Justice and Licensing (Scotland) Act, replacing several confusingly similar community sentences: the Probation Order, Supervised Attendance Order and Community Service Order and the pilot Community Reparation Order for young people.

The CPO is a single sentence that offers sentencers a 'menu' of ten requirements. The sentencer can impose a combination of these on the convicted person, detailed in Table 6.1. CPOs can be imposed by any criminal court, but Justice of the Peace (JP) courts can only impose some requirements.

Table 6.1 Community Payback Order requirements

Imposed by	*Requirement*	*Explanation*
Any court	Offender supervision	Mandatory supervision by social work, with regular scheduled meetings, over six months to three years. **Must be imposed alongside these other requirements.*
	Compensation*	Pay compensation to the victim (instalments or lump sum). Distinct from a compensation order (Chapter 5) but set at the same levels (up to £2,500 by JP court, £10,000 by sheriff summary, unlimited in solemn trials).
	Unpaid work or other activity	Undertake 20–300 hours of unpaid work or another 'purposeful activity', arranged and supervised by the local authority.
	Residence*	Live in a specific place for the duration of the supervision period.
	Conduct*	Do or refrain from doing something, e.g. avoid particular places/people. Cannot be imposed where another requirement would meet the same objective, or as an injunction against further offending.
Sheriff and High Court only	Programme*	Participate in a specific programme designed to address offending behaviour.
	Mental health treatment*	Treatment for a mental health problem.
	Drug treatment*	Residential or non-residential treatment programme for drug use. *Distinct from a DTTO, discussed below.*
	Alcohol treatment*	Residential or non-residential treatment programme for alcohol use.
	Restricted movement*	Movement restrictions, enforced by EM. *Distinct from an RLO, discussed below.* *Until May 2022, this could only be imposed where somebody had already breached their CPO (2019 Management of Offenders (Scotland) Act).*

The CPO is intended to combine the simplicity of a single sentence with the flexibility to tailor it to individual circumstances. For instance, a person whose offending is thought to be related to alcohol use could be issued with alcohol treatment and supervision requirements. By requiring a supervision requirement to be imposed alongside most other requirements, the sentence seeks to combine treatment with support. In practice, the most common requirements are supervision (imposed in 68% of CPOs in 2023–24) and unpaid work (68%). As part of supervision (see below), the supervising social worker can refer the person formally or informally to a range of programmes, e.g. for drug use, mental health treatment or to address problem behaviours. Engagement with programmes or treatment does not have to be an explicit requirement of the CPO itself.

Unpaid work is arranged and supervised by a professional Community Payback supervisor (not a supervising social worker) and the public can propose unpaid work activities to benefit their local community. Common forms of unpaid work include gardening, clearing snow and ice, cleaning or restoring public spaces, and working in charity shops.

6.1.3 *Other community sentences: the DTTO and RLO*

There are two other community sentences in Scotland: the **Drug Treatment and Testing Order (DTTO)** and **Restriction of Liberty Order (RLO)**. DTTOs were introduced by the (UK-wide) Crime and Disorder Act 1998 and rolled out in 2003; they aim to address crime committed to enable drug use. They can last up to three years and entail medical treatment for dependent drug use with support and supervision from JSW, as well as regular court hearings to monitor progress. Although DTTOs entail regular, random drug testing, evidence of drug taking is not necessarily grounds for breach of the order; periods of relapse are to be expected.

RLOs, introduced by the 1997 Crime and Punishment (Scotland) Act, require people to be or refrain from being in a specified place within certain specified times (for up to 12 hours, though these hours can be dispersed) and are usually enforced through electronic monitoring (Chapter 7). RLOs and DTTOs can be imposed as standalone sentences or alongside a CPO.

6.1.4 *Dealing with breaches*

For various reasons, the sentenced person might not be able – or willing – to comply with the terms of their order. They might **breach** it – for instance, by missing appointments with their social worker. The supervising social worker has significant discretion here; if they report the breach, the person would be returned to court and the case considered. The court may (a) take no further action (b) vary the order (e.g. by adding further conditions) or (c) revoke the CPO and impose an alternative sentence – including imprisonment. In this way, the 'carrot' of (conditional and supervised) freedom is paired with the 'stick' of further sanction for non-compliance (but see Section 6.4).

6.1.5 *Agencies of community justice*

The main professional grouping involved in community justice is **Justice Social Work (JSW)** – local authority social workers who specialise in criminal justice. JSW supervise people on community sentences, including by risk assessing, making referrals and working with people to address issues believed to cause their offending (i.e. seen as 'criminogenic'). In smaller local authorities with lower criminal justice caseloads, Justice Social Workers may split their time with other social work roles. All social workers must have a social work degree and be accredited with the **Scottish Social Services Council**, but 'paraprofessionals' without these qualifications are increasingly employed to assist social workers.

JSW plays several other important roles. First, justice social workers investigate the social circumstances of convicted people to assist courts in the sentencing decision (see Chapter 4). The Justice Social Work Report includes information on the person's history, their prior and current offending, and an assessment of their risk of recidivism including criminogenic and protective factors. It assesses the person's suitability for various community sentences and specific CPO requirements, but should not recommend any particular sentence – only inform the sentencer's decision. Where diversion from prosecution is being considered, JSW may perform a similar reporting function for the Crown Office. JSW also supervises some people released by the court on bail. Finally, JSW works with people in prison, before and after release, to monitor them and assist their reintegration into the community – sometimes known as 'throughcare' or 'aftercare' (discussed further in Chapter 10).

Working with people in the community to address the issues related to their offending is a complex task, so the work of community justice involves a range of agencies and professionals beyond JSW. Other local authority departments are needed to resolve specific problems – for instance, JSW might liaise with housing officers to ensure a person released from prison returns to a secure tenancy or refer people with dependent substance use to treatment programmes. The voluntary sector is often involved as well; this includes large national organisations like Sacro and Apex Scotland as well as smaller local charities and social enterprises. These might be commissioned by local authorities to provide services to people under supervision or might do so through charitable funding. Where a person under supervision is subject to electronic monitoring, JSW might liaise with the private EM provider (Chapter 7).

The 2016 Community Justice (Scotland) Act created formal partnerships at the local authority level, usually called **Community Justice Partnerships** or **Reducing Reoffending Partnerships**. These do not engage in 'frontline' criminal justice work; instead, they coordinate partnership working. They produce regular plans to reduce reoffending and may commission specific services (e.g. programmes run by charities) to address particular needs. Local authorities are political bodies, as well as service providers, and can exercise significant political influence on community justice policy (see Section 6.2.3).

JSW are also key partners in **Multi-Agency Public Protection Arrangements (MAPPA)**, a set of regional partnerships established by the 2005 Management of Offenders etc. (Scotland) Act, following similar developments in England and Wales and amid the wider risk management agenda. MAPPA partners include social work, the police, the Scottish Prison Service (SPS) and other agencies, with the intention to coordinate risk management in supervising specific groups: people subject to sex offender notification requirements (Section 10.1.3), who constitute over 90% of MAPPA cases, people subject to restrictive mental health orders, and a small number thought to pose a high risk of serious harm. Most people supervised under MAPPA are surveilled routinely by a single agency (usually JSW or the police), but for the small group thought to pose the highest risk, there is intensive multiagency supervision and surveillance. While the stated intention of MAPPA is to prevent harm rather than punish, the distinction in practice may not be clear-cut.

Community Justice Scotland was created by the 2016 Act and launched in April 2017 to serve as a national 'leadership' body for the sector, promoting and sharing best practices and trying to change the public 'conversation' about crime and justice. It is not a 'frontline' body either – it provides advice and guidance to the local partnerships and aims to promote community justice to sentencers and the public. Finally, JSW is inspected by the **Care Inspectorate**, serving a function analogous to His Majesty's Inspectorate of Probation in England and Wales, but working across *all* social work and social care.

Community justice in Scotland is therefore something of a patchwork, with no single agency having total and singular responsibility. We turn now to the historical development of this distinctive institutional structure.

6.2 Policy, politics and the development of community justice

This section looks at the history of community justice policy in Scotland and how the system has developed since the 1968 Social Work (Scotland) Act established the 'generic social work' model. We focus on two key contextual features. First, developments in community justice have often been shaped by concerns about imprisonment, particularly efforts to reduce it. Second, because of the distinctive role of local authorities, Scottish community justice has been shaped not only by national politics but also by dynamics around local government.

6.2.1 The 1968 Social Work (Scotland) Act and 'generic' social work

The most distinctive and important feature of the Scottish approach to community penalties developed from the 1964 Kilbrandon Report. Kilbrandon was focused on youth justice (Chapter 9), but the idea that offending should be treated alongside other social welfare issues was influential on services for adults. The 1966 report *Social Work and the Community* argued for a 'generic' social work profession in which various disciplines could be unified (Brodie et al., 2008). The result was the **1968 Social Work (Scotland) Act**, one of the most important pieces of legislation in Scottish criminal justice. The Act abolished Scotland's probation service (set up in 1931), merging it into 'generic' local authority social work departments. (See McNeill, 2005; Kelly, 2017 for discussions of early-20th century Scottish probation.)

All this should be understood in the context of what was in the 1960s the dominant way of thinking about punishment in the UK and much of the West – **penal welfarism**. Centred on a positivist understanding of the causes of crime as social and psychological, penal welfarism saw the institutions and professions of a strong postwar welfare state (mental healthcare, social work, psychiatry, probation) as key in addressing these causes. England and Wales came close to achieving a similar probation-social work 'merger' in the 1960s, but in the end, proved politically unable to do so.

One effect of the 1968 Act, particularly according to supporters of the Scottish model, has been to keep a welfarist, social work ethos in Scottish community justice, despite its systematic erosion in other jurisdictions by a stronger emphasis on risk and punishment. This is not to say that the approach in Scotland has not changed – as discussed below (Section 6.3), shifting ideas about rehabilitation and punishment have had significant impacts.

6.2.2 The 1970s and 1980s

Despite the intentions of the 1968 Act, people on probation were soon getting a barely adequate service. The system of generic social work budgets – which granted local authorities wide discretion over spending priorities – meant that when allocating money for social work, people under community sentences lost out to groups perceived as more 'deserving' of support, such as children and older people (Moore, 1978).

Meanwhile, rising prison populations and a wave of violence and protests across prisons in the UK (including Scotland) in the 1980s drew attention to the issue of prison overcrowding. Community penalties were increasingly seen as a way to resolve this issue – since if people who would otherwise be imprisoned receive community sentences instead, this avoids the harmful consequences of imprisonment *and* reduces prison overcrowding.

Achieving this goal, however, required resolving the budget issue. In 1989 it was announced that social work funding for criminal justice work would be 'ringfenced' – local authorities would *have* to spend it on supervising people serving community penalties or released on licence (Rifkind, 1989). At the same time, in 1991, the 'National Objectives and Standards' (now 'National Outcomes and Standards') were introduced, to ensure a good level of service, standardise practice across local authorities and institute accountability mechanisms for social work. Together these measures were intended to ensure that social work departments would be able to rehabilitate people under their supervision, thus reducing reoffending and taking pressure off prisons – but they were, at best, only partly successful.

6.2.3 *Local and central control since 1989*

Since ringfencing, Scottish community justice has been repeatedly reorganised, largely focused not on frontline JSW but on the *management and organisation* of the system, specifically how far it should be centralised or localised (Morrison, 2015).

A 2003 Scottish Labour manifesto proposal to merge JSW with the SPS met with fierce resistance from local government and social work – who feared it would endanger the social work ethos of JSW, increase control by central government rather than local communities, and diminish the distinctiveness of Scottish approaches (McNeill, 2005). This, alongside the moderating influence of the Liberal Democrats as Labour's coalition partners, led to a compromise between central and local interests – *regional* bodies called Community Justice Authorities (CJAs) established by the 2005 Management of Offenders etc. (Scotland) Act. CJAs were meant to act as an intermediate layer of governance between local authorities and central government, but the compromises which produced them ultimately rendered them unable to hold local authorities to account (Buchan and Morrison, 2020).

In the 2011 election, the Scottish National Party (SNP) achieved an overall majority – unusual in our Parliamentary system – and was keen to consolidate power and emphasise Scottish distinctiveness in criminal justice. Meanwhile, there was renewed pressure to drive down imprisonment. Particular concern centred on women's criminal justice experiences, leading to the establishment of a Commission on Women Offenders (2012). Alongside its recommendations for women's community justice services (see Box 6.3), the Commission's report was critical of the CJA model; alongside a contemporaneous report by Audit Scotland (2012), it created the impetus to reorganise once again. After just over a decade of operation, CJAs were abolished and replaced with a new system under the 2016 Community Justice (Scotland) Act – another compromise between local and central government, this time with two 'tiers' – the local partnerships and the national body, Community Justice Scotland (see Section 6.1.5).

The appropriate balance between local and central organisation is more than simply political wrangling. Scotland's geographic diversity prompts consideration of locally oriented forms of justice. A person living in central Glasgow and a person living in a village in Shetland, each sentenced for a similar offence, to a CPO with the same requirements, may still have very different experiences. They may differ in terms of what unpaid work they do (working in a charity shop or shovelling snow), whether there are enough other people locally for group work sessions to take place, and how they travel to their supervision (a short walk or lengthy boat ride). These can't be easily separated from the wider context of socioeconomic inequalities between areas – differences in cost of living, rates and forms of poverty and area deprivation. Supervising agencies and local authorities in each area must tailor their approach to local conditions while dealing with very different levels of resources and workload. This however is in tension with liberal 'justice model' arguments that criminal justice should treat people the same way, regardless of who they are or where they live.

While a *local social work* service might better respond to local needs and support desistance from crime (see Section 6.3.4) in its social context, a more *centralised criminal justice* service could potentially promote consistency of outcomes, realise efficiencies of scale and facilitate coordination with other (national) justice agencies. Navigating and reconciling these contradictory impulses is not straightforward, even if we could somehow separate it from political conflicts and compromises.

Meanwhile, the longstanding problem of insufficient JSW funding continues. Far from a solution, the ringfencing instituted in 1989 created further inequalities between areas and services; the model used to allocate funding between local areas is now very old and does not take account of subsequent social and demographic changes. While some authorities have enough money to commission 'extras' like restorative justice (see Box 6.1), others can barely cover their statutory obligations and must make up the shortfall from elsewhere in their budgets. The ringfenced nature of the funding has also created tensions in partnerships since many services – especially charities – experience greater financial insecurity.

6.2.4 Community penalties and the unfulfilled promise of decarceration

Community penalties are sometimes referred to as 'alternatives to imprisonment'. For sentencers, community penalties offer a way to punish offending without inflicting the harms of imprisonment, allowing them to take better account of mitigating factors and adapt the punishment to the person's individual circumstances. The idea is also attractive to policymakers because imprisonment offers little social benefit at extraordinary expense – community penalties generally cost only a small fraction of the cost of a prison place.

Diverting cases away from imprisonment and into community penalties, would, in theory, make a better and cheaper justice system. Increasing the use of community penalties thus appears as a penal policy 'lever' for reducing imprisonment. In 2008, the report *Scotland's Choice* (Scottish Prisons Commission, 2008: 3) advocated that "paying back in the community should become the default position in dealing with less serious offenders" (echoing the language, if not the reality, of the 1980s reforms discussed in Section 6.2.2). This coincided with two political developments – the SNP's rise to power with a policy agenda centred on re-asserting Scottish distinctiveness in criminal justice, and pressure to reduce public spending created by the 2008 financial crisis.

The logic implicit in this approach is that, if community penalties can be made more 'credible', sentencers will choose them over imprisonment, so will imprison fewer people and the imprisonment rate will fall (for a comprehensive critique of this see Tata, 2020). The creation of the CPO and the restructuring in 2016–17 were justified in policy rhetoric partly in terms of making community penalties more effective and 'credible', to reduce imprisonment.

So far, the promise of decarceration has not been met. Over 15 years since *Scotland's Choice*, the imprisonment rate remains stubbornly high – similar to that of England and Wales. While there has been an upward trend in the 'share' of sentences accounted for by community penalties, the share accounted for by imprisonment has not fallen. Rising numbers of people under criminal justice supervision (in various forms), *alongside* rising imprisonment, have led McNeill (2019) to decry the rise of American-style 'mass supervision' in Scotland. This echoes the argument of some theorists, notably Cohen (1985), that measures created to divert people *away* from the criminal justice system (or at least the 'deep end' of it) can end up having the exact opposite effect.

Failures to decarcerate may arise from political sensitivities and culture. Scottish policy's emphasis has been on using community penalties to reduce *short* prison sentences, more politically acceptable than reducing numbers of longer sentences. However, short prison sentences are often imposed on those who have already repeatedly breached community penalties (see Box 4.2). Buchan (2020) and Buchan and McNeill (2023) argue that Scottish efforts to decarcerate fail to substantively address the drivers of imprisonment, because the policy environment is set up to favour managerial and administrative solutions over a more substantively political approach (such as limiting sentencers' discretion). Again, how justice gets done is inseparable from the political context.

Box 6.1 Restorative justice in Scotland

In recent years, Scottish justice policy has outwardly embraced **restorative justice (RJ)** – the use of mediated communication between people involved in an offence or an act of harm, with the intention of finding a way to deal with the impact of it and move forward from the incident (Marshall, 1999). RJ can include apologies and forgiveness but does not have to (see our Blether with David Russell – Box 6.4).

In light of evidence highlighting lower reoffending rates associated with RJ, its potential for giving a voice to victims, and a European movement towards using RJ as part of victims' services (EU Directive 29/2012), the Scottish Government decided in 2017 to expand the use of RJ in criminal justice, issuing national guidance, followed by the ambitious goal of making RJ available to everyone, nationwide, by 2023 (Scottish Government, 2019). Up until this point, RJ had generally taken the form of short-term, small-scale pilot projects (Kirkwood and Kritikos, 2025).

Since RJ is not custodial (though it may take place in prison) and seeks to involve communities in dealing with crime, it is relevant to community justice. At the national level, the work of promoting RJ within the system has fallen to a new hub within Community Justice Scotland. Local provision of RJ in response to crime might involve JSW directly in arranging or facilitating RJ meetings, or local community justice partners commissioning RJ services from other organisations and referring cases to them.

RJ has tended to be used in Scotland mainly as a diversionary measure (see Section 4.3.2) to deal with minor offending by young people under the Whole System Approach (Maglione et al., 2020; see Chapter 9) – despite evidence that consistently shows the value of RJ in cases of serious crime involving adults (Keenan and Zinsstag, 2022). In response to a demand from victim-survivors, a national service has been developed to provide RJ in response to sexual offending – but some victims' groups argue RJ is never appropriate for such harms and risks deepening the trauma further.

The Scottish Government's 2023 goal was not met, though there remains an appetite to 'grow' RJ in Scottish criminal justice. Efforts to expand provision beyond small-scale local projects have encountered familiar systemic problems: a concern about how to balance local responsivity with centralised support and coordination, issues with information sharing across agencies, lack of knowledge among practitioners and inadequate funding (Maglione et al., 2020).

Currently, it is unclear how JSW and others will navigate ongoing debates around RJ and its relationship with criminal justice (Butler et al., 2022). Kirkwood and Hamad (2019) suggest that a 'restorative justice informed criminal justice social work' could entail more use of RJ in community justice, but also rethinking JSW through a restorative 'lens' to promote restoration for all people and communities affected by crime. This is a compelling idea but challenging to implement in practice, particularly given more immediate challenges for Scottish community justice. Finally, it is worth noting that many theorists of RJ are critical of its integration with criminal justice, noting that RJ – which emerged as a critique of criminal justice institutions – must remain separate from them to be true to its ideals (Maglione et al., 2024).

Questions to consider

- What are some arguments for and against using restorative justice in cases of serious crime?
- What are some possible implications of incorporating restorative justice into criminal justice institutions?

6.3 The changing face of rehabilitation

Having discussed procedural and organisational aspects, we now turn our attention to how community justice *practice* has changed. Community justice has largely been centred around 'rehabilitation', but looking at its history reveals different ideas about what this means. Many theorists are also sceptical about the idea of 'rehabilitation'. Some interpretations of the term and ensuing practices imply that offending is a feature of the person which can be eradicated through intervention, ignoring the social and structural context of offending and the social construction of 'crime', 'criminals' or 'offenders'. Nevertheless, it remains important and persistent and changing ideas about what 'rehabilitation' is and how to do it are vital to understanding what community justice looks like 'on the ground' – for practitioners and people under supervision.

Here we look at several ways of thinking about rehabilitation. Although each is most strongly associated with a particular period in recent history, all remain relevant today.

6.3.1 Welfarism and treatment

The 1968 Social Work (Scotland) Act established the system of generic social work alongside the Children's Hearings System (Chapter 9), marking a high point of **penal welfarism** – a discourse that situates the institutions of punishment as part of the wider postwar welfare state project. This entailed a particular prominence for a 'treatment' model of 'rehabilitation' and community justice practice, characterised by an emphasis on professional diagnosis and treatment of the supervised person's psychological or social problems.

The fortunes of penal welfarism waned significantly from the 1970s onwards, across much of the English-speaking world. Partly this resulted from a loss of faith in rehabilitation itself as rates of recorded crime continued rising, but there were also radical critiques of the often-coercive nature of rehabilitative 'treatment' (Bottoms and McWilliams, 1979; Cohen, 1985). The decline of penal welfarism has at least as much to do with wider political developments – particularly the shift towards neoliberalism in the 1970s (see Section 1.3.1), accompanied by an increasingly punitive tendency in justice policy, with a greater focus on punishment and control in community penalties and stricter sanctions for failure to comply.

England and Wales since about the 1980s has pursued an increasingly risk-focused and punitive approach to probation (McWilliams, 1990), with tougher enforcement for breach, a 'de-social worked' approach to training, and a disastrous part-privatisation between 2013 and 2020 (Annison, 2019). But while Scotland has experienced the rising imprisonment seen in other jurisdictions, community penalties have to an extent been protected by the 1968 Act – and, as discussed above, by social work and local government interests resistant to any effort to abstract Scottish community justice from its social work roots.

Aspects of the treatment ideal remain alive and well, though now underpinned by cognitive behavioural therapy (CBT) approaches (which have also become popular elsewhere). The supervising social worker can refer a person under supervision to a range of programmes intended to address specific needs, problems and behaviours. Reflecting the 'generic social work' approach, these are often only indirectly connected to criminal justice – they may be run by the NHS, other social work or charities, and open to a wide range of people. For instance, a person whose offending is linked to dependent use of alcohol might be referred to a group work programme for reducing alcohol use but would carry out that programme alongside others who are simply seeking to reduce their alcohol use (without having been convicted of anything). Some programmes are more closely offending-focused and may be delivered within JSW, such as the Caledonian System which uses individual and group work with men who have abused their partners (Ormston et al., 2016).

For all forms of social work (not only justice), even the most apparently welfare-oriented intervention may still be experienced by the people subject to it as an intrusive, stigmatising form of state social control rather than support (see below). Furthermore, the persistence of welfarist rhetoric is in tension with a different aspect of community justice practice – an emphasis on assessing and managing risk.

6.3.2 Risk

Scotland has not been fully insulated from developments affecting community penalties in other English-speaking jurisdictions. Reflecting a wider social preoccupation with risk (Beck, 1992), risk management through statistically driven **actuarial** systems has been a major part of community justice in Scotland since the 1990s. As in England and Wales and elsewhere, we can locate the origins of this approach in rising concern about serious violent and sexual crime, alongside the rise of **managerial** approaches to justice – in which administrative and efficiency concerns become significant – and an emphasis on 'What Works?' to reduce crime.

This approach uses statistical data to attempt to predict a person's risk of further offending. Rehabilitation – in this way of thinking – develops from the premise that statistical correlates ('risk factors') are in fact *causes* of crime and targets interventions at those risk factors that are dynamic, i.e. amenable to change – sometimes referred to as addressing 'criminogenic needs'. Since 2010, the principal risk assessment tool used in JSW is the Level of Service/Case Management Inventory (LS/CMI), developed by the Canadian psychologists Andrews et al. (2004). Social workers use a short preliminary LS/CMI at the pre-sentence reporting stage and conduct a full analysis when supervision starts.

This premise, as well as the subsequent move from prediction to intervention, is disputed. Despite the *apparently* scientific and 'neutral' character of actuarial risk assessment, some risk factors are not straightforward to measure and in practice often depend on social workers' subjective opinions and professional judgements – for example, whether someone's family are viewed as supportive or as 'pro-criminal' associates (McNeill et al., 2009). Since actuarial risk assessment relies for its prediction on data gathered by criminal justice, it can reproduce the biases of criminal justice while appearing scientific.

Other than in social work practice itself, the rise of actuarialism is associated with significant institutional and sentencing developments in Scotland – the creation of the Risk Management Authority, the Order for Lifelong Restriction (both discussed in Chapter 10) and MAPPA (Section 6.1.5).

6.3.3 Payback

Efforts to use community penalties for rehabilitation and welfare, in preference to imprisonment, coexisted awkwardly with the persistence of punitive political rhetoric on crime. The notion of **'payback'** offered a possible means of reconciling these apparent opposites – at least in political discourse, if not necessarily always in practice. This idea became prominent in the late 2000s and remains so in much of the practice – and name – of the CPO.

Underlying much of the political language surrounding the CPO was the idea of payback in retributive, punitive terms – connotations of vengeance, with someone suffering pain to 'pay back' for the harm caused by their offence (Maruna and King, 2008). Despite the range of possible requirements (Section 6.1.2), the emphasis was on unpaid work, especially its difficult and demanding nature. Unpaid work is still far more often imposed than most other CPO requirements.

In England and Wales, 'community payback' usually only refers to unpaid work on a community sentence, where special high-visibility clothing is used to identify people doing it as part of a sentence. This is supposed to inform the public and improve the legitimacy of community penalties but has punitive undertones of public shaming (Maruna and King, 2008). Unpaid work in Scotland seeks to avoid the stigmatising features of its counterparts elsewhere. Ordinary (or generic high-vis) clothing is worn, with public engagement efforts including allowing local communities to suggest projects, and plaques to indicate when work on a local site (such as a park or playground) has been done by people working on community payback (Figure 6.1). However, the actual experience of 'payback' may still be painful – Williams' (2019) ethnographic study of Scottish unpaid work found that although for some it was a valuable and reintegrative experience, for others it consisted of repetitive, tedious 'odd jobs' with little reparative or personal value.

Instead of revenge, we can think of 'payback' as *reparation* – people making amends to their victim or the wider community for their offence. This may still be painful, but a more reparative way of thinking sees 'paying back'

Figure 6.1 A community Payback sign in Fife.

as part of a redemption narrative which concludes with the person being welcomed back into the community, seen no longer as an 'offender' but as a contributor to wellbeing (McNeill, 2010). For instance, the work a person undertakes in treatment to address problems with substance use could also be seen as a way of paying back. This has more in common with the welfarist traditions at the root of community justice and dovetails with the rise of desistance in Scottish criminal justice.

6.3.4 Desistance

The concept and practices of 'rehabilitation' – particularly their welfare and treatment, and risk management forms – have long come under academic critique. Critiques relate to:

- Rehabilitation's (much contested) positivist understanding of crime as resulting from deficits in the person;
- So seeing the role of the criminal justice system as intervening (often coercively) to treat this;
- Relying on expert judgements about how this should be done and when the process is complete.

In the 2000s, a group of academics argued that the process of change – known as **desistance** from crime – was individual and subjective, so must be led by the person, attending to the needs that they (not professionals) felt were important and building on their strengths and resources, especially relationships. The criminal justice system is not the driver of change, but it can help *or* get in the way. Understandings of desistance are discussed more in Box 6.2, but research suggests not only that living in a profoundly unequal and individualistic society can inhibit desistance, but that criminal justice institutions can hinder desistance even while claiming to promote it.

The concept of desistance had an enthusiastic uptake in Scotland, especially during the late 2000s and 2010s. The work of academic researchers, especially Fergus McNeill and Beth Weaver, was important in promoting desistance to Scottish policymakers as well as for its research insights (especially Weaver and McNeill, 2007). In 2010, the National Outcomes and Standards were reformulated to include "social inclusion to support desistance from offending" as a key outcome, and desistance is prominent in the National Strategy for Community Justice. Motivational interviewing and 'strengths-based' approaches have become increasingly prominent in JSW practice, and there has been an effort to shift the language of criminal justice to reduce the stigma associated with criminal justice involvement. Practitioners now rarely describe people as 'criminals' and increasingly avoid 'offenders'; instead, terms like 'people with convictions', 'people under supervision' or 'people in conflict with the law' might be used. This spurred the use of 'Justice Social Work' rather than 'Criminal Justice Social Work' (you will see 'CJSW' used in all but the most recent sources). The language of desistance became commonplace across much of Scottish criminal justice (see Chapter 8 on prisons). However, Fenton (2013) argued that risk-averse, managerial practice within JSW presented serious challenges for truly embracing the insights of desistance research.

The extent to which a change in language has reflected a genuine change of approach has been debated. Some academics argue that the concept inhibits more radical change, retaining fundamental misunderstandings about the nature of crime, still emphasising the need for the person to change and construing the criminal justice system as a positive influence (without sufficiently attending to its harms). Others suggest that this merely reflects problems with implementation: as theory has been translated into practice, some factors in desistance have received more weight than others, with an emphasis on developing agency, assets, skills and interpersonal relationships, rather than on the role of criminal justice, social structures and communities in co-creating (re)offending and wider harms.

While desistance research was an extremely influential development in Scottish criminal justice, the interaction with other rehabilitative logics, alongside the impact of wider social inequalities, is critical in people's experience of community justice and life after punishment (Chapter 10).

Box 6.2 Understandings of desistance

'Desistance' is the name given to the process of moving away from crime or criminalisation. It is not just a period of not offending – even people who offend prolifically don't offend all the time. It is the achievement of identities, social roles (e.g. ties to family, work and education), relationships and resources which support someone to *continue* not offending (see Weaver (2019) for a review of theories of desistance). Some scholars have emphasised that this doesn't only require the person to make changes but also requires recognition and acceptance of change by society (McNeill, 2015; Weaver, 2015; Nugent and Schinkel, 2016).

The process of desisting from crime, even where deemed 'successful', can be lonely and painful. In Nugent and Schinkel's (2016) study, the lives of 'desisters' in the community were marked not by successful 're-integration' but rather by feeling 'stuck', free from prison, but not fully members of society. These 'pains of desistance' include isolation: having to avoid friends (even family) with whom they risked getting into trouble or running into contact with the police. They described being unable to achieve their goals for a successful life, leading to feelings of hopelessness. The stigma of offending and the collateral consequences of criminal records can continue to impact efforts to desist long after formal criminal justice involvement has ended (Anderson, 2019; Chapter 10), making it hard to find employment (Weaver and Jardine, 2022) and leading to targeting by police (Schinkel et al., 2019).

While social and community bonds have long been seen as significant to desistance, contemporary research emphasises the importance of access to community *resources and opportunities* in sustaining it (Barry, 2013). Earlier desistance scholarship has been critiqued for paying insufficient attention to the challenging structural contexts of desistance, ignoring "the central and intersecting roles of racism, sexism, class and other related fields that maintain inequalities" (Glynn, 2013: 125) in sustaining criminal justice involvement. More recent desistance research has attended more to the structural aspects and the connection between individual experiences and social inequalities (Weaver et al., 2023). A significant body of work exists on gender and desistance (discussed in Boxes 6.3 and 10.2), although less exists on the connection between desistance and other identities, especially ethnicity (although see Glynn 2013; Calverley, 2013).

Questions to consider

- Make a short list of factors you think might be relevant to someone's desistance from crime. For each factor you write down, consider:
  - How might these vary between individuals?

    - How might these link to structural issues and inequalities in wider society?
    - How does or can criminal justice in Scotland affect these?
- What are the implications of Nugent and Schinkel's (2016) findings for criminal justice and wider society?

6.4 Experiencing community penalties

Different ideas about rehabilitation can play out in different ways for the people subject to community penalties.

Given that supervision involves regular interactions between the person under supervision and their supervising justice social worker (or probation officer, etc.), this experience is heavily affected by the quality of the supervision relationship (Shapland et al., 2012). Where the supervisor listens and shows respect, it seems that talking can help (to an extent) (McCulloch, 2005). Where the supervisory relationship is not positive, the interaction can instead feel distrustful, degrading, and neglectful (Weaver et al., 2021). Other concerns relate to the impact on families and potential intrusion by social workers into family life (Ditton and Ford, 1994). While contemporary social work practice should centre non-coercive approaches that actively involve people in decision-making, this sits uneasily with the innately coercive nature of punishment (Weaver, 2011).

The rise of risk logics in criminal justice contributes to experiences of stigma; people under supervision may experience feelings of 'misrecognition' at being reduced to 'risk factors' that may not correspond to their experience or rated as 'riskier' than they are or believe themselves to be (McNeill, 2019). The emphasis of addressing risk factors falls not on changing wider social structures but on the individual under supervision, whose efforts are not always recognised; people under supervision may thus have to edit their own presentation to be 'recognised' as less risky.

Contrary to some characterisations of community penalties as an 'easy ride', research from Romania (Durnescu, 2011; see also Hayes, 2018) emphasises the deprivation of autonomy and privacy for people so punished: the loss of choice about what to do, being asked to share personal details, having to reorganise their life to fit the requirements of the order (such as appointments), and losing time and money (e.g. by missing work) – and the shame of having to explain why to their employer. The person will probably have to talk about the offence repeatedly, returning to a moment that could be uncomfortable, distressing and shameful.

Box 6.3 Women's experiences of community sentences

Efforts to use community penalties as a tool for reducing imprisonment have sometimes centred on women's offending, spurred by concern over conditions for women in prison and arguments that women are primarily victims of harm. The Commission on Women Offenders (2012) was key in setting this agenda.

Recorded crime by women tends to be less serious, while women who become involved in the criminal justice system face poverty, unemployment and dependent substance use at rates even higher than among men involved in the justice system – but also more clearly *gendered* factors such as pregnancy, single parenthood and victimisation in abusive relationships. These can affect women's desistance from crime in complex, sometimes contradictory ways (Malloch and McIvor, 2011, Schinkel, 2019), which mainstream desistance explanations (and justice institutions) have tended to distort or ignore (Barr, 2019). Women may be especially aware of the stigma of being labelled as an offender – which different people may experience as an incentive for or barrier to desistance, or both.

The Commission on Women Offenders (2012) report highlighted that gendered factors affect women's compliance with community sentences (e.g. caring responsibilities might prevent them from attending JSW appointments). To address the complex challenges women experience and support them to comply with community sentences, it recommended establishing multiagency 'one stop shops' across Scotland for women involved in the justice system.

This was inspired by existing services, notably the 218 Centre in Glasgow and the Willow Project in Edinburgh and Midlothian. These projects used medical and psychological treatment, mentoring, group work, and education workshops, co-located within the same building, to support women involved in the criminal justice system or otherwise at risk of harm. The idea is to provide holistic treatment to address what are often complex problems and overlapping deprivation and marginalisation affecting these women. Following the Commission's report, the Scottish Government provided money in 2013 to fund new and existing community justice services specifically for women.

An evaluation of these services (IRISS, 2015) found overall positive effects, particularly in helping service users to achieve shorter-term outcomes around stability, mental health, housing and substance use, but noted less progress towards longer-term and community-oriented outcomes of the type associated with longer-term desistance – stable employment, meaningful activities and strong relationships. While some women's services (particularly the Shine mentoring programme) are available nationally, many serve specific local communities and thus arguably raise the same questions around local provision as discussed above (Section 6.2.3). Many of these services suffered from unstable and short-term funding and were not able to act sustainably as the 'one-stop shops' envisioned by the Commission. The 218 Centre has since closed due to heavily reduced funding, at a time when so-called 'community' provision for women was opening inside the prison estate (see Box 8.1 and Cleary, forthcoming). Related issues are discussed further in Box 10.2.

Questions to consider

- What should be done to support women in the criminal justice system?
- What are some arguments for and against gender-specific community justice services for women?

Although often seen as preferable to prison, community penalties come with the threat of prison for failure to comply, placing people under a 'shadow' we will return to in Chapter 10. Velasquez Valenzuela (2018) observed that with the Presumption Against Short Sentences (see Box 4.2), some Sheriffs were increasing the number of requirements on community orders to 'toughen' them up, no doubt increasing the associated pains and the fear of breach. He warns that at some point, the lengthy and requirement-heavy restriction of a community sentence may actually be perceived as worse than a prison sentence.

These experiences can help us to understand why some people fail to comply with community orders. Weaver et al. (2021) found a range of interacting reasons for non-compliance. For some, non-compliance was related to an active indifference towards the requirements of the order or rejection of authority (sometimes linked to perceptions of unfair treatment arising earlier in the justice process). For others, overwhelming challenges within their social circumstances (mental ill-health, poverty or drug use) made complying with the order's conditions seem unachievable or assumed greater priority. Finally, non-compliance could also arise from perceptions of demeaning, hostile, unfair or seemingly pointless (e.g. very short, non-meaningful) interactions with supervisors where challenging life circumstances were apparently not recognised, let alone addressed. Halsey et al. (2017) describe people reoffending when an accumulation of life difficulties, and a failure of supervisors to provide help when requested leads to an act of self-sabotage – a "fuck it" moment.

All of this research shows that community penalties can be experienced as painful, stigmatising and threatening, and emphasises the importance of respectful and constructive supervisory relationships.

Box 6.4 A Blether with ... David Russell, Community Safety and Justice Manager, Midlothian Community Safety and Justice Partnership

Interview by Gerda-Liis Nurmjoe, BA Social Sciences, Edinburgh Napier University

Can you tell us a bit about your work?

"I sit in the JSW team, but my role is a bit different; Midlothian Community Safety & Justice Partnership has oversight of justice services, but we also have collective responsibility for the Community Justice Outcome Improvement Plan. We work with partners including Police Scotland, Justice Social Work, Children and Families social work, and a wide range of charities. We don't have an operational role, but we advocate for desistance approaches, a reduction in short-term sentencing and community justice values".

Tell us a bit about your work in relation to restorative justice?

"When the national approach to restorative justice came out, I was keen to be involved in developing RJ around sexual harm cases, so we partnered with Thriving Survivors, who have the national role of developing RJ in cases of sexual harms; I now chair their advisory panel and I've contributed to their risk assessment tools. They have a survivor-focused approach, and one of the things we as partners agreed early on was that if survivors are asking for restorative justice, they should have the opportunity to have it. The other thing for me was thinking about 'what's the risk of *not* taking part?' Arguably, it's that people try and do it themselves – unsupported.

The biggest challenge we've faced with restorative justice is the lack of understanding. We had some backlash against using restorative justice in sexual offences, because people thought we were just going to put the parties together in a room and leave them to it – that's not the case. We have many different approaches such as surrogacy models, indirect conferencing and letter-writing. It's not always about apology and forgiveness – it can simply be an agreement like "You go to Tesco and I'll go to Asda". What I mean is that if you've got people in the same community, it might be about giving a person the reassurance that they'll not bump into the other person".

How did the COVID-19 pandemic influence your work?

"The increase in social isolation had a huge impact – we're still dealing with that. The pandemic had a huge impact on children's learning, including their sexual development – we're seeing younger people getting charged for offences like image-based sexual abuse. That's a priority area for our action plan, and we're working with the charity Stop It Now! Scotland to develop local responses and interventions to prevent it.

We've been really fortunate in not being badly affected by the backlog of unpaid work hours – our backlog is actually lower than it was before Covid, because we've been creative in our approach – for instance, using unpaid work to help with food parcels in the community".

How would someone get into this line of work?

"One of my biggest and proudest achievements is coming from an unconventional approach. I started off as a prison officer in HMP Edinburgh, and I really owe a lot to that in understanding how to manage conflict – particularly how to manage violence and help people desist from it. I then went into Barnardo's, supporting victims of child sexual abuse and children who displayed harmful sexual behaviour, then did a postgraduate certificate in Child Protection at the University of Stirling.

I'm an advocate for bringing in people from different backgrounds and lived and living experiences of the justice system. When I was at school, I couldn't wait to get out – I hated school! But now I'm writing research papers with the University of Birmingham, which I'm incredibly proud of".

This is just a short excerpt – listen to the full podcast at https://www.sccjr.ac.uk/project/criminal-justice-in-scotland/. David's research is listed at *https://uk.linkedin.com/in/david-russell-53894119a*.

Conclusion

This chapter has discussed Scottish community justice and community sentences. The role of local authority social work is an unusual structural feature that has arguably enabled the continuation of a more welfarist ethos, protecting Scottish community justice from some of the punitive and managerialist tendencies found in other Anglophone jurisdictions. However, it has also enmeshed Scottish community justice with political dynamics around devolution and local government. Scottish policy around community justice has been shaped by efforts to reduce imprisonment, which have so far failed, despite claims to a distinctively Scottish approach.

We have discussed the repeated restructuring since the late 1980s. In 2022–23, amid wider social care reforms, the Scottish Government suggested a further change: the local partnerships established in 2016 could be brought under a proposed 'National Care Service', which could encompass all social work and social care. These proposals gave little sense of what the new service might look like or what it might mean for JSW. After two years of uncertainty, the proposal – having lost much of its initial political support – was scrapped in January 2025. Meanwhile, questions persist over inadequate funding for JSW and local authority services generally.

The COVID-19 pandemic exacerbated an existing backlog in unpaid work imposed by the courts and not yet completed. This relates to staffing and resource pressures on local authorities and the challenges of organising community payback placements in communities. To mitigate the backlog, the Scottish Government 'wrote off' about 250,000 hours, but the courts' efforts to tackle *their* backlog of cases returned the unpaid work backlog back to pandemic levels. At the end of 2024, there remained nearly three-quarters of a million hours to be worked across Scotland (Johnson, 2024).

Media reporting of this situation, and community sentencing generally, tends to imply that only custody is sufficiently punitive, while some supporters of community penalties admire their emphasis on rehabilitation. Both arguments can miss an important point: community penalties *are* punishment and can be stigmatising and painful, particularly in the context of longstanding social inequalities and marginalisation which create significant barriers to desisting from crime.

We have seen that rehabilitation means different things to different people, creating tensions in social work practice. But practice ideas of 'rehabilitation' and even desistance usually emphasise that work needs to be done to, by or with the person. Far less attention is given to the role of social workers in being vocal about the harms and oppressions people have experienced and being active in resisting these (Anderson, 2016). Community justice is too often seen in narrow terms.

We return to some of the themes and agencies discussed in this chapter when we discuss supervision on licence (Chapter 10). The next chapter however focuses on a specific form of supervision in the community – the use of electronic monitoring.

Critical questions

- Think about the rationales for punishment: retribution, deterrence, rehabilitation, denunciation, reparation and incapacitation (Box 4.3). Can you highlight examples of each in Scottish community justice?
- What is the significance of 'community' in 'community justice'?
- Does it matter how community justice services are organised? What are the implications of changing organisational structures for practice?
- Are you able to find any information (perhaps through your local authority) about community payback work in your area? If so – do you think the projects taking place are useful to the community and/or the people on community sentences?
- Is it realistic to expect JSW to bring about 'social inclusion to support desistance from offending'? What could they do, and what would the implications be for people under supervision? Are there other ways to achieve this?

Key resources

British Journal of Community Justice special issue on Community Justice in Scotland.

This collection of articles will be available by the time this book is published or shortly after – see https://mmuperu.co.uk/bjcj/issues/.

Grant, S., Buchan, J. and O'Donnell, A. (2020). Scotland. In: *Probation in Europe* (updated online chapter). Confederation of European Probation. https://www.cep-probation.org/wp-content/uploads/2020/11/Scotland-chapter-final-version.pdf

Explains the procedural and organisational detail surrounding community justice in Scotland in depth.

McNeill, F. (2019) *Pervasive Punishment: Making Sense of Mass Supervision*. Emerald Publishing.

A discussion of the expansion of community penalties in Scotland and in the USA includes a short story exploring this from the perspectives of a person under supervision and their supervising social worker.

The Road from Crime. https://www.iriss.org.uk/resources/videos/road-crime.

This film discusses desistance research alongside the real story of Allan Weaver, who desisted from crime and became a Justice Social Worker.

Weaver, B. (2019) Understanding desistance: a critical review of theories of desistance. *Psychology, Crime and Law* 25(6): 641–658.

A recent, concise overview of different theories of desistance.

References

Anderson, S. (2016) The value of 'bearing witness' to desistance. *Probation Journal* 63(4): 408–424.

Anderson, S. (2019) Frustrating desistance: Stigma as a barrier to change. In Best, D. and Colman, C. (eds) *Strengths-Based Approaches to Crime and Substance Use*. Routledge. 159–177.

Andrews, D.A., Bonta, J. and Wormith, S.J. (2004). *The Level of Service/Case Management Inventory (LS/CMI)*. Multi-Health Systems.

Annison, H. (2019) Transforming Rehabilitation as 'policy disaster': Unbalanced policy-making and probation reform. *Probation Journal* 66(1): 43–59.

Audit Scotland (2012) *Reducing Reoffending in Scotland*. Audit Scotland.

Barr, U. (2019) *Desisting Sisters: Gender, Power and Desistance in the Criminal (In) Justice System*. Palgrave Macmillan.

Barry, M. (2013). Desistance by design: Offenders' reflections on criminal justice theory, policy and practice. *European Journal of Probation* 5(2): 47–65.

Beck, U. (1992) *Risk Society: Towards a New Modernity*. Sage Publications.

Bottoms, A.E. and McWilliams, W. (1979) A non-treatment paradigm for probation practice. *British Journal of Social Work* 9(2): 159–202.

Brodie, I., Nottingham, C. and Plunkett, S. (2008) A tale of two reports: Social work in Scotland from social work and the community (1966) to changing lives (2006). *British Journal of Social Work* 38(4): 697–715.

Buchan, J. (2020) The struggle is real: Theorising community justice restructuring agonistically. *European Journal of Probation* 12(2): 73–90.

Buchan, J. and McNeill, F. (2023) Progressive penality as performance. *Howard Journal of Crime and Justice* 62(3): 325–340.

Buchan, J. and Morrison, K. (2020) Compromise, partnership, control: Community justice authorities in Scotland. *Criminology & Criminal Justice* 20(2): 226–243.
Butler, S., Maglione, G. and Buchan, J. (2022) Institutionalising restorative justice for adults in Scotland: An empirical study of practitioners' perspectives. *Criminology and Criminal Justice* 24(1): 269–290.
Calverley, A. (2013) *Cultures of Desistance: Rehabilitation, Reintegration and Ethnic Minorities*. Routledge.
Cleary, J. (forthcoming) Scottish community justice and women: Progress or peripheral concern? *British Journal of Community Justice*.
Cohen, S. (1985) *Visions of Social Control: Crime, Punishment and Classification*. Polity.
Commission on Women Offenders (2012) *Commission on Women Offenders: Final Report*, April 2012. Scottish Government.
Ditton, J. and Ford, R. (1994) *The Reality of Probation: A Formal Ethnography of Process and Practice*. Avebury.
Durnescu, I. (2011) Pains of probation: Effective practice and human rights. *International Journal of Offender Therapy and Comparative Criminology* 55(4): 530–545.
Fenton, J. (2013) Aversion and anxiety in Scottish criminal justice social work: Can desistance and human rights agendas have an impact? *Howard Journal of Criminal Justice* 52(1): 77–90.
Glynn, M. (2013) *Black Men, Invisibility and Crime: A Critical Race Theory of Desistance*. Routledge.
Halsey, M., Armstrong, R. and Wright, S. (2017) 'F*ck It!': Matza and the mood of fatalism in the desistance process. *British Journal of Criminology* 57(5): 1041–1060.
Hayes, D. (2018). Proximity, pain, and state punishment. *Punishment & Society* 20(2): 235–254.
IRISS (Institute for Research and Innovation in Social Services) (2015) *Evaluation of Sixteen Women's Community Justice Services in Scotland*. Scottish Government.
Johnson, S. (2024) 'Backlog' of unpaid work not carried out by Scottish criminals rises. *Telegraph*, 20 December. Available at https://www.telegraph.co.uk/news/2024/12/20/backlog-unpaid-work-not-carried-out-scottish-criminals-rise/
Keenan, M. and Zinsstag, E. (2022) *Sexual Violence and Restorative Justice*. Oxford University Press.
Kelly, C. (2017) Probation officers for young offenders in 1920s Scotland. *European Journal of Probation* 9(2): 169–191.
Kirkwood, S. and Hamad, R. (2019) Restorative justice informed criminal justice social work. *Probation Journal* 66(4): 398–415.
Kirkwood, S. and Kritikos, L. (2025) A history of restorative justice in Scotland: The evolving nature of an innovation in criminal justice policy and practice. *Howard Journal of Crime and Justice*, 64(1): 61–76.
Maglione, G., Buchan, J. and Robertson, L. (2020) The local provision of restorative justice in Scotland: An exploratory empirical study. *European Journal on Criminal Policy and Research* 28: 617–640.
Maglione, G., Marder, I. and Pali, B. (eds) (2024) *Restorative Justice at a Crossroads: Dilemmas of Institutionalisation*. Routledge.
Malloch, M. and McIvor, G. (2011) Women and community sentences. *Criminology & Criminal Justice* 11(4): 325–344.
Marshall, T. (1999) *Restorative Justice: An Overview*. Home Office.

Maruna, S. and King, A. (2008) Selling the public on probation: Beyond the Bib. *Probation Journal* 55(4): 337–351.

McCulloch, T. (2005) Probation, social context and desistance: Retracing the relationship. *Probation Journal* 52(1): 8–22.

McNeill, F. (2005) Remembering probation in Scotland. *Probation Journal* 52(1): 23–38.

McNeill, F. (2010) *Community Payback and the new National Standards for Criminal Justice Social Work*. SCCJR Briefing Paper No 02/2010. https://www.sccjr.ac.uk/wp-content/uploads/2012/11/Briefing_Paper_2010_02_community_payback.pdf

McNeill, F. (2015) Desistance and criminal justice in Scotland. In Croall, H. Mooney, G. and Munro, M. (eds) *Crime, Justice and Society in Scotland*. Routledge. 200–215.

McNeill, F. (2019). Mass supervision, misrecognition and the 'Malopticon'. *Punishment and Society*, 21(2), 207–230.

McNeill, F., Burns, N., Halliday, S., Hutton, N. and Tata, C. (2009) Risk, responsibility and reconfiguration: Penal adaptation and misadaptation. *Punishment and Society* 11(4): 419–442.

McWilliams, W. (1990) Probation Practice and the Management Ideal. *Probation Journal* 37(1): 60–7.

Moore, G. (1978) Crisis in Scotland. *Howard Journal of Criminal Justice* 17(1): 32–40.

Morrison, K. (2015) The management of community justice services in Scotland: Policy-making and the dynamics of central and local control. In Wasik, M., Santatzoglou, S. (eds) *The Management of Change in Criminal Justice: Who Knows Best?* Palgrave Macmillan. 152–169.

Nugent, B. and Schinkel, M. (2016) The pains of desistance. *Criminology and Criminal Justice* 16(5): 568–584.

Ormston, R., Mulholland, C. and Setterfield, L. (2016) *Caledonian System Evaluation: Analysis of a Programme for Tackling Domestic Abuse in Scotland*. Ipsos MORI Scotland.

Rifkind, M. (1989) Penal policy: The way ahead. *Howard Journal of Criminal Justice* 28(2): 81–90.

Schinkel, M. (2019) Rethinking turning points: Trajectories of parenthood and desistance. *Journal of Developmental and Life-Course Criminology* 5: 366–386.

Schinkel, M., Atkinson, C. and Anderson, S. (2019) 'Well-Kent Faces': Policing persistent offenders and the possibility for desistance. *British Journal of Criminology* 59(3): 634–652.

Scottish Government (2014) *Future Model for Community Justice in Scotland*. Scottish Government.

Scottish Government (2019) *Restorative Justice Action Plan*. Scottish Government.

Scottish Government (2022) *National Strategy for Community Justice*. Scottish Government.

Scottish Government (2024) *Criminal Proceedings in Scotland 2022–3*. Scottish Government.

Scottish Prisons Commission (2008) *Scotland's Choice: Report of the Scottish Prisons Commission*. Scottish Prisons Commission.

Shapland, J., Bottoms, A., Farrall, S., McNeill, F., Priede, C. and Robinson, G. (2012) *The Quality of Probation Supervision – A Literature Review*. Centre for Criminological Research, University of Sheffield.

Tata, C. (2020) *Sentencing: A Social Process – Re-Thinking Research and Policy*. Palgrave Macmillan.

Velasquez Valenzuela, J. (2018) *Doing Justice: Sentencing Practice in Scottish Sheriff Courts*. PhD thesis, University of Glasgow.

Weaver, B. (2011) Co-Producing community justice: The transformative potential of personalisation for penal sanctions. *British Journal of Social Work* 41: 1038–1057.

Weaver, B. (2015) *Offending and Desistance: The Importance of Social Relations*. Routledge.

Weaver, B. (2019) Understanding desistance: A critical review of theories of desistance. *Psychology, Crime and Law* 25(6): 641–658.

Weaver, B., Graham, H. and Maruna, S. (2023) Turning Over a New Leaf: Desistance Research for a New Generation. In Liebling, A., Maruna, S. and McAra, L. (eds) *The Oxford Handbook of Criminology*. Seventh edition. Oxford University Press. 146–165.

Weaver, B. and Jardine, C. (2022) Citizenship on probation: Understanding the labour market exclusion of criminalized people in Scotland. *Probation Journal* 69(3): 296–317.

Weaver, B. and McNeill, F. (2007) *Giving Up Crime: Directions for Policy*. SCCCJ.

Weaver, B., Piacentini, L., Moodie, K., and Barry, M. (2021) Exploring and explaining non-compliance with community supervision. *British Journal of Criminology* 61(2): 434–455.

Williams, R.G. (2019) *Tripartite Interaction in the Community Payback Order*. PhD thesis, University of Edinburgh.

7 Electronic monitoring in Scotland

Key ideas

- In Scotland, electronic monitoring (EM, often called 'tagging') can be used in various ways across the criminal justice process, from bail to supervised release from prison.
- EM in Scotland is contracted out to a private provider; it is the only part of Scottish criminal justice that is mostly privatised.
- Scottish EM has until recently been limited to radio-frequency technology, but is starting to expand into GPS and may in future employ alcohol monitoring.
- EM has become prominent alongside the rise of risk management from the 1990s onwards; the dramatic developments around electronically monitored Home Detention Curfews illustrate the issues around risk and risk aversion in criminal justice.
- The evidence for EM's effect on reoffending and desistance is mixed. The technology appears to offer a way of ensuring compliance while supporting positive relationships, but there are significant harms going beyond the restriction on movement.

Introduction

Electronic monitoring (EM) includes a range of technologies to ensure compliance with an order or conditions imposed through the criminal justice system, although the exact rationale for this may vary depending on how it is used. In this chapter and in much of the criminological literature, the emphasis is on the use of body-worn devices ('tags') capable of collecting and remotely transmitting data about a person, principally their location and movements. In theory, EM allows close monitoring and control of movements and schedules, without too much interference with the monitored person's home, family and work life.

EM is not the only way in which criminal justice systems use electronic and digital technology to monitor people. Furthermore, outside of the criminal justice system, we are all subject to extensive technological surveillance. The collection and monitoring of extensive personal data about us is widespread

DOI: 10.4324/9781003372882-7

in the technologies we use throughout our daily lives (for example, the CCTV that captures us, the phones we use to navigate, wearable fitness technology, etc.). However, while we are all increasingly electronically monitored, the use of EM within criminal justice is distinct – particularly since it is used to monitor compliance and (as with community sentences) may come with the threat of imprisonment for breach of conditions.

We begin this chapter by explaining the technologies used for EM in Scotland and outlining the key agencies involved, principally the private security company G4S. We then give a brief history of the introduction and development of EM in Scotland and how it fits into wider penal and political trends. By examining the changing use of electronic monitoring as part of Home Detention Curfew (HDC), we highlight the intersection of politics, risk assessment and criminal justice. Finally, we consider what is known about the effect of EM on reoffending, and recent Scottish research on the lived experience of being electronically monitored.

7.1 Electronic monitoring in Scotland

Within Scotland, EM can be used at different points in the criminal justice system: for legally innocent people (on EM bail awaiting trial), people convicted of less or moderately serious offences (community sentences), and people serving sentences for serious offences (supervised release from prison).

- While awaiting trial (EM bail), under an **Electronic Monitoring Order (EMO)**.
- In community sentences:
  - To enforce a **Restriction of Liberty Order (RLO)**, a community sentence requiring a person to stay at a particular place during particular hours (often their home, and overnight). Less commonly, RLOs can require people to stay *away* from a place at particular times;
  - Optionally, as a **Restricted Movement Requirement** on a Community Payback Order (CPO) or a Drug Treatment and Testing Order (DTTO) (see Chapter 6).
- In youth justice: as part of a **Movement Restriction Condition (MRC)** imposed by a children's hearing.
- During/after imprisonment: to monitor people on **Home Detention Curfew (HDC)**, parole or non-parole licences (see Chapter 10).

As of late 2024, there were over 2,100 people electronically monitored by Scottish criminal justice (Constance, 2024). Over the last decade, there have been significant shifts in the proportions accounted for by the various measures. There has been a steady rise in RLOs, which have tended to form the bulk of the EM caseload. Restricted movement requirements on CPOs have increased but continue to account for smaller numbers. MRCs are very rare, and electronically monitored DTTOs are even rarer. Meanwhile, as discussed in Section 7.2.2, the use of HDCs has fallen significantly since 2018 and has yet to recover. Most recently, there has been a significant rise in EM bail.

7.1.1 Technologies of electronic monitoring

Electronic monitoring in a Scottish/UK context has generally been used to monitor someone's presence at a particular location during particular times. The usual method in the UK uses **radio frequency (RF)**. This works with a device attached to the person (usually an ankle bracelet, often called a 'tag') which communicates by radio with a receiver (officially a Home Monitoring Unit or HMU) placed in that location (usually the person's home) and connected to the monitoring centre via the mobile or landline phone network. This receiver can detect when the device (the radio signal) is present, and hence when it is not.

Usually, RF monitoring is used to ensure someone is at home during certain hours; if the signal is not detected when it should be, the HMU sends an alert to the monitoring organisation (the EM service provider). The monitoring organisation then attempts to contact the person and decides on the appropriate response. Much less frequently, if someone is required to *avoid* a location, an HMU can be installed there as an 'away from' box. The ankle bracelet is designed to be waterproof, impossible to remove without special equipment, and to set off an alert if tampered with (although as with any product, the reality may not always match the manufacturers' claims).

More recently, technological advances have offered more flexible and expansive ways to monitor someone's geographical location, using **global positioning system (GPS)** technology. This technology is now ubiquitous (notably in smartphones) and allows monitoring not just whether someone is in a particular place at a particular time, but also *where* they move over time – all without any need for an HMU. This more fine-grained surveillance is likely to impact how EM is experienced – potentially either greater freedom of movement (if it facilitates a *less* restrictive curfew), or an increase in the restrictive and punitive experience of EM. From 2025 onwards, under the 2019 Management of Offenders (Scotland) Act, GPS monitoring has been adopted in Scotland but only to enforce Home Detention Curfews (Section 7.2.2).

The only other currently relevant technology in Scotland is remote alcohol monitoring, specifically **trans-dermal alcohol monitoring (TAM)**. This involves the person wearing devices which can measure alcohol levels in their sweat and remotely transmit this information. This allows for remote testing and enforcement of licence requirements to abstain from alcohol (currently available as part of a parole or non-parole licence – see Section 10.2.1). In 2025, TAM is legally permitted but not currently used in Scotland, despite longstanding interest in it amid wider concerns about the role of alcohol in offending (see Section 2.2). However, it raises various issues – including the possibility that TAM evidence could lead to increased sentences (since intoxication at the time of the offence may be considered aggravating) (Andreangeli, 2020).

Other existing and developing technologies could be, and in some places are, employed for the surveillance of people under criminal justice orders (see for instance Nellis et al., 2013). While commonly used for promoting compliance with orders, we can imagine other uses within criminal justice of technologically enabled remote monitoring. In January 2025, the Fatal Accident Inquiry (FAI) into the deaths of Katie Allan and William Brown (Lindsay) in HMYOI Polmont recommended that the Scottish Prison Service (SPS) pilot electronic 'signs of life' monitoring technology *inside* prison cells to prevent self-inflicted deaths (Determination by Sheriff S.G. Collins KC, 2025).

7.1.2 Key agencies

In Scotland, a private provider is contracted by the Scottish Government to deliver EM (**the EM service provider**). As of early 2025, EM is provided by the multinational private security provider G4S, under a contract closely managed by the Scottish Government. G4S was first awarded the contract for EM services in Scotland in 2012 (McIvor and Graham, 2016) and secured a further five-year contract in 2019 – despite a scandal in the 2010s in which G4S were found to have systematically overcharged the UK government for EM contracts in England and Wales. Before G4S, the contract was held by Reliance Monitoring Services (2001–06), then Serco (2006–12).

G4S installs and removes equipment in people's homes, visits people under EM, and monitors and processes 'events' (e.g. where a signal is not detected when it should be). This is coordinated via the company's National Electronic Monitoring Centre near Glasgow.

In ensuring compliance with orders, the service provider works in partnership with other agencies. In the event of a breach, G4S must inform **Police Scotland**, who take the next steps in responding to the breach. For RLOs, G4S is responsible for reporting breaches to the court; in other types of supervision, including CPOs and DTTOs, this is the responsibility of the supervising social worker. Although they do not do the actual monitoring, **justice social work (JSW)** also has an important role to play in conducting risk assessments and assessing the suitability of someone's home for curfew. Decision-making around HDCs involves the **Scottish Prison Service** and sometimes the **Parole Board for Scotland**, while in the rare cases of electronic monitoring imposed by children's hearings (see Chapter 7), non-compliance (not called 'breach') is referred to the **Children's Reporter**.

It is worth noting here that 'events' flagged up by the machines, which may initially appear to be breaches, can have other causes – including equipment or software failure. In determining what is or isn't a 'breach', the discretion of those supervising the order is nearly as important here as in other forms of supervisory punishment. Minor or first-time 'time violations' (typically an absence during curfew) do not always trigger this process. McIvor and Graham (2016) found significant variation between courts around breaches, with some Sheriffs establishing especially close oversight through their working relationships with G4S.

While many European jurisdictions have incorporated EM into *public*-sector justice services, Scotland appears – despite much more limited justice privatisation than in England and Wales (notably a minimal use of privately run prisons), to have adopted a privatised 'Anglo-American' model of EM with little controversy.

7.2 Understanding the development of EM in Scotland

7.2.1 A brief history of electronic monitoring in Scotland

As discussed elsewhere, the late 20th century is typically understood as a time when social democracy declined in favour of neoliberalism. One feature of criminal justice under neoliberalism was the rise of risk management approaches (see Section 6.3.2), in what Feeley and Simon (1992) have termed 'the new penology'. These practices purport to assess people in the criminal justice system, categorise them into groups by risk, and then seek to manage this risk in the most efficient and cost-effective way possible. EM can be understood as a tool of this new penology, one which prioritises management over rehabilitation, and makes people responsible for their compliance with punishment (Laurie and Maglione, 2020). The emphasis on private-sector provision of the technology also aligns with neoliberal support for privatisation.

The earliest electronic tag was patented in 1969, and the use of EM in criminal justice gathered momentum in the 1980s (Smith, 2001). EM was piloted in England and Wales in 1988 for people on bail, then introduced as part of a sentence (a curfew order) through the Criminal Justice Act, 1991 and a national rollout in 1999. The impetus for EM down south has been attributed to a range of converging factors, including high prison populations and associated costs, an emphasis on alternatives to custody (but dissatisfaction with existing options), and lobbying from proponents, including the companies producing the relevant equipment (Mair and Nellis, 2013).

The subsequent introduction of EM in Scotland was arguably modelled on England and Wales and fuelled by similar concerns (Nellis, 2015). The Crime and Punishment (Scotland) Act 1997 (s.5) introduced the RLO, and the use of EM to enforce RLOs was piloted in 1998. Although evaluations suggested it would have little impact on the prison population or on reducing costs (Smith, 2001), electronically monitored RLOs were rolled out in 2002.

EM was then expanded through the Criminal Justice (Scotland) Act 2003, which enabled its use as part of a DTTO and the (now defunct) probation order. In 2010, when the probation order was replaced by the CPO (see Chapter 6), EM could initially only be imposed as part of a CPO where there had already been a breach of that order. The 2003 Act also introduced the use of EM to monitor people released from prison on licence (see Chapter 10).

Following this, the Management of Offenders etc (Scotland) Act 2005 allowed for EM as part of arrangements for the temporary release of people from prison under HDC, following similar arrangements in England and Wales (Mair and Nellis, 2013). Around this time, there were pilots experimenting with EM to monitor bail conditions, with the intention of reducing the use of prison remand. However, these stopped after unpromising evaluations (Barry et al., 2007; Casey, 2023). Within youth justice, the post-devolutionary shift towards more punitive and risk-focused approaches (see Chapter 9) included powers for children's hearings to impose EM on children – initially called Intensive Support and Monitoring and now Movement Restriction Conditions. However, as with some of the other youth justice measures introduced at that time (Section 9.3.1), actual uptake was low and it is now used rarely.

The use of EM fluctuated in the early 2000s, then held steady at around 3,000 cases a year (mostly RLOs and HDCs) until the collapse of HDC (Section 7.2.2).

Characterising the 'Scottish approach' to EM as it developed after the initial pilots, Graham and McIvor (2017: 68–69) suggested that "from 2002 to 2016, the national picture of the uses of EM in Scotland can broadly be understood as relatively simple, standardised, stable and small in scale". It used just RF technology, with a fairly standardised regime (curfews usually running from 7 pm to 7 am). It was less common than other community sentences or imprisonment, and generally imposed as a standalone intervention (not integrated with other support or supervision). This led to concerns that without accompanying supportive interventions, the potential of EM to facilitate desistance from crime was underexplored (Nellis, 2015).

Since then, Scottish policy has shifted gradually towards a model which seeks to integrate risk management with rehabilitation and 'desistance' from crime (see Section 6.3.4). This is reflected in the final report of the EM Working Group (2016), whose vision for EM explicitly includes more integration of EM with other supportive measures and an emphasis on reducing offending and promoting desistance.

These proposals were incorporated into the Management of Offenders (Scotland) Act 2019. As well as expanding the types of technology available to include GPS and TAM (Section 7.1.1), this Act extended the use of EM as part of a CPO (allowing a Restricted Movement Requirement to be imposed without the person having first breached the order) and widened the range of post-release measures where it can be used. Provisions of the Act not yet commenced in 2024 may further extend the use of EM to enforce other orders, including Supervised Release Orders.

In response to concerns about the high numbers of people imprisoned on remand (Chapter 8), the 2019 Act reintroduced electronically monitored bail. This was intended to increase confidence that people would comply with bail conditions and hence the willingness of prosecutors and judges to release people on bail rather than remanding them. Resolving one problem identified in the 2007 evaluation (Barry et al., 2007), the Bail and Release from Custody (Scotland) Act 2023 allows for time spent on EM bail to be taken into account when imposing a custodial sentence (with two days on EM bail reducing the prison sentence by one day, unless the court decides otherwise). Where bail is refused, the court must justify why EM bail was not considered appropriate.

It is yet to be seen whether this time, EM bail will fulfil policymakers' hopes of reducing the remand population and easing pressure on overcrowded prisons. Research following its introduction highlighted issues with insufficient provision in some (especially rural) areas, and variations in awareness and support among relevant justice decision-makers (Scottish Government, 2023). It does appear however that EM bail has risen significantly in its first few years to account for about 20% of electronic monitoring orders in 2023–24 (G4S, 2024). Returning to other uses of EM in Scotland, there has been a steady growth in the use of RLOs over the past decade (Casey, 2023). For HDC, it has been a very different story, discussed just below.

While neoliberalism and risk management agendas have had important influences in Scotland, Laurie and Maglione (2020) underscore the importance of attending to local contexts. Scotland has remained part of a neoliberal polity while successive Scottish National Party (SNP) governments have at least *outwardly* espoused social democratic ideals and claims to a progressive *civic* rather than ethnic nationalism. This contributes to "a paradoxical policy based on a performative yet unstable tangle of political motives" (Laurie and Maglione, 2020: 697). There has been a clear policy commitment to the continued expansion of EM use in Scotland, notably in the 2022 Vision for Justice and the 2022 National Strategy for Community Justice – but this 'tangle' has influenced how EM has come to look in practice in Scotland, as exemplified in the changing fortunes of the HDC.

7.2.2 *The rise and fall of Home Detention Curfew*

HDC was introduced in Scotland by the 2005 Management of Offenders etc. (Scotland) Act, with the stated aim of ensuring that people leaving prison have a "managed return to their communities" (Scottish Government, n.d.). The Act gave prisons the power to release two groups of prisoners on HDC, for a period of between 14 and 180 days. The first is those serving a short sentence (three months to four years), who have served at least a quarter of their sentence. The second group is those serving a long sentence (defined as four years or over), following a recommendation at the halfway point of their sentence by the Parole Board after their first review (this is different from release on parole, which can also be electronically monitored). A prisoner on HDC serves part of their sentence in the community, subject to an electronically monitored curfew.

Certain groups are excluded from HDC: people subject to Sex Offender Notification Requirements, sentenced to a Supervised Release Order or Extended Sentence (see Section 10.2.1), people subject to compulsory mental health treatment, prisoners recalled from parole, and foreign nationals liable to deportation (see Chapter 11).

The power to grant HDC rests with the SPS, usually the Deputy Governor of the relevant prison. Their decision is informed by a JSW report into the suitability of the person's curfew address for HDC. For longer-term prisoners, it relies on the recommendation of the Parole Board. In deciding to release someone on HDC, SPS must consider the protection of the public, preventing reoffending, and the successful reintegration of the person into the community. SPS may also decide it is in the public interest to revoke an HDC licence, with Police Scotland then tasked with returning the person to prison.

In 2017, a murder was committed in Paisley by someone on an HDC, who had breached his conditions some time previously but had not been returned to prison. The incident received considerable press attention and led to independent reviews of HDC arrangements by the HM Inspectorate of Constabulary in Scotland (HMICS) and HM Inspectorate of Prisons for Scotland (HMIPS), with significant consequences for the use of HDC in Scotland, and so for time served by people in custody.

As well as improved information sharing and timely responses, the HMICS (2018) review recommended the introduction of a new offence of being 'unlawfully at large' following a breach of HDC conditions. This offence was created by the Management of Offenders (Scotland) Act 2019; a person convicted of it would not only be recalled to prison but also face further punishment (up to two years' imprisonment) for the breach.

These reviews also recommended improved risk assessment processes to be developed alongside the Risk Management Authority (see Chapter 10), and a presumption *against* release for certain groups of prisoners: where the conviction relates to violence, possession of an offensive weapon or having links to organised crime (HMICS, 2018).

The consequence of all this was plummeting use of HDC in Scotland – from 300 people living on HDC in the community in 2018 to fewer than 60 in 2019 (HMIPS, 2019). The presumption against release remained until April 2020, by which point the COVID-19 pandemic was creating pressure to reduce the prison population, and risk assessment processes had been revised; under the 2019 HDC Operating Protocol, prisoners usually must already be held at the lowest level of security within the prison to be deemed suitable for HDC.

The history of HDC in Scotland reflects wider issues with risk management approaches to justice, in prison and the community (see Sections 8.2.2 and 6.3.2). One repeated problem for criminal justice is how to deliver on the promise that it will – and can – accurately assess and manage risk, despite problems with the evidence and assumptions that underpin much risk assessment practice (Prins and Reich, 2021). The intention of these approaches is to prevent harm by identifying 'risky' people and situations and putting them under close surveillance and control. Among other things, this puts acute pressure on decision-makers in the criminal justice system. Even *before* the 2017 murder, people working within the SPS had adopted a "cautious approach" to HDC use and recall (McIvor and Graham, 2016). The response to the murder reflects a common system – and political – response to failures of this (unachievable) promise of risk management: falling back on increased use of incapacitation. The number of people living on HDC at any given time has not recovered to pre-2018 levels.

However, amid ongoing concern over prison overcrowding, the Scottish Government returned to the issue of HDC. In November 2024, Scottish Ministers laid before Parliament the Electronic Monitoring (Approved Devices) (Scotland) Amendment Regulations, 2024, enabling the use of GPS devices specifically to monitor compliance with HDC. Alongside this, the eligibility criteria for HDC are set to be changed. These measures seek to reduce overcrowding by making HDC a 'safer' option – but as with the bail reforms, it remains to be seen whether they will have the intended effect. It also represents a new development in the technologies available to Scotland's electronic monitoring regime. More generally, there remain questions as to whether EM can support desistance and about its effect on monitored people and their families – as we discuss in the next section.

7.3 Evaluating electronic monitoring

7.3.1 Electronic monitoring and desistance

As part of the work of the EM Working Group and subsequent developments, greater consideration has been given as to how EM can be used to facilitate desistance from crime (McIvor and Graham, 2016; see Box 6.2 on desistance). There are various 'common-sense' rationales and criminological theories that suggest EM may prevent further offending, although the evidence base has historically been mixed at best. A series of systematic reviews of international evidence found insufficient evidence to support the conclusion that EM reduces reoffending when compared to either community sentences with less intensive monitoring or prison (Renzema and Mayo-Wilson, 2005; Mackenzie, 2006). Other studies have drawn more positive conclusions about the effectiveness of EM, at least when used as an alternative to prison (Andersen and Telle, 2022; Henneguelle et al., 2016), although they disagree as to how long the effect on reoffending lasts beyond the monitoring period.

One of the main challenges in determining whether EM has any effect on reoffending is that internationally the use of EM varies considerably. As well as being used at different stages of the criminal justice process, it is used with different target groups (e.g. people deemed low risk who might not have reoffended anyway, or those deemed high risk for reoffending). Moreover, EM is often combined with other interventions (e.g. treatment) or requirements (e.g. curfews, but also, in some jurisdictions, requirements to work), so that it is hard to establish the impact (if any) of the monitoring aspect, as opposed to the other conditions. As with other 'alternatives to imprisonment', the example of EM raises the question of what an EM order, as actually imposed, constitutes an alternative *to*.

This means it is essential to carefully consider the evidence for specific schemes, and the rationale through which change is envisaged in particular schemes, so that this can be evaluated; however, no equivalent studies of Scottish EM have been commissioned. The problems with evaluation are compounded by the fact that, as we have seen, Scotland uses EM at various stages of the justice process and with different rationales. Research with Sheriffs suggests that some employ EM specifically as a mechanism for punishment, with less regard for any potential to support changes in behaviour (Graham and McIvor, 2017) – and often without integration with more traditional measures widely held to be more supportive of desistance (though, as noted in Chapter 6, not without restrictive and punitive aspects).

Of course, reducing reoffending is not the only concern when deciding whether to employ EM in criminal justice. There are many other considerations such as cost, the desire to punish the person, and the impact that each sentence might have on the person being sentenced and their family – to which we now turn.

7.3.2 *The experience of electronic monitoring*

The way in which EM is experienced will vary across places and times, depending on factors such as the forms of technology used, the details of the sentence or process it forms part of, and how these interact with the circumstances of those people involved (Richter et al., 2021). Thinking about these factors can help us understand how the experience of EM in Scotland compares to its use in other places. Two recent ethnographies of EM in Scotland (Casey, 2021, 2023; Gacek, 2019), provide important insights into how the process is experienced by the people involved.

When someone is placed on an EM order in Scotland, a field officer from the service provider must attend the property where the person will be under curfew (this may be their own home, or, for example, that of a family member). During this first 'induction' visit, the HMU is installed at the property, and the tag is fitted to the person. After this, there is a process of digitally mapping out the spatial 'range' of the box to fit the boundaries of the property (Casey, 2021). The monitored person walks around the property, placing a foot in every corner of every room, and even underwater in the bath or shower. This information is transferred digitally to the monitoring centre, where officers monitor the person. Following installation, if the person is not detected at the right place at the right time, these officers receive an alert and follow up with the person, for example by phone call. A record is kept of the timing and duration of these incidents; one incident might not necessarily constitute a breach, though there is little transparency about the threshold for breach proceedings to be initiated. During their time under EM, people must not only stay in the property but be ready to answer phone calls to check up on them. If they don't answer the phone, the assumption is often made that they are breaking the rules (Casey, 2021). They may also get visits at very short notice from Field Officers who expect to be able to enter the property, for example, to check equipment.

Limitations in the technology can have important effects, resulting in more restrictive conditions than prescribed by the courts. Casey (2021) observes that the digital range and the physical boundaries of the property may not fit onto one another – so someone can appear to be 'outside' their curfew area, while actually inside at home. To avoid appearing to breach the conditions of their curfew, they might have to avoid certain spaces *in their own home* during curfew hours. If they don't do this and the Monitoring Officer is alerted, the onus is often on them to prove they have not breached conditions.

As with other forms of punishment, EM can be stigmatising and embarrassing (Gacek, 2019) – an experience which may disproportionately affect women, given the equipment is designed for men, and whose (generally) tighter clothes may make the tag more obvious (Holdsworth and Hucklesby, 2014). People with certain illnesses or injuries may also experience *physical* discomfort from the tag (Casey, 2021).

Many people under EM live with others, who also experience aspects of this punishment. This includes the intrusion of monitoring (field officers visiting, phone calls at antisocial hours, etc.) (Payne et al., 2014). Family members can come to feel responsible for the person being monitored and their compliance with the order, putting strain on family ties (Smith, 2001; Casey, 2023). Both Hucklesby (2008) in England and Deuchar (2012) with young people in Scotland found mixed impacts on family relationships – sometimes for the better (e.g. spending more time with children), but sometimes for the worse, as tensions were exacerbated by having to spend long periods in shared space, with no option to introduce physical distance when conflict arose. EM can also make it harder to visit family members the person does not live with (Hucklesby, 2008).

While women are statistically much less likely to be monitored, our knowledge of gendered patterns of family life suggests that they may suffer more from EM, whether they are monitored themselves or are family members of people so monitored. Evidence from England (Holdsworth and Hucklesby, 2014) highlights that since women are more likely to do domestic chores and much more likely to be single parents, they may need to 'breach' more often, e.g. late-night trips to get things for children. As with other feminist critiques, this shows the impact of a system designed for (and around) men 'carried over' to women without recognition of the impact of gender on their lives.

While a curfew may seek to reduce (what is viewed as negative) peer contact, young adults in Scotland with experience of EM nevertheless talked about the negative emotional impacts of being isolated by EM from their peer network and social supports (Miller and Anderson, 2021). Being confined to one's home is not only isolating but may be boring and frustrating (Gacek, 2019).

Finally, ethnographic data call into question the claim that EM supports employment (Laurie and Maglione, 2020). Both Hucklesby (2008) and Casey (2023) have highlighted the ways in which being subject to EM can *negatively* impact employment, for example, the stigma of the tag, limitations on hours available to work, and the lack of flexibility. An EM curfew might fit with a standard '9 to 5' job, but not with shift work, precarious employment or jobs that require travel to sites.

Casey (2023) argues that when we pay attention to the lived reality for those who are subject to EM, this can undermine many of the assumptions and claims of policymakers about the benefits and rationale for EM, for example around its possibilities to support desistance from crime (Hucklesby, 2008).

Conclusion

This chapter has shown that the electronic monitoring of people under supervision fits into the criminal justice system at various stages – before and during trial, under community sentences and as part of supervised release from prison. This chapter has focused on the uses of EM by the criminal justice system, but there are examples of it being used in other settings adjacent to criminal justice such as immigration enforcement (Bhatia, 2021). The development of EM in Scotland initially proceeded along similar lines to that of England and Wales, but more recently there has been policy interest in integrating EM with other measures and using it to ease pressure on the prison system.

Advocates of EM argue that it offers a cheaper and less punitive alternative to imprisonment, with round-the-clock surveillance and technological enforcement of restrictions, managing risk without interfering unduly with 'prosocial' bonds to work and family life. However, the ethnography of EM 'on the ground' (Casey, 2021, 2023) calls this into question and highlights the gap between what is expected by justice policy and how monitored people live their lives. In the next chapter, we will address in detail the most intensive form of punishment administered by criminal justice – imprisonment.

Critical questions

- Think about the ways in which EM has been used in Scotland and could be used in future. How might these different uses work to support desistance from crime? Are there ways in which EM might actually hinder desistance?
- What are some arguments for and against privatising criminal justice services, including EM? Why do you think Scotland adopted privatised EM with relatively little controversy?

- What are the ethical implications of criminal justice monitoring health data – such as a person's alcohol intake or 'signs of life' – remotely? In what ways do the purpose of monitoring and the criminal justice context affect the ethical implications?
- Can electronic monitoring achieve the goal of managing and reducing 'risk' in the community?
- Unlike other agencies discussed in this book, there are no regular inspections of electronic monitoring and little clarity as to which body should inspect it. Which scrutiny bodies should be responsible for EM?
- Beyond RF/GPS tagging and trans-dermal alcohol monitoring, can you think of other technologies that could be used to monitor people in the criminal justice system? What are some implications of these?

Key resources

Casey, R. (2023) (Un)making penal electronic monitoring policy in Scotland. In Maier, K., Ricciardelli, R. and McNeill, F. (Eds) *Punishment, Probation and Parole: Mapping Out 'Mass Supervision' In International Contexts*. Emerald Publishing Limited. 79–99.

A key recent source on electronic monitoring in Scotland.

Daems, T. (2020) *Electronic Monitoring: Tagging Offenders in a Culture of Surveillance*. Palgrave Macmillan.

An overview of the various functions of electronic monitoring as used in European jurisdictions.

McIvor, G. and Graham, H. (2016) *Electronic Monitoring in Scotland*. SCCJR. https://www.sccjr.ac.uk/wp-content/uploads/2016/06/Electronic-Monitoring-in-Scotland-Report.pdf

A comprehensive review of EM in Scotland (albeit before important legislative changes).

References

Andersen, S.N. and Telle, K. (2022) Better out than in? The effect on recidivism of replacing incarceration with electronic monitoring in Norway. *European Journal of Criminology* 19(1): 55–76.

Andreangeli, A. (2020) *'Sobriety Tagging': What is it, and What Issues Does it Raise in the Scottish Context?* https://www.shaap.org.uk/blog/318-sobriety-tagging-arianna-andreangelli.html

Barry, M., Malloch, M., Moodie, K., Nellis, M., Knapp, M., Romeo, R. and Dhanasiri, S. (2007) *An Evaluation of the Use of Electronic Monitoring as a Condition of Bail in Scotland: Final Report*. Scottish Executive.

Bhatia, M. (2021) Racial surveillance and the mental health impacts of electronic monitoring on migrants. *Race and Class* 62(3): 18–36.

Casey, R. (2021) *Left to Their Own Devices: A Technosocial Ethnography of Penal Electronic Monitoring in Scotland*. PhD thesis, University of Glasgow.

Casey, R. (2023) (Un)making penal electronic monitoring policy in Scotland. In Maier, K., Ricciardelli, R. and McNeill, F. (eds) *Punishment, Probation and*

Parole: Mapping Out 'Mass Supervision' in International Contexts. Emerald Publishing Limited. 79–99.

Constance, A. (2024) *Justice Secretary: Statement on Scotland's Prison Population*. Scottish Government. https://www.gov.scot/publications/justice-secretary-statement-on-scotlands-prison-population/

Determination By Sheriff S.G. Collins KC under *The Inquiries Into Fatal Accidents and Sudden Deaths etc (Scotland) Act 2016 into the Deaths of Katie Allan and William Brown*, 13 January 2025. https://www.scotcourts.gov.uk/media/1olg15np/2025fai006-fai-katie-allan-william-brown.pdf

Deuchar, R. (2012) The impact of curfews and electronic monitoring on the social strains, support and capital experienced by youth gang members and offenders in the west of Scotland. *Criminology & Criminal Justice* 12(2): 113–128.

Electronic Monitoring Working Group (2016) *Electronic Monitoring in Scotland: Working Group Final Report*. Scottish Government.

Feeley, M.M. and Simon, J. (1992) The new penology: Notes on the emerging strategy of corrections and its implications. *Criminology* 30(4): 449–474.

G4S (2024) *Statistical Bulletin: Electronic Monitoring to the Criminal and Youth Justice Systems in Scotland, 1st* April 2023–31st March 2024. G4S.

Gacek, J. (2019) Stuck in the carceral web: Prisoners' experiences of electronic monitoring. *Criminological Encounters* 2(1): 35–52.

Graham, H. and McIvor, G. (2017) Advancing electronic monitoring in Scotland: Understanding the influences of localism and professional ideologies. *European Journal of Probation* 9(1): 62–79.

Henneguelle, A., Monnery, B. and Kensey, A. (2016) Better at home than in prison? The effects of electronic monitoring on recidivism in France. *Journal of Law and Economics* 59(3): 629–667.

HM Inspectorate of Constabulary in Scotland (HMICS) (2018) *Strategic Review – An Independent Assessment of Police Scotland's Response to a Breach of Home Detention Curfew (HDC)*. HMICS.

HM Inspectorate of Prisons for Scotland (2019) *Report on the Review of the Arrangements for Home Detention Curfew within the Scottish Prison Service – Progress Review*. HMIPS.

Holdsworth, E. and Hucklesby, A. (2014) Designed for men, but also worn by women. *Criminal Justice Matters* 95(1): 14–15.

Hucklesby, A. (2008) Vehicles of desistance?: The impact of electronically monitored curfew orders. *Criminology & Criminal Justice* 8(1): 51–71.

Laurie, E. and Maglione, G. (2020) The electronic monitoring of offenders in context: From policy to political logics. *Critical Criminology* 28: 685–702.

Mackenzie, D.L. (2006) *What Works in Corrections: Reducing the Criminal Activities of Offenders and Delinquents*. Cambridge University Press.

Mair, G. and Nellis, M. (2013) 'Parallel tracks': Probation and electronic monitoring in England, Wales and Scotland. In Nellis, M., Beyens, K. and Kaminski, D. (eds) *Electronically Monitored Punishment: International and Critical Perspectives*. Routledge. 63–81.

McIvor, G. and Graham, H. (2016) *Electronic Monitoring in Scotland*. SCCJR. https://www.sccjr.ac.uk/wp-content/uploads/2016/06/Electronic-Monitoring-in-Scotland-Report.pdf

Miller, J. and Anderson, S. (2021) *A Qualitative Exploration of the Attitudes of Young People to the Sentencing of Young People in Scotland*. Scottish Sentencing Council.

Nellis, M. (2015) The strategic failure of electronic monitoring in Scotland. In Croall, H. and Mooney, G. and Munro, M. (eds) *Crime, Justice and Society in Scotland.* Routledge. 182–199.

Nellis, M., Beyens, K. and Kaminski, D. (eds) (2013) *Electronically Monitored Punishment.* Routledge.

Payne, B.K., May, D.C. and Wood, P.B. (2014) The 'pains' of electronic monitoring: A slap on the wrist or just as bad as prison? *Criminal Justice Studies* 27(2): 133–148.

Prins, S.J. and Reich, A. (2021) Criminogenic risk assessment: A meta-review and critical analysis. *Punishment and Society* 23(4): 578–604.

Renzema, M. and Mayo-Wilson, E. (2005) Can electronic monitoring reduce crime for moderate to high-risk offenders? *Journal of Experimental Criminology* 1(2): 215–237.

Richter, M., Ryser, B. and Hostettler, U. (2021) Punitiveness of electronic monitoring: Perception and experience of an alternative sanction. *European Journal of Probation* 13(3): 262–281.

Scottish Government (no date) *Reducing Reoffending: Home Detention Curfew.* https://www.gov.scot/policies/reducing-reoffending/home-detention-curfew/

Scottish Government (2023) *Decision-Making on Bail and Remand in Scotland: Final Report* December 2023. Scottish Government.

Smith, D. (2001) Electronic monitoring of offenders: The Scottish experience. *Criminology and Criminal Justice* 1(2): 201–214.

8 Prisons and imprisonment in Scotland

Key ideas

- The history of imprisonment in Scotland, as in many other jurisdictions, contains historical and recent examples of deep isolation and psychological brutalisation, alongside more innovative regimes.
- Over recent decades, the framing and lexicon of Scottish imprisonment has sought to cast it as an institution which can 'unlock the potential' (SPS, 2013) of all those in its custody.
- This framing did not sufficiently acknowledge the harms of imprisonment and despite improvements in some areas, these aspirations were not achieved.
- Scottish imprisonment currently faces multiple challenges including overcrowding, the fabric of the estate, healthcare, high rates of deaths in custody and the overrepresentation of people experiencing different types of marginalisation within its population.
- It is essential to consider Scottish imprisonment in the wider criminal justice context since factors elsewhere influence flows into and out of prison.

Introduction

Prisons in Scotland reflect many themes discussed elsewhere in this book, namely that of a purportedly distinctive approach, alongside many apparent similarities, to prison systems in the rest of Western Europe; the challenges of operating in a heated politicised environment; the over-involvement of those experiencing socioeconomic and health inequalities; and the disjuncture between punishment and welfare in a penal setting. Imprisonment as a social institution is totemic in its symbolism of state power to punish, though it is used less frequently than either financial penalties or community sentences in Scotland. Only about 14% of sentences are prison sentences (Scottish Government, 2023), but imprisonment represents the best-known, most severe and perhaps most problematic sanction available. As outlined in earlier chapters, every penal sanction results in pain, but the 'pain' experienced by those in prison is particularly pronounced and long-lasting, in Scotland as elsewhere.

DOI: 10.4324/9781003372882-8

It is important to note that there are other carceral spaces in Scotland which perform similar or related functions and raise some of the same issues, including police custody (Section 3.3.3), secure care (Section 9.2.4), immigration detention (Section 11.1.2) and secure mental health settings (beyond the scope of this book).

We turn next to the key agencies in imprisonment in Scotland.

8.1 Key agencies and the prison estate

The **Scottish Prison Service (SPS)** runs all but one of Scotland's 17 prisons. SPS is an Executive Agency, so formally part of the Scottish Government

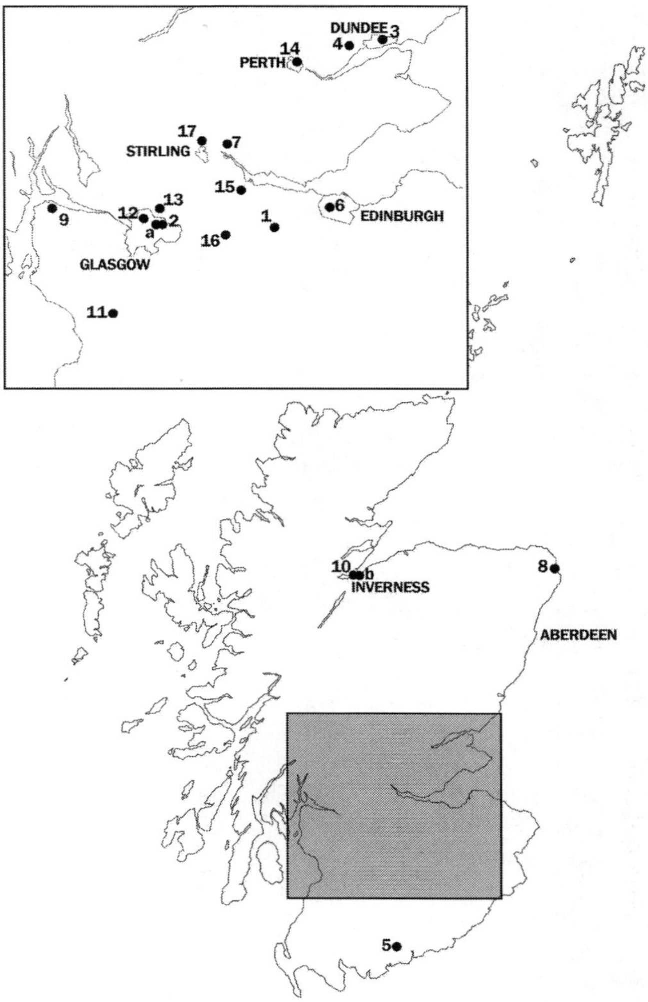

Figure 8.1 A map and outline of the Scottish prison estate.

Table 8.1 Key information on Scottish prisons (in alphabetical order)

Number	*Name*	*Opened*	*Design capacity*	*Population (from CJSVF1)*	*Population type*
1	HMP Addiewell	2008	702	750	All except women and convicted young people
2	HMP Barlinnie	1882	987	1,328	Men – remand and convicted (all sentence lengths) Receiving prison – people arriving straight from court National Top End for life/long-term sentence prisoners approaching potential release date
3	The Bella Centre	2022	16	14	Adult and young (aged 18–21) women (low supervision)
4	HMP Castle Huntly	1946 (first as borstal, some parts of the site pre-dates this)	284	167	Adult males (at the end of their sentence) Open prison – lower security
5	HMP Dumfries	1863	176	185	Men – remand, convicted (short-term sentences)
6	HMP Edinburgh	1920	867	926	Men – remand, convicted (short-term, long-term, life, OLRs, offence protection prisoners)
7	HMP Glenochil	1960s (first as detention centre)	668	700	Men – convicted (short-term, long-term, life sentence, extended sentence, offence protection prisoners and OLRs)
8	HMP & YOI Grampian	2014	552	481	Men and women – remand, convicted (short-term, long-term, extended)
9	HMP Greenock	1910	249	230	Men and women – remand and convicted (short- and long-term sentences) National Top End – long-term prisoners at the end of their sentence on low supervision
10	HMP Inverness	1902	93	111	Remand adult and young person (aged 18–21); convicted adults (short-term, prisoners awaiting allocation, long-term or life)
11	HMP Kilmarnock	1999	502	620	Range of prisoner populations

(Continued)

Table 8.1 (Continued)

Number	*Name*	*Opened*	*Design capacity*	*Population (from CJSVF1)*	*Population type*
12	The Lilias Centre	2022	24	22	Convicted adult and young (aged 18–21) women – low supervision
13	HMP Low Moss	2012	785	839	Men, remand, convicted (short-term, long-term, life and extended sentence)
14	HMP Perth	1840	631	685	Men, remand, (convicted), short-term, long-term, life and extended sentence (OLRs)
15	HMP & YOI Polmont	1911 (first as borstal)	758	537	Young men (aged 18–21) remand, convicted (short, long, life) Adult women aged 21 and over, (remand, convicted, short- or long-term sentence) Adult men (convicted, short-term, low supervision)
16	HMP Shotts	2012	538	541	Adult men – long-term adult male National Integration Centre: adult men in initial stages of sentences of over 8 yrs
17	HMP & YOI Stirling	2023	117 (+ mother and baby unit with two spaces)	78	Adult and young (aged 18–21) women
a	HMP Glasgow	*Under construction*	1,344		Replacement for HMP Barlinnie
b	HMP Highland	*Under construction*	200		Replacement for HMP Inverness

Design capacity and population (as of 1 January 2025) from the Criminal Justice Voluntary Sector Forum (unpublished).

(all SPS employees are civil servants) but operating at 'arm's length' from it. Policy and strategic direction must align with the Scottish Government's Justice Strategy, while 'operational decisions' are left to SPS. Individual prisons have some autonomy, to reflect varying size, geography and prisoner profiles. Each is governed by a Governor and their Deputy, and these roles have significant ability to shape the prison's life and culture.

The use of private prisons has never really taken off in Scotland (unlike in the United States, Australia and England and Wales). There is now only one private prison, HMP Addiewell, operated by Sodexo. HMP Kilmarnock was brought back into public ownership in 2024 at the end of its contract with the private security company Serco, and the Scottish Government have pledged to do the same with Addiewell at the end of its contract in December 2033.

There are currently 17 prisons in Scotland (see Table 8.1 and Figure 8.1). The prison estate is never static; over the past 20 years, old prisons have been closed, new ones built, and existing prisons repurposed. Calls to house people close to their loved ones and communities have often been in tension with economic pressures for 'efficiencies of scale' which centralise services needed for specific populations (e.g. a regime[1] for men starting long sentences). Legally, men and women must be kept separate (though sometimes within the same prison), and those aged 21 and under separated from older prisoners (in Young Offender Institutions).

Prisons vary significantly in scale and architecture. The largest men's prison, HMP Barlinnie, is chronically overcrowded (with capacity for around 1,000 people but holding 1,400 prisoners throughout 2024) and repeatedly deemed 'not fit for purpose' due to its Victorian architecture. Barlinnie's replacement – a new large prison, HMP Glasgow – is scheduled for completion by 2028. Conversely, two Community Custody Units (CCUs) for women, the Lilias and Bella Centres, opened in 2022, consisting of small house units with capacity for 24 and 16 individuals respectively. There is one 'open prison' for men at the end of their sentence.

The rest of Scotland's prisons exist between these two extremes (though the norm is probably much closer to Barlinnie than the CCUs). Much has been made of the new 'progressive', 'community-facing', 'desistance' and 'trauma-informed' design of newer prisons (especially for a small number of women – Jewkes and Moran, 2017), and while these offer an improvement in living conditions from prisons like Barlinnie, there has been pushback both in terms of the suitability of some design aspects, but also to claims that these design features ameliorate or remove the harms of imprisonment.

Box 8.1 Women in prison in Scotland

Throughout the first part of the 21st century, concern grew about the national prison for women, HMP Cornton Vale, with repeated

Her (now His) Majesty's Inspectorate of Prisons for Scotland (HMIPS) reports finding it "in a state of crisis". This was driven in part by a sharp rise in the female prison population (sharper than that of the male prison population at this time), as well as the inability of staff to properly care for this population who tend to have deeper and more entrenched vulnerabilities (e.g. relating to addictions and mental health difficulties) than their (already vulnerable) male counterparts.

Reflecting these concerns and the progressive visions of the Scottish National Party (SNP)-led administration at the time (See Chapter 1), the Scottish Government established the **Commission on Women Offenders in Scotland** in 2011, whose report was published in 2012 (sometimes known as the Angiolini report after the Commission's Chair, Dame Elish Angiolini, who also produced important reports on policing – see Section 3.2.3). Among other things, the report recommended closing Cornton Vale, replacing it with one smaller national prison for longer-term and higher-risk prisoners and other very small, regional prisons for lower-risk women in custody (Commission on Women Offenders, 2012). It took over a decade before Cornton Vale was finally closed, during which time the Scottish Government first planned, then cancelled (at very short notice) a replacement at Inverclyde.

HMP Stirling, opened in 2023, is now the national prison replacing Cornton Vale for longer-term sentenced women. Two new Community Custody Units (CCUs), the Lilias and Bella Centres, opened in 2022, designed for women assessed as low risk, usually reaching the end of their sentence, to help them prepare for release.

These new prisons are built for much smaller populations than the prisons for men – HMP Stirling can house 100 women, while the Lilias and Bella Centres have 24 and 16 places respectively. These prisons were designed to be small to provide a more supportive, 'trauma-informed' approach to working with women in custody. The architecture of the prisons is also noteworthy. They are built with minimal visible security – there are no grill gates, and the spaces are bright and open. The two CCUs each consist of a series of 'houses' in which women live together and are encouraged to budget and cook for themselves, with supervised release for some into the community. The CCUs in particular were much celebrated when they opened and regarded by some as heralding a more progressive approach to female imprisonment. At present, an evaluation of them (the SPAROW project) is underway; its findings may be available by the time this book is published and should give us more of a sense of whether the reality lives up to the aspiration.

While HMP Stirling and the two CCUs are certainly an improvement in conditions compared to Cornton Vale (a very low bar, however), there are two critical points worth considering. First, no matter how 'trauma-informed' these prisons may be, they remain carceral spaces – places in which people lose their liberty, are separated from their community and are subject to practices of control. The Inspectorate has critiqued the use of routine body-searching, contravening this approach (HMIPS, 2024). It will be important to ensure that vulnerable women are not 'up-tariffed' to prison as part of 'therapeutic sentencing' practices. Second, these new prisons can only house 140 women in total, and the female prison population (in the latter half of 2024) is around 340, so most Scottish women prisoners are not kept in the new facilities.

Questions to consider

- Do you think the design of a prison can be trauma-informed? What might this look like? (You may find it useful to look up some pictures of the Lilias and Bella Centres)

8.1.1 Accountability bodies

Accountability mechanisms are required to ensure prisons operate with regard to human rights standards and to minimise the inevitable harms of imprisonment. Established in 1981, **HM Inspectorate of Prisons for Scotland (HMIPS)** carries out scheduled prison inspections and produces thematic reports on cross-cutting issues. HMIPS use volunteers – **Independent Prison Monitors (IPMs)** – to provide current and ongoing monitoring throughout the estate (unlike in England and Wales, where this role is undertaken through a separate organisation), and who work alongside professional inspectors. However, HMIPS can only raise awareness of problems, it has no power to compel any changes – and some concerns (e.g. conditions in Barlinnie and overcrowding) have repeatedly recurred. HMIPS must strike a difficult balance: it must independently hold SPS to account, but also rely on its cooperation, without which prison inspecting would be difficult if not impossible.

The UK, as a signatory to United Nations Optional Protocol to the Convention Against Torture (OPCAT) and other Cruel, Inhumane and Degrading Treatment or Punishment, adheres to human rights-based inspection standards through mechanisms like the **National Preventative Mechanism (NPM)**, including HMIPS, and is also subject to recommendations from bodies like the **European Committee for the Prevention of Torture and Inhuman or Degrading Treatment or Punishment (CPT)**.

Where there has been a death in custody, the **courts** and **Crown Office and Procurator Fiscal Service** also play a role in holding **Fatal Accident Inquiries (FAIs)**. However, FAIs into deaths in custody rarely make recommendations to prevent future deaths (Armstrong et al., 2021, 2024 and Section 8.3.4) and their recommendations are not legally binding.

8.2 The history of imprisonment in Scotland

The history of imprisonment in Scotland bears many similarities to that of other Western jurisdictions, with some notable exceptions. Claims have been made about a distinctive and progressive 'Scottish approach' to imprisonment (e.g. McAra, 2005), while others argue these claims mask a more complex mix of often countervailing principles (Munro et al., 2010; Brangan, 2019).

Scottish prisons emerged in the mid-18th century to hold those awaiting transportation or unpaid debtors and only began to be used as a punishment in their own right in Scotland in the 19th century. Cameron (1983) describes a shift from disparate local organisation to centralisation and control by the Home Office; between 1839 and 1898, the number of prisons in Scotland reduced from 178 to 14.

In 19th and early 20th century Scotland, prison life was characterised by harsh labour, a strict privilege system, and prisoner isolation, but the 1895 Gladstone Committee reforms shifted the focus towards prisoner reform (Cameron, 1983), albeit without a swift transition to penal welfarism (see Section 1.3.1).

8.2.1 The 1970s and 1980s: 'dangerous' prisoners, segregation and innovation

The 1970s were an increasingly challenging time for prisons in Scotland (Brangan, 2021; Coyle, 1991). By the late 1970s, Scotland had the highest rate of imprisonment in Europe, creating pressures across the system. There was also concern over a small group of longer-term prisoners who were deemed impervious to the usual system of incentive-driven compliance (Coyle, 1991).

From the 1960s to the 1980s, units within Inverness and Peterhead prisons were built to hold this new class of prisoner. These units were marked by the depth of their restrictions and isolation from the rest of the prison, subjecting those held there to 'extreme deprivation and mortification' (Brangan 2021: 117; Sparks, 2002). Contrary to intentions for greater control, this approach led to a series of violent incidents, particularly after peaceful protests against conditions in these units (O'Carroll, 2022) went unheard. Famously, the British army was deployed in Peterhead prison in 1987 after two prison officers were taken hostage by prisoners in these units.

Responding to the failure of these exclusionary regimes to reduce violent incidents, a third unit established in 1973 took a different approach. Seeking inspiration from therapeutic communities in England and Wales, the Barlinnie Special Unit was established in the empty women's unit at Scotland's largest prison (Brangan, 2021; Anderson, 2024) as a distinct institution for those prisoners deemed 'unmanageable', formerly held in Inverness and Peterhead.

This unit operated on an entirely different regime from any other Scottish prison at the time, or since. With a far less pronounced hierarchy and much greater mutual trust, it operated more as a community of peers. Instead of the drag of manual labour, much of the days were spent invested in arts, facilitated by on-site art therapists and psychiatrists (Anderson, 2024). Prisoners' families and professions of various sorts could visit the unit freely, including prisoners' cells (Sparks, 2002). Most men flourished in this looser environment, although there were frustrations that it was never integrated with the rest of the prison system.

In its 21-year operation, this unit saw only two serious incidents (one violent assault, one suicide), and the overall reduction in violence and disorder could certainly be regarded as a success (Coyle, 1991). Despite a positive evaluation it was closed suddenly in 1994, amidst waning support and increasing discomfort from some within the prison system (Anderson, 2024; Brangan, 2021; Sparks, 2002).

Although highly praised within Scottish criminal justice and criminology (see e.g. McAra, 2005), it is important to note that this was a 'special' unit; a one-off, never replicated, and subsequent developments within SPS seemed almost embarrassed by this penal innovation (see also Brangan 2021; Munro et al., 2010). It tells us little about the wider nature of imprisonment in Scotland – and indeed, was a response to particularly extreme forms of isolation elsewhere in the system.

8.2.2 *The 1990s and 2000s: Opportunity and Responsibility and devolution*

During the 1980s, disturbances were increasingly dispersed throughout the Scottish prison estate driven by the drugs market in prison, the redistribution of prisoners across the estate, and overcrowding – the latter driven by longer sentences and restrictions to parole (Chapter 10) in the 1980s (Coyle, 1991; Brangan, 2021). Consideration began to focus on how conditions for *all* prisoners might affect their behaviour, rather than a focus on a small number of specialist units.

At the same time, there was also growing support across Scotland for devolution and for the articulation of a distinctly Scottish political and policy identity. This led to the transformation in the 1990s of the Prisons Division of the Scottish Office into an arm's-length 'agency' – the SPS – with a new more corporate logo, headquarters and greater autonomy and power in the production of policy (Brangan, 2021).

With the new organisation came a new direction (Brangan, 2021). The SPS (1990) policy *Opportunity and Responsibility* reimagined the prisoner as a 'responsible' individual, imbued with rational thought and agency, but who must be provided with 'opportunities' for personal development, initially education and vocational training, to teach them how to "manage their own risks and potential" (Brangan, 2021: 154).

The ideas within *Opportunity and Responsibility* subsequently became enmeshed with actuarial and managerial approaches (see Section 6.3.2) emerging from North America, focused particularly on assessing risk and targeting **'criminogenic needs'** – those needs where evidence was deemed strongest of a causal link to involvement in offending. Although not dominant within the *Opportunity and Responsibility* policy, in SPS, there was a shift in language towards managing prisoners' perceived risk and the formalisation of existing education and work into 'offending behaviour programmes', intended to address specific 'needs' and thus reduce risks. In this framing, the 'responsible' prisoner makes the right choices as viewed by the prison – increasingly to take the relevant programmes – in order to progress through the system or face the consequences.

Of course, this logic relies on and relays a certain story about who prisoners are, how offending happens, and what the role of the prison is, and like all stories of this type it needs to be interrogated. It is worth noting that the leap from statistical prediction to causal explanation in understandings of 'criminogenic needs', the effectiveness of offender behaviour programmes at addressing these, treating risk as a meaningful characteristic of a person that can and should be measured, and reoffending as something that originates from individual deficits are all influential ideas but have also all been subject to challenge.

The managerialism affecting prison systems throughout much of the West at the time began to permeate Scotland; throughout the 1990s, prisoners were even referred to as 'customers'. For Brangan (2021) the idea of a 'responsible prisoner' reflected the ascendant neoliberal policy agenda across Britain – even as Scottish approaches *outwardly* rejected the punitive rhetoric of England and Wales. Brangan (2019: 781) argues that this apparently more benign approach to imprisonment "denies the pains of imprisonment", separating itself from critiques of more punitive institutions, making it *seem* more 'civilised' rather than *being* more 'humane' (by imprisoning fewer people).

Prisons in Scotland faced practical difficulties at the turn of the century (and the beginning of devolution). Prisons were severely overcrowded meaning prisoners spent more time locked in cells, with reduced or no access to rehabilitative activities and work, and nearly a quarter of prisoners lacking in-cell sanitation, meaning they had to endure the unhygienic and degrading conditions of 'slopping out' – using a container as a toilet (often in shared cells where meals were eaten) and emptying it every morning (HMIPS, 2003).

The response from the new Scottish Executive was two-fold. First, an unprecedented prison building and refurbishment programme in the 2000s and 2010s. Second, prison privatisation, with the opening of two privately run prisons: HMP Kilmarnock in 1999 and HMP Addiewell in 2008. Improving the physical structure of the estate gradually enabled the cessation of 'slopping out', though this only finally ended completely in 2013 when HMP

Peterhead prison was finally closed down, bringing to an end a notorious chapter in Scottish penal history.

Towards the end of the 2000s, an important report by the Scottish Prisons Commission (2008), *Scotland's Choice*, advocated dramatic reduction in the prison population to 5,000, and a shift towards using community sentences instead. While the reforms that followed *Scotland's Choice* failed to have the intended effect on imprisonment (see Box 4.2 and Section 6.2.4), the report did shape the tone of policy discussions about imprisonment in the 2010s.

8.2.3 *The 2010s: unlocking potential, transforming lives?*

There was considerable support for reform across the justice system by the early 2010s, particularly where this could align with nation-building narratives of a 'progressive' Scotland in the context of an ascendant SNP and the 2014 independence referendum. As part of this agenda, a new SPS Chief Executive was hired in 2012 who had formerly overseen significant reforms in the Northern Irish Prison Service. In 2013, the *Organisational Review: Unlocking Potential Transforming Lives (UPTL)* claimed to herald "a golden age for the Scottish Prison Service" (SPS, 2013: 3).

The story told about prisoners, crime and prisons had shifted, with UPTL proposing a more optimistic vision of imprisonment in Scotland. Two key areas are worth mentioning here. First, it contained a changing way of talking about prisoners and their 'rehabilitation'. The review leant heavily on the vocabulary and principles from theories of desistance from crime (see Section 6.3.4/Box 6.2), having engaged with some key thinkers in the field (McNeill, 2015). 'Rehabilitation' and 'reoffending' were gone, replaced with the language of 'citizenship' and 'reintegration'; indeed, in a follow-up document published in 2016, SPS even referred to itself as a 'citizenship recovery service' (SPS, 2016). The second key area of the review was a renewed focus on training and 'professionalising' prison staff, including a plan for a university-accredited qualification for prison officers, to marry their operational 'knowhow' with professional ethics and latest knowledge and theory relevant to their role (Morrison, 2018).

While UPTL was never properly evaluated, it would be fair to say that the aspirations it contained were not realised, though some positive changes did occur (e.g. to staff training). The intentions of the professionalisation agenda were often worn down by the realities of prison working life, the working culture that operated throughout the estate, and resistance from the prison officers' union (POAS) (Morrison and Maycock, 2021). Furthermore, counter to much of the learning from desistance research, UPTL focused on the individual, rather than the wider social contexts in which prisoners operate (McNeill, 2015). Piacentini et al. (2018) argued that the fundamental ethos of the Review still operated through a paradigm of 'risk', in which people are viewed as 'requiring' transformation by the prison to fulfil their potential. HMIPS reports praised SPS' efforts to improve the experiences of prisoners' families, including the introduction of numerous Visitor Centres and specific roles within the prison to support families (see e.g. HMIPS, 2018). Jardine (2019) found that while families valued contact visits, they sometimes experienced rules as simultaneously rigid and inconsistently applied, and some interactions with officers as stigmatising. Families were tasked with supporting desistance but were unable to meaningfully influence decisions and the collateral harms to them of imprisonment were often ignored.

This speaks to a broader critique of UPTL: reframing the prison as a space of transformation underplays the harms of imprisonment. Some of these harms could be seen starkly in the period following the review, including rising violence between prisoners and decreased time spent in purposeful activity[2] and education. The SPS was sharply criticised for its use of conditions akin to solitary confinement for prisoners in need of healthcare (Russo, 2024) and the vast availability of drugs throughout the estate. Deaths in prison from suicide increased dramatically over the 2010s (Armstrong et al., 2024), and in 2015, while on remand, Allan Marshall died following a brutal restraint by prison officers at HMP Edinburgh. The subsequent FAI found his death was "entirely preventable", and in 2023, SPS came under police investigation for Corporate Homicide in relation to the incident.

The publication of UPTL in 2013 and the subsequent years of implementation took place in an increasingly fraught and challenging environment marked by a chronically and critically overcrowded estate, rising costs but decreased budget due to austerity, and rising staff absence rates. Previous initiatives were discontinued (for example, Throughcare Support Officers – a role introduced after the review for prison officers to work with short-term prisoners after release (see Chapter 10)). Since then, amid growing and consistent pressures on the system, the legacies of the Organisational Review now seem largely forgotten.

8.2.4 The 2020s: COVID-19 and the post-pandemic 'normal'

The pandemic, and the lockdown to contain the spread of the virus, were experienced particularly acutely by those in prison, compounding the isolation of imprisonment and existing hardships, particularly related to mental health (Gormley et al., 2020, Russo, 2024). Early in lockdown, Scottish prisoners were locked in their cells for up to 23 hours a day. Family visits ceased immediately, and prisoners could not always access, or clean, communal phones on prison landings (Gormley et al., 2020). Prisoners complained of poor communication and that infection control measures (e.g. mask wearing) were not always in place (Gormley et al., 2020). Prisoners were also unable to access offending behaviour programmes, with implications for their release on parole (see Section 8.3.2). Prisons received some praise for keeping infection rates low during the early phases of the pandemic, but it was ultimately felt that they had not balanced their different human rights obligations, prioritising Article 2 (right to life), over Article 3 (protection from ill-treatment) (HMIPS, 2022).

Against this bleak backdrop, the Government announced an emergency early release of 348 people serving sentences for non-serious offences in May 2020, and the introduction of 7,500 'dumb', i.e. not internet enabled, mobile phones throughout the estate to improve contact with families, a policy widely welcomed by charities and the Inspectorate of Prisons (and now replaced with in-cell telephony) (Morrison and Graham, 2022).

The pandemic normalised a more 'locked down' regime – meaning prisoners now spent much more time in their cells – which would have been unthinkable previously. By summer 2024, prisons had entered a 'new normal' of prisoners spending on average only seven hours per day out of their cells, (though in some prisons this is far less). While SPS has tried to justify this on the grounds of budgetary pressures and high rates of staff absence (it takes fewer staff to run a prison if people spend more time in their cells), these much more restricted regimes have significant implications for prisoners' wellbeing and progression through sentence and reflect policy priorities within the system.

Meanwhile, the new Corporate Plan 2023–28 (SPS, 2023) replaces the language of 'desistance' with a commitment to "person-centred, inclusive, trauma-informed and rights-based" services (p.18). Once again, it promises prisons which promote improved health and wellbeing. New language brings with it a now familiar critique: that this obscures the harms of imprisonment and frames prisons as places of recovery and rehabilitation (Anderson, 2025) – claims which are (at the very least) problematised by research and the recurring challenges facing Scottish prisons.

8.3 Challenges and controversies

There are numerous challenges facing prisons in Scotland today, as a cursory overview of HMIPS reports will highlight.

8.3.1 Overcrowding

Prisons have been overcrowded, or nearly overcrowded, more or less continually since the start of the 21st century. In 2024, in response to population levels deemed at crisis point again, the Scottish Parliament approved an emergency release scheme releasing circa 450 people towards the end of their sentence and introduced legislation to allow the earlier release of some short-term prisoners. However, these measures had little to no effect on the population, and longer-term problems causing overcrowding remain unresolved.

An overall prison population matters for practical as well as moral reasons (though the two are closely connected). Practically, an overcrowded prison estate doesn't function properly. There is not enough staff or space for prisoners to access 'the regime' so they spend more time locked in their cells. Violence also tends to increase, as more people must double up or triple up in cells. In addition, any effort within prisons to support people in custody

Figure 8.2 A simulated prison landing at the SPS Training College.

is made substantially more difficult if their emotional, healthcare, and vocational needs are unmet or worsened. Morally, it is even harder to meet the Inspectorate's standards of human rights and dignity in an overcrowded prison estate.

Managing an overcrowded prison is not only about the overall *numbers* of prisoners and spaces available. It's also about *who* is in prison and *where* they can be placed (or 'housed'). Some prisoners must be separated from the 'mainstream' population, for their own protection, for example, those serving sentences for sexual crimes or for harming children, or those under 'non-offence protection' for reasons such as debts to others in prison (see Cornish, 2022 for decision-making around this). People from different Serious and Organised Crime (SOC) groups must be kept separate for their own protection. Custodial sentences for both sexual and SOC offences have been rising sharply due to changes in policing and sentencing, placing additional pressures on an overcrowded system, because there are fewer free places in the estate to move people to, if required. Finally, the growing number of people with social care needs due to the ageing prison population (see Box 8.2) places further challenges on sentence management, since their health needs can sometimes only be met in specially adapted cells (HMIPS, 2020). Therefore, pressures of the very high population level are further compounded by the diversity of needs and requirements of different groups in prison.

The persistence of prison overcrowding is perhaps surprising given that there has been little change in the share of sentences accounted for by custody since 2014. Overcrowding appears instead to be affected by several other factors.

Box 8.2 Demographics and inequalities in prison

As we have seen (see Box 3.1), Scottish data on demographics and inequalities in criminal justice are limited. We have more data related to imprisonment than other areas since SPS must collect significant quantities of information on people in prison, although since data are often collected for prison operational – rather than research – purposes there can be problems with data quality. Data come from two main sources: the Scottish Government Prison Statistics Interactive Analysis Tool (which takes data from the prison service data platforms, though these data are unstable), and the SPS Quarterly Information Pages (see under Key Resources for both). These tell us several interesting things.

First, the prison population is ageing, driven both by increases in the number of older prisoners and a dramatic fall in young adult prisoners (and an end to the imprisonment of children – see Section 9.2.4). The ageing prison population creates significant challenges for prison staff, who must now support a different group of prisoners than before, whose needs (particularly healthcare) are often poorly met (HMIPS, 2020).

An SPS (2024a) report suggests that 10% of people in Scottish prisons have a disability, though this may be a significant underestimate (Hatcher et al., 2022). Gormley's (2022) research suggests that for people with learning disabilities, imprisonment can be especially hard to bear, and potentially difficult to justify morally. Some of her participants did not understand the basic facts of their sentence or know how long they had been in prison.

Overall, 95% of the prison population are men and 4% are women (a reduction from 8% in 2021–22) (SPS, 2024a and see Box 8.1). This slight change might reflect the change in sentence types committed to custody, with a reduction in imprisonment for more minor crimes, and an increase in custody for more serious offences including sexual violence. Transgender, non-binary or gender-fluid people represent less than 1% of the overall prison population (but see Box 8.3). Moreover, 89% of prisoners reported they were heterosexual (SPS, 2024a).

Looking at ethnicity (including religion) in Scottish prisons directs our attention to now-familiar methodological challenges. Overall, 94% of the prison population declared themselves as White; 2% as Asian, Asian Scottish or Asian British; 1% as Caribbean and Black, and 1%

as African, 1% as 'other' (SPS, 2024a). These figures broadly reflect the proportion of ethnicities in the Scottish population, but imprisonment *rates* appear markedly higher for African, Caribbean, Black and Other ethnic groups – that is, members of those groups in Scotland are more likely to be imprisoned (Scottish Government, 2024b).

There is insufficient data on the religious affiliation of those in prison; data quality problems mean that recent data are not available from SPS. Past data suggest Catholics may be over-represented in Scottish prisons, in line with their experience of greater levels of deprivation historically (McBride et al., 2025). Figures from 2013/14 show a significant overrepresentation of Scottish Muslims in prison (Sturge, 2024). As with other discussions of ethnicity in the justice system (Box 3.1), this highlights the limitations of Scottish data, as well as the importance of a nuanced and intersectional understanding of the different experiences of different ethnic groups.

People in Scottish prisons are more likely to have lived in more disadvantaged geographic areas in Scotland prior to imprisonment. Certain local authorities around the Central Belt (particularly in the West) have much higher rates of imprisonment. While only 3% of the prison population comes from the least deprived areas of Scotland, 43% comes from the most deprived (SPS, 2024a). The link between imprisonment and deprivation, first identified empirically by Houchin (2005), remains as entrenched as ever.

Questions to consider

- What does the above suggest about the relationship/s between inequalities, offending and punishment in society?
- What difficulties might arise in measuring less 'visible' characteristics like sexuality, disability or religion in prisons?

8.3.2 Long sentences and progression

At the 'front door' of the prison, there has been a change in the offence profile of prisoners, alongside increases in sentence lengths. Even though the *number* of custodial sentences passed has decreased over the past ten years (especially for shorter sentences), the *length* of these sentences has increased over this time. This partly reflects not only the changing profile of offences for which people are sentenced to custody (a reduction in minor crimes, and an increase in e.g. sexual crimes), but also a general increase in sentence length *for the same crimes* (e.g. an increase by 40% for drug possession and 38% for sexual assault over a ten-year period, and an increase by 33% for the 'punishment part' of a life sentence over the last 17 years (Scottish Government, 2023)). Furthermore, despite a presumption against sentences of less than 12 months being in place for nearly five years (Box 4.2) and a reduction in short custodial sentences over the past decade, there remained 700 people in prison in Scotland serving sentences of less than 12 months (8% of the overall population) in summer 2024.

At the 'back door', issues concerning prisoners' ability to *progress* through their sentence ('**progression**') towards release and (relatedly) the decisions of the Parole Board for Scotland mean that prisoners on longer sentences are less likely to be released on licence (see Chapter 10). SPS (drawing on advice from other professionals) is responsible for progression before someone's consideration for release by the Parole Board for Scotland. Critically, to progress through a sentence, a person must be able to access relevant offending behaviour programmes according to their assessed needs, as well as other types of 'purposeful activity' (including education, training, work and exercise). Concerns about access to purposeful activity are longstanding in Scotland, and in Autumn 2023, prisoners in two of the largest prisons were receiving as little as 12 hours a week (an average of just under 1 ¾ hours per day). The average over the estate at this time was only 21 hours per week (three hours a day) (Scottish Parliament, 2023). Chapter 10 discusses the challenges of achieving parole.

Sentence progression may sound like a technical aspect of the prison system, but if it does not work adequately, people spend years longer in prison than they otherwise might. Extending the deprivation of someone's liberty due to bureaucratic problems is an unacceptable injustice.

8.3.3 Remand

To remand someone in custody means to send them to prison prior to their trial or (less commonly) after trial but before sentencing. People's liberty is taken away even though they are usually, in the eyes of the law, still innocent, with no guarantee that they will be found guilty at trial. As such, we might hope that remanding someone in custody should happen only in the most serious of cases where there is a real risk of causing further serious harm. Unfortunately, this is not the case in Scotland, and there is evidence of people continuing to be remanded for very minor crimes including shoplifting and theft from a vehicle (Howard League Scotland, 2021).

The proportion of people on remand in Scottish prisons (as of summer 2024) stands at 28% (of which 4% have been convicted and are awaiting sentence). The numbers are even higher for women – 40% of the female population is on remand (Scottish Government, 2024a), due in part to an increase in time on remand prior to trial.

Within the prison, the remand population is very 'fluid' – remand prisoners enter and leave custody at far higher rates than those arriving following sentence and account for over 80% of arrivals at prison (Scottish

Government, 2024a). This 'flow' of people is hard for the prison to manage and extremely disruptive for the individuals concerned, whose lives are upset by even short periods in custody. High remand numbers are problematic not only because of the moral question about imprisoning people who have not been (and may never be) found guilty but also because the regime is different for remand prisoners – with (even) less time out of cells, and much less, if any, access to purposeful activity. Because statutory services are not in place for non-sentenced individuals, remanded people are also frequently released without support in place.

There have been recent attempts to encourage a greater use of bail rather than remand with the passing of the Bail and Release from Custody Act (Scotland) 2023. However, the way this legislation was eventually framed meant that sentencers continued to have wide discretion over whether to grant bail or not. As of January 2025, not all of the legislation has been implemented, and numbers on remand have continued to rise.

Box 8.3 Transgender people in prison in Scotland

The debate around transgender people in Scottish prisons both reflects the wider culture war around the rights of transgender people in society and played a central part in fuelling this war in the early 2020s. SPS (2014) introduced its first policy for the management of transgender people in prison in the aspirational era following the publication of UPTL.

The policy's overall framing was how to ensure the human rights and dignity of transgender people in prison were met by SPS. The key tenet was that transgender people in Scottish prisons did not require a Gender Recognition Certificate (GRC) to be housed according to their expressed gender; if they self-declared as a woman, they could be considered to live in the female estate. Its operation *in practice* was more nuanced. Governors and senior managers would individually risk-assess each transgender person in custody and house them accordingly – if a person self-identified as a woman, but was regarded as posing a risk to women in custody (for example due to their offending history), they would be housed separately in the male estate (while continuing to live as a woman and use feminine pronouns). Indeed, in 2020, only half the transgender women in prison in Scotland were housed in the female estate.

Ten years later, the 2014 policy reads as well-intentioned but perhaps naïve in not explicitly discussing the complex decision-making involved in managing transgender people in custody. Neither did it recognise the potential opposition to this policy, although the cultural environment surrounding transgender people in society was much less heightened then. As the debate about transgender people's and women's rights became more fractious, attention from gender-critical campaign groups focused on the 2014 policy. A summary of arguments against it is contained in Murray and Hunter Blackburn (2019), who argued that SPS had consulted only a narrow group of interested parties and not properly noted the potential adverse impact of housing a pre-operation transgender woman in the female estate. Wider concerns were that women in prison are disproportionately likely to have been the victim of gender-based violence and abuse, and it was, therefore, essential to ensure there were no male-bodied people in that environment (though male staff have long worked in the women's estate).

Considering these criticisms, the SPS agreed to review the policy in the late 2010s. This review was delayed by numerous factors including COVID-19, the political fallout surrounding the passage of the Gender Recognition (Reform) Bill, and a high-profile case of a transwoman prisoner convicted of multiple offences of sexual violence against women. When initially remanded in custody, she had been held in Cornton Vale (then the national women's prison), but in isolation, separate from other women prisoners. It is extremely unlikely she would have been subsequently housed in the female estate. These details were lost in the ensuing outcry, with the case becoming a lightning rod for opposition to gender recognition reform and arguably contributing to the resignation of Nicola Sturgeon as First Minister in 2023.

The new SPS policy for managing transgender people in custody was published in December 2024 after an extensive consultation exercise with all interested parties. The new policy did not change the fundamentals of the previous approach, stating that transgender women 'could be admitted to the women's estate but only if they do not meet any VAWG [violence against women and girls] criteria … and there is no other basis to suppose that they pose an unacceptable risk of harm to those housed in the women's estate' (SPS, 2024b). Individual risk assessment continues to form the basis of decision-making. Thus, SPS seeks to balance the rights of transgender people in prison to live according to their gender, with the rights of all women to live in a safe environment. While welcome, there remains a gap in the discussion of, and attention to, the needs and experiences of non-binary people in prison in Scotland, as elsewhere (Cairns, 2024). The approach in Scotland differs from the more restrictive policy of England and Wales, where pre-operation transgender women cannot be housed in the women's estate, even with a GRC and no record of gender-based or sexual violence. However, the implications on SPS policy and practice of the April 2025 UK Supreme Court judgment on the definition of 'woman' within the Equality Act are not yet clear and may be significant.

The experience of being transgender in prison results in particular pains (Maycock, 2022; see also Cairns, 2024), often due to the lack of community sharing their experience: extreme isolation, the practical difficulties of securing accommodation in their lived gender, and the serious mental health impacts that can result from these. These are exemplified in the case of a transwoman prisoner who died by suicide in 2019 while held in segregation at the men's prison, HMP Perth, as the SPS had been unable to secure appropriate accommodation.

Questions to consider

- How can prison regimes best accommodate transgender and non-binary prisoners?
- Given that these constitute a tiny minority of prisoners, why do you think the debate around transgender prisoners has been so heated?

8.3.4 Healthcare and deaths in custody

Please note that this section discusses drug use, mental illness and suicide.

People in prison have poorer health outcomes and age faster than people in the community. It is difficult to unpick the causal relationship; people in prison come disproportionately from more disadvantaged areas which have poorer health outcomes, but this is further exacerbated by imprisonment and problems with prison healthcare provision (Hatcher et al., 2022), which does not have parity with services in the community.

People in Scottish prisons have worse physical health, including in relation to cardiovascular disease, diabetes, epilepsy, asthma and related conditions, blood-borne viruses and STIs (Hatcher et al., 2022). They have a higher rate of past brain injury (often requiring hospitalisation), usually due to sustained domestic violence for women, and repeated violent interactions for men; in a study by McMillan et al. (2021) 78% of women in four Scottish prisons reported having sustained a significant head injury.

Factors like these contribute to a higher rate of so-called 'natural deaths' in prison than in the community. But while 'natural' might suggest 'unavoidable', research shows these deaths could have been prevented with the right treatment in prison (Barkas et al., 2021). This relates not only to people's ability to access healthcare support when they report symptoms but also wider support to live healthily in prison, given challenges accessing nutritious food and activity (Barkas et al., 2021). As Barkas et al (2021: 10) put it in relation to the 'natural' death of a 51-year-old who had been in prison since the age of 16: "*When a person dies so young, who has known only prison [their entire adult] life, what could this reveal about the quality of care and lifestyle management in prisons?*"

Similar themes are found when considering mental health. While no firm data are captured at a national level, modelling (using data about the prevalence of conditions from prisoners' demographics in the community) found that between 15% and 20% of the Scottish prison population had a long-term mental health condition, history of self-harm, symptoms of anxiety and/or depression. The same method estimated that 30% would have a current alcohol use disorder (McIntosh et al., 2022). However, this method does not capture the *effect of being in prison* on mental health, only what their mental health would have been had they not been put in prison. As such, we suggest it is likely a (serious) underestimate of the true scale of mental health needs in Scottish prisons. The same research found that younger, female and remand prisoners were particularly affected.

Improving support for physical and mental health in prison has been the subject of repeated calls from HMIPS and human rights bodies over the years. For example, the Scottish Human Rights Commission (2024) found there were too many very mentally unwell people in prison who should be in a secure hospital setting, and that segregation units were used to house prisoners too mentally unwell to be held in mainstream accommodation, an experience which only worsened their mental health.

A large proportion of prisoners test positive for illicit substances on entry to prison, while nearly half report having been under the influence of drugs and/or alcohol at the time of the offence (Toomey et al., 2022). There are security implications around preventing (as far as possible) the entry of drugs into prisons, dealing with intoxicated people in prison, and connections between drug dealing and organised crime. Furthermore, drugs present challenges for prison healthcare, which include not only direct impacts like preventing overdoses, but also addressing other health concerns, for instance, the mental and physical health impacts of withdrawal from drug use.

It is understandable that people in prison may use drugs or alcohol as self-medication for mental illness or simply to make the time pass faster (especially given the lack of meaningful engagement in work or education). Toomey et al. (2022) suggest that one in ten people who use drugs in Scottish prisons *start* doing so in prison. A range of treatment options are available in prison, but the limited data suggest that most drug treatment is via opioid replacement therapy using methadone (as opposed to psychosocial interventions). All this is taking place in the context of Scotland's crisis of drug-related deaths (see Box 1.1). The rate of drug-related deaths in prison is rising, with 44 drug-related deaths in prison between 2017 and 2022 (Armstrong et al., 2024), and drug use implicated in several FAIs into deaths in custody (Barkas et al., 2021). These include not only overdoses but deaths by suicide during withdrawal, and cases in which seriously ill prisoners were refused treatment because staff assumed they were drug-seeking.

The most serious outcome of physical and mental ill-health is death, including deaths by suicide. Sadly, but perhaps not surprisingly, rates of death in Scottish prisons are high and rising, with deaths by suicide increasing by

42% between 2008 and 2022 (Armstrong et al., 2024). The same analysis also found a strikingly higher rate of deaths by suicide in Scotland than in England and Wales.

Since 2017, it has been mandatory to hold a FAI for all deaths in custody. This is a judicial inquiry chaired by a Sheriff, carried out whenever anyone dies in an accident at work, or in legal custody or secure accommodation. The purpose of an FAI is to investigate the circumstances of the death and to 'consider what steps (if any) might be taken to prevent other deaths in similar circumstances'. The main mechanism for this is if the FAI makes a 'finding' either about a defect in the system or about whether any 'reasonable precautions' could have been taken that would have prevented this death (Armstrong et al., 2024). Still, FAIs otherwise operate much like a trial, where witnesses are called and give evidence under oath.

Valuable research into deaths in custody using FAI reports has been recently undertaken (see Armstrong et al., 2021, 2024; Barkas et al., 2021), which we have drawn on above. However, this research also raises concerns about the suitability of FAIs to hold the state to account for deaths in custody. FAIs cannot establish legal civil or criminal liability or punish wrongdoing. Instead, their rulings provide public scrutiny which *should* lead to changes in practice, but which cannot be enforced. Armstrong et al (2025) argued that the FAI process focuses too narrowly on the legal provisions which underpin them. As a result, each FAI addresses each death in isolation, so cannot see general trends or reoccurring issues. FAIs are not concerned with dignity in dying or the alleviation of suffering prior to death, but only about the prevention of death from occurring. This research also found that 'findings' (from which recommendations can be made), were only made in 6% of cases between 2005 and 2019, while families of the deceased are rarely involved meaningfully in the process (Armstrong et al., 2024).

Conclusion

This chapter has provided an overview of the Scottish prison system. While the formal institutions have changed with evolving political and social climates, many of the problems of imprisonment remain the same. There exist significant contrasts and contradictions – most obviously between the aspirational language of 'unlocking potential' and 'trauma-informed' approaches and the often dehumanising, isolating and harmful reality of imprisonment. Relatedly, examples of innovative practice in a few small units for specific groups coexist with the continued use of very large prisons, including the future HMP Glasgow which is set to replace HMP Barlinnie. While there has been political commitment to reduce imprisonment and some political will to address the less contentious short-term prisoner population (see Box 4.2), there has been less will to address the (growing) longer-term population and little progress in reducing remand.

We cannot look at imprisonment as an institution without discussing questions of its 'justice' and 'efficacy'. We believe this chapter has provided ample evidence of the *in*justice of imprisonment. Imprisonment clearly reflects (and arguably perpetuates) wider socioeconomic and health inequalities. Despite the language of 'rights-respecting' prisons, prisoners' rights are routinely infringed; accountability mechanisms intended to safeguard them can draw our attention to these issues but have little power to compel action. The often-lifelong stigma of a prison sentence (see Chapter 10) may mean punishment continues long after the sentence has been served.

Whether prison is 'effective' is difficult, if not impossible, to answer because of the inherent contradictions in the purposes of punishment to simultaneously incapacitate, punish, rehabilitate, denunciate, deter and repair harm (see Box 4.3). While we could say that the only one of these aims which is successfully achieved is 'incapacitation' in that prison should stop crime from occurring – even this is questionable upon closer analysis, because crime continues in prison (with thousands of assaults committed on people within a prison setting each year), and can spill out from the prison into the community and vice versa. For rehabilitation, the statistics are clear; the most recent figures not affected by COVID (although much else has happened since then) show that prison has the highest rate of reoffending of any disposal with 43.8% of people released from prison in 2018/19 committing further crimes within one year (Scottish Government, 2021). However, reoffending rates vary considerably by the length of the sentence, being far higher for short sentences than longer sentences (explanations for this likely involve various factors beyond the sentence itself).

There is widespread agreement that prisons in Scotland face serious problems. Many people have called for much greater political commitment and resources to address these longstanding issues, although with different views about how this should be done, including by radically reducing the use of prison. There are others in Scotland who think these problems are insurmountable, and that societal responses to harm are not best approached through a system which inevitably inflicts further pain. For these voices, directing more resources into prisons is counterproductive, with resources and energy better directed into alternative approaches and the community. While the prospect of moving away from a reliance on prison in Scotland seems distant, there is one area in which Scotland has had apparent success in moving away from carceral approaches – its approach to dealing with children's offending, the focus of our next chapter.

Critical questions

- Do you think prisons in Scotland can be places of transformation and healing? Why/why not?
- Choose one of the prisons in Scotland and look at the HMIPS reports on them (see under https://prisonsinspectoratescotland.gov.uk/publications and search by 'Establishment'). What sort of issues and themes are raised in the reports?

- How can problems like overcrowding and progression be addressed? Do you think it is in fact possible to 'solve' these?
- Given the many problems with imprisonment, why do you think it persists in Scotland?

Key resources

Armstrong, S., Barkas, B., Allan, L., Allan, S. and Cairns, D. (2024) *Nothing to See Here? Deaths in Custody and FAIs in Scotland* – 2023. SCCJR. https://www.sccjr.ac.uk/wp-content/uploads/2024/02/Nothing-to-See-Here-2023-FINAL.pdf

One of a series of reports on deaths in custody in Scotland.

Brangan, L. (2019) Civilizing imprisonment: The limits of Scottish penal exceptionalism. *The British Journal of Criminology* 59(4): 780–799.

Historical account of Scotland's prison system, which evaluates claims of Scottish exceptionalism.

His Majesty's Inspectorate of Prisons for Scotland – Publications. https://prisonsinspectoratescotland.gov.uk/publications

HMIPS reports provide one of the best ways of keeping up to date with developments in prisons in Scotland, drawing attention to important concerns.

Schinkel, M. (2015) Hook for change or shaky peg? Imprisonment, narratives and desistance. *European Journal of Probation* 7(1): 5–20.

Schinkel, M. and Lives Sentenced Participants (2021) Persistent short-term imprisonment: Belonging as a lens to understand its shifting meanings over the life course. *Incarceration* 2(1):1–20.

Two important articles on how prisoners in Scotland make sense of their imprisonment.

Scottish Prisons Interactive Analysis Tool. https://scotland.shinyapps.io/sg-prison-population-statistics/

Scottish Prison Service Quarterly Information Pages. https://www.sps.gov.uk/about-us/transparency/publications?combine=&field_category_target_id=73

A useful online dashboard for exploring prison population stats online, and more robust but less frequently available data from SPS.

Notes

1 The prison 'regime' refers to the organisation of prison activities, programmes, education, outdoor space, visits, etc.

2 Purposeful activity includes any activity which might have a beneficial value for prisoners, but which can include such basic things as a job mopping floors in the prison.

References

Anderson, K. (ed) (2024) *The Barlinnie Special Unit: Art, Punishment & Innovation*. Waterside Press.

Anderson, S. (2025) The trouble with trauma: Interconnected forms of violence in the lives of repeatedly criminalised men. *Howard Journal of Crime and Justice* 64: 24–43.

Armstrong, S., Allan, L., Allan, S., Barkas, B. and Kinnear, D. (2021) *Nothing to See Here? Statistical Briefing on 15 Years of Fatal Accident Inquiries into Deaths in Custody*. SCCJR. https://www.sccjr.ac.uk/publication/nothing-to-see-here-statistical-briefing/

Armstrong, S., Barkas, B., Allan, L., Allan, S. and Cairns, D. (2024) *Nothing to See Here? Deaths in Custody and FAIs in Scotland – 2023*. SCCJR. https://www.sccjr.ac.uk/wp-content/uploads/2024/02/Nothing-to-See-Here-2023-FINAL.pdf

Barkas, B., Allan, L., Allan, S., Armstrong, S. and Kinnear, D. (2021) *A Defective System: Case Analysis of 15 Years of Fatal Accident Inquiries after Deaths in Prison*. SCCJR. https://www.sccjr.ac.uk/wp-content/uploads/2021/10/A-Defective-System.pdf

Brangan, L. (2019) Civilizing imprisonment: The limits of Scottish penal exceptionalism. *British Journal of Criminology* 59(4): 780–799.

Brangan, L. (2021) *The Politics of Punishment: A Comparative Study of Imprisonment and Political Culture*. Routledge.

Cairns, B., (2024) Transgender perspectives on the Scottish Prison System: On the Subject of the Legal Subject. In Maycock, M., O'Shea, S., and Jenness, V. (eds) *Transgender People Involved with Carceral Systems*. Routledge. 319–334.

Cameron, J. (1983) *Prisons and Punishment in Scotland: From the Middle Ages to the Present*. Canongate.

Commission on Women Offenders (2012) *Commission on Women Offenders: Final Report*. Commission on Women Offenders.

Cornish, N. (2022) *Vulnerability, Decision-Making and the Protection of Prisoners in Scotland and England*. PhD thesis, University of Glasgow.

Coyle, A. (1991) *Inside: Rethinking Scotland's Prisons*. Scottish Child.

Gormley, C. (2022) The hidden harms of prison life for people with learning disabilities. *British Journal of Criminology* 62(2): 261–278.

Gormley, C., Schinkel, M., Barkas, B., Casey, R., Cornish, N. and McNeill, F. (2020) Criminal justice involved. In Armstrong, S., and Pickering, L. (eds) *Left Out and Locked Down: Impact of COVID-19 Pandemic for Marginalised Groups in Scotland*. University of Glasgow. 61–73.

Hatcher, R.M., Tonkin, M.J., Palmer, E.J. and Blackmore, C. (2022) *Understanding the Physical Health Care Needs of Scotland's Prison Population*. Scottish Government.

HM Inspectorate of Prisons for Scotland (HMIPS) (2003) *HM Chief Inspector of Prisons for Scotland: Report for 2002–2003*. Scottish Executive Justice Department.

HMIPS (2018) *HM Chief Inspector of Prisons for Scotland: Annual Report 2017–2018*. HMIPS.

HMIPS (2020). *Who Cares? A Follow-Up Review of the Lived Experience of Older Prisoners in Scotland's Prisons*. HMIPS.

HMIPS (2022) *HM Chief Inspector's Annual Report 2021–22*. HMIPS.

HMIPS (2024) HM Inspection of Bellas and Lilias Community Custody Units. HMIPS.

Houchin, R. (2005) *Social Exclusion and Imprisonment in Scotland: A Report*. Glasgow Caledonian University.

Howard League Scotland (2021) *The Scandal of Remand in Scotland: A Report by Howard League Scotland* – May 2021. Howard League Scotland. https://howardleague.scot/news/2021/may/scandal-remand-scotland-report-howard-league-scotland-%E2%80%93-may-2021#:~:text=In%20the%20early%20months%20of,a%20total%20population%20of%207%2C394.

Jardine, C. (2019) *Families, Imprisonment and Legitimacy: The Cost of Custodial Penalties*. Routledge.

Jewkes, Y. and Moran, D. (2017) Prison architecture and design: Perspectives from criminology and carceral geography. In Liebling, A., Maruna, S. and McAra, L. (eds) *The Oxford Handbook of Criminology*. Sixth edition. Oxford University Press. 541–561.

Maycock, M. (2022) The transgender pains of imprisonment. *European Journal of Criminology* 19(6): 1521–1541.

McAra, L. (2005) Modelling penal transformation. *Punishment and Society* 7(3): 277–302.

McBride, M., Anderson, S. and O'Donnell, E. (2025) *No Problem (In) Here?: A scoping study of Catholics in Scottish Prisons*. SCCJR. https://www.sccjr.ac.uk/wp-content/uploads/2025/02/No-Problem-In-Here-Scoping-the-Experiences-of-Catholics-in-Scottish-Prisons-250225-FINAL-DOC.pdf

McIntosh, L.G., Rees, C., Kelly, C., Howitt, S. and Thomson, L.D.G. (2022) *Understanding the Mental Health Needs of Scotland's Prison Population*. Scottish Government.

McMillan, T.M., Aslam, H., Crowe, E., Seddon, E. and Barry, S.J.E. (2021) Associations between significant head injury and persisting disability and violent crime in women in prison in Scotland, UK: A cross-sectional study. *The Lancet Psychiatry* 8(6): 512–520.

McNeill, F. (2015) Desistance and criminal justice in Scotland. In Croall, H., Mooney, G. and Munro, M. (eds) *Crime, Justice and Society in Scotland*. Routledge. 200–215.

Morrison, K. (2018) Professionalism and affective learning for new prison officers: learning values, attitudes and behaviours in training at the Scottish Prison Service. In Loo, S. (ed) *Multiple Dimensions of Teaching and Learning for Occupational Practice*. Routledge. 150–169.

Morrison, K. and Graham, H. (2022) Scotland. In Dünkel, F., Harrendorf, S. and van Zyl Smit, D. (eds) *The Impact of Covid-19 on Prison Conditions and Penal Policy*. Routledge. 443–454.

Morrison, K. and Maycock, M. (2021) Becoming a prison officer: An analysis of the early development of prison officer cultures. *Howard Journal of Crime and Justice* 60(1): 3–24.

Munro, M., Mooney, G. and Croall, H. (2010) Criminal justice in Scotland: overview and prospects. In Croall, H., Mooney, G. and Munro, M. (eds) *Criminal Justice in Scotland*. Willan. 261–278.

Murray, K. and Hunter Blackburn, L. (2019) Losing sight of women's rights: The unregulated introduction of gender self-identification as a case study of policy capture in Scotland. *Scottish Affairs* 28(3): 262–289.

O'Carroll, M. (2022) *Is There Anybody Out There? Prison Activism and Abolition in Scotland 1972–87*. SCCJR. https://www.sccjr.ac.uk/wp-content/uploads/2022/12/Is-there-Anybody-Out-There.pdf

Piacentini, L., Weaver, B. and Jardine, C. (2018) *Employment and Employability in Scottish Prisons: A Research Briefing Paper*. SCCJR. https://www.sccjr.ac.uk/publication/employment-and-employability-in-scottish-prisons-a-research-briefing-paper-feb-2018/

Russo, D. (2024) *Isolation in Scottish Prisons – What Does It Mean to Be Alone Inside? A Socio-Legal Analysis*. PhD thesis, University of Edinburgh.

Scottish Government (2021) *Reconviction Rates in Scotland: 2018–19 Offender Cohort*. Scottish Government. https://www.gov.scot/publications/reconviction-rates-scotland-2018-19-offender-cohort/

Scottish Government (2023) *Criminal Proceedings in Scotland, 2021–22 – Updated*. Scottish Government. https://www.gov.scot/publications/criminal-proceedings-scotland-2021-22-updated/ (and see accompanying experimental statistics)

Scottish Government (2024a) *Safer Communities and Justice Statistics Monthly Data Report*. July 2024 edition. Scottish Government. https://www.gov.scot/publications/safer-communities-justice-statistics-monthly-data-report-july-2024-edition/

Scottish Government (2024b) *Scottish Prison Population Statistics 2023–24*. Scottish Government.

Scottish Human Rights Commission (2024) *Review... Recommend... Repeat... An Assessment of Where Human Rights Have Stalled in Places of Detention*. SHRC.

Scottish Parliament (2023) *Parliamentary Question Reference S6W-21395*. https://www.parliament.scot/chamber-and-committees/questions-and-answers/question?ref=S6W-21395

Scottish Prison Service (1990) *Opportunity and Responsibility – Developing New Approaches to the Management of the Long Term Prison System in Scotland*. Scottish Prison Service.

Scottish Prison Service (2013) *Unlocking Potential, Transforming Lives: Report of the Scottish Prison Service Organisational Review*. Scottish Prison Service.

Scottish Prison Service (2014) *Gender Identity and Gender Reassignment Policy for Those in our Custody*. SPS.

Scottish Prison Service (2016) *Unlocking Our Potential: A Value Proposition*. Scottish Prison Service.

Scottish Prison Service (2023) *Corporate Plan 2023–2028*. Scottish Prison Service. https://www.sps.gov.uk/sites/default/files/2024-02/CorporatePlan_2023-2028_CorporateReports.pdf

Scottish Prison Service (2024a) *SPS Quarterly Public Information Page: Prison by Numbers Quarter 3 (October–December 2023)*. SPS.

Scottish Prison Service (2024b) *SPS Policy for the Management of Transgender People in Custody: Operational Guidance*. SPS.

Scottish Prisons Commission (2008) *Scotland's Choice: Report of the Scottish Prisons Commission*. Scottish Prisons Commission.

Sparks, R. (2002) Out of the 'digger': The warrior's honour and the guilty observer. *Ethnography* 3: 556–581.

Sturge, G. (2024) *UK Prison Population Statistics*. House of Commons Library.

Toomey, C., Fotopoulou, M. and Armstrong, S. (2022) *Mapping Drug Use, Interventions and Treatment Needs in Scottish Prisons: A Literature Review*. SCCJR.

9 The youth justice system in Scotland

Key ideas

- The main Scottish youth justice institution is the unique system of 'children's hearings' – where volunteer panel members aim to promote the welfare of all children (not just children who offend), rather than punishing. They were set up following the 1964 Kilbrandon Report.
- The 'Kilbrandon philosophy' is the idea that children who offend should be treated not as offenders but as 'children in trouble'. This is often seen as emblematic of Scotland's distinctiveness in youth justice.
- Youth justice is closely connected to other areas of policy that aim to promote child welfare, which has been a focus for successive Scottish Governments.
- In Scotland as elsewhere, debates over youth justice reflect questions about how we should respond to children's offending. Most recently, diversionary approaches and children's rights have had a significant impact on Scottish youth justice.
- These debates also reflect *political* developments in terms of Scotland's relationship with the rest of the UK, sometimes moving closer to English policies and sometimes further away.

Introduction

A central element of Scotland's response to youth offending is the **Children's Hearings System**. This unique system, admired around the world, is underpinned by a philosophy of treating young people who offend not as offenders but as children with unmet needs, and centred on welfare rather than punishment. Yet Scotland is also a country where children are routinely criminalised and over-policed, which until very recently had the lowest age of criminal responsibility in Europe.

Youth justice contains paradoxes and is deeply connected with questions of child welfare and what Scottish society wants for its children. The history of Scottish youth justice also shows very well how political developments in our devolutionary settlement have shaped criminal justice in complex ways.

DOI: 10.4324/9781003372882-9

In this chapter, we discuss first of all how the Scottish youth justice system works and what makes it different to other systems, in particular the 'Kilbrandon philosophy'. We then consider how our approach to youth justice has changed, with a particular focus on developments since devolution. We conclude by considering how developments in contemporary youth justice have been shaped by Scotland's efforts to improve outcomes for children and embed children's rights in the system while responding to (arguably overdue) concern about the welfare of children in institutional settings.

9.1 Background: the Kilbrandon Report

The contemporary history of Scottish youth justice begins in 1964 with a report by Lord Kilbrandon on juvenile offending and youth courts in Scotland. This report was written at the peak of the welfare- and rehabilitation-oriented approach to justice (**penal welfarism**), which dominated UK justice for much of the 20th century. Prior to the Kilbrandon Report, the 1908 Children Act had already specified – in line with mainstream opinion – that young people who offend must be treated differently to adults. In the context of penal welfarism, Kilbrandon was able to go further, arguing that young people who come into conflict with the law should be treated not as offenders or delinquents, but as 'children in trouble' – just like children who are victims of abuse, neglect, poverty or illness. It is this principle – not the emphasis on welfare in itself – that makes Scotland's system special.

Kilbrandon argued that proper investigation of a child's circumstances requires an inquisitorial approach, rather than the traditional adversarial trial used to determine guilt (see Section 4.3.4), which was potentially alienating and frightening for children. Kilbrandon recommended that *all* children in trouble – whether they had offended or not – be dealt with by a system of 'hearings', in which the child's welfare would be paramount. The '**children's hearings**' were established by the 1968 Social Work (Scotland) Act and began operating in 1971 (the same Act set up the use of social work to supervise community penalties, as discussed in Chapter 6). Scotland is unusual, then, in that its main youth justice institution is not really a criminal justice agency. However, as we shall see, it is not clear that the Kilbrandon philosophy has ever been consistently and thoroughly implemented in practice.

Box 9.1 Needs, deeds or something else?

Youth justice systems can be understood as being underpinned by various 'discourses' – theories and ideas about what childhood is, what young people are like, what causes their offending and how it should be dealt with.

A fundamental debate across youth justice is between the 'welfare' and 'justice' discourses. In essence, this is the question of whether youth justice should attempt to treat the underlying needs of children who offend (and thus, in theory, rehabilitate them) or hold children to account, by fairly and consistently punishing the offences they have committed (the justice model). This is commonly summarised as **'needs versus deeds'**. This is a significant question, which echoes a key debate in criminology: whether people offend by choice (associated with classical criminology) or because of some circumstance beyond their control (genetics, psychology, socioeconomic circumstances, etc.) (associated with positivist criminology). In youth justice, there is a tendency to lean more towards 'needs' than when dealing with adults, reflecting the special status and lesser culpability of children.

As children came to be seen as distinct from adults (and accepted understandings of the age range of 'childhood' itself gradually 'extended' to include older children), this allowed for children to be seen either as vulnerable and in need of protection or as dangerous, irrational and requiring punishment. Both framings, however, present children as lacking agency and requiring intervention from the justice system. Other perspectives would reject the terms of this debate, redirecting attention instead to young people's relative lack of power to determine laws or direct criminal justice activity, and society's tendency to direct criminal justice activity against and criminalise the harms perpetrated by (especially working-class) young people, while permitting many harms committed by powerful adults.

The history of youth justice has been defined by shifting discourses, with welfare being prominent across the UK for most of the 20th century, but continuing to characterise *Scottish* youth justice in the late-modern era, even as other parts of the UK embraced different approaches. Alongside the central 'needs versus deeds' question, there are various other discourses – principles of diversion underpin the Whole System Approach (Section 9.3.3) and, more recently, we have seen children understood as rights bearers, deserving of care and support, while still able to participate in decisions about their own lives (Section 9.3.4). Another recent current draws on neurological ideas to frame children as having not fully developed brains, as impulsive and lacking maturity, up until the age of 25.

Ideals and principles rarely survive contact with the real world unscathed; real justice systems are full of complexity and contradictions, and real-world youth justice doesn't fit neatly with any one discourse. But we can use this sort of theorising to deepen our understanding and make the link between criminological theory and the 'on the ground' reality of criminal justice.

For a closer look at youth justice discourses, see Muncie and Hughes (2002); Carr and Smith (2023) give a recent overview of how these play out in a range of youth justice systems.

Questions to consider

- Thinking about the discourses of youth justice discussed here – welfare, justice, diversion, rights, etc. – how do these play out in the historical developments discussed in this chapter?
- What do you think distinguishes childhood from adulthood? How might this be relevant for thinking about how to deal with young people's offending?

9.2 Overview of Scottish youth justice: key agencies and process

As with other groups, **police** are often the initial contact with the youth justice system (controversy about the over-policing of young people is discussed in Chapter 3), but the system involves various criminal justice and child welfare bodies (often working in partnership) and its own distinct institutional arrangements.

9.2.1 *Early and Effective Intervention (EEI) and diversion from prosecution*

Under the Whole System Approach (Section 9.3.3), much of youth justice seeks to divert cases away from the system at an early stage, diverting out of the youth justice system wherever possible.

Early and Effective Intervention (EEI) is a system that aims to ensure proportionate responses to offending by children, identifying problems in a child's life that might be causing their offending. Each local authority has its own EEI arrangements but they usually involve the police and social workers (often specialists in 'Children and Families' rather than Criminal Justice), and sometimes other agencies. The police can refer a child suspected of an offence to EEI, which can take various diversionary measures. The child can be referred to specific support agencies (such as social work or mental health) or targeted 'intervention' programmes. EEI can also refer the child to police 'direct measures' (a formal warning from police) or even take no action at all.

Diversionary measures are well-intentioned, but, since most children referred to EEI have no previous concerns about their wellbeing, there remains the risk of net-widening (i.e. drawing more children into involvement with the youth and criminal justice agencies) (Gillon, 2021). Given efforts to embed children's rights in Scottish youth justice (see Section 9.3.4), there are also questions about the extent to which EEI measures recognise children's rights, including the right to have family involved in the process.

For more serious offending, the child would be referred to a children's hearing (see below) or – in a minority of cases – referred for prosecution by the **Crown Office and Procurator Fiscal Service (COPFS)**. Even at this stage, there can still be a way out. The Procurator Fiscal (PF) (see Chapter 4) can decide to refer a child to a diversionary programme instead of charging. This can include restorative justice, social work programmes and others. The PF may also impose a 'direct measure' (a warning, fiscal fine or compensation – see Section 5.1.2), similar to cases of adults diverted from prosecution.

9.2.2 The Children's Hearings System (CHS)

When there is concern about a child's welfare or their behaviour, a referral can be made (usually by the police, social work or education) to a **Children's Reporter**, an official who investigates and decides what the grounds are for the hearing and whether compulsory measures may be needed. Where this is the case, a children's hearing is convened – although in most cases a hearing is not considered necessary. Reporters' work is coordinated and supported by the **Scottish Children's Reporter Administration (SCRA).**

There has been a dramatic fall in the number of cases referred to the Children's Reporter – referrals declined from a peak of about 55,000 in 2006–07 to around a fifth of that figure by the 2020s. Within this there has been an especially sharp fall in the number of referrals on offence grounds, which made up only about a quarter of referrals in 2023/24. Even in offence referrals, the child's welfare should come first. Donnelly's (2019) research highlights an age dynamic in the grounds for referral, with younger children more likely to be referred on care and protection grounds while older children are more likely to be referred on 'conduct' grounds (e.g. substance use or being out of parental control) and offence grounds. Since these are often the same children this raises questions about the effectiveness of the CHS' earlier interventions.

The child may not agree with the grounds given for a hearing, and so a formal process is needed where this is disputed. The longstanding process has been that a decision is sought from a local **Sheriff** (see Chapter 4). In cases of offence grounds *only*, this resembles a criminal trial, with witnesses, cross-examination and the criminal standard of proof ("beyond a reasonable doubt") (again, see Chapter 4). This means that children referred on offence grounds *are* in fact treated differently, despite Kilbrandon's intentions, and this adversarial element can feel distressing. Sheriffs might also be called on to resolve legal or factual disagreements in children's hearings (e.g. about where a child habitually resides).

The hearing has traditionally comprised lay panel members, ordinary people who volunteer their time to hear cases: they hear about the child's circumstances and they (not the Reporter or Sheriff) make decisions about outcomes, including involuntary care. While intended to be from the community, they may nevertheless have very different backgrounds to those of the children they work with.

The hearing is a formal legal process, regardless of the grounds for referral, but members are expected to try to create an informal atmosphere – so the child feels safe, supported and able to participate, although the Independent Care Review (2020) and Hearings System Working Group (2023) reports suggest this is not always realised in practice. The child has the right to attend and the hearing is also attended by 'relevant persons' including parents or others with "significant involvement in the upbringing of the child". The child may also have an independent advocacy worker (to support the young person and ensure their rights are respected and their voice heard), a designated independent 'safeguarder' (to protect the child's best interests) and the child's representatives – a lawyer and/or a friend or other trusted person. (For more on the procedure of children's hearings, see Norrie, 2022). Social workers in local authorities (often specialists in 'Children and Families') might also attend. The *Hearings for Children* review (Hearings System Working Group, 2023) highlighted concerns about animosity and conflict, and an increasingly adversarial-feeling system. Despite the common focus on the child's best interests, people in different roles might see the functions of the panel in very different ways (Porter et al., 2016).

The panel have a range of options, including to 'discharge' the referral if they disagree that formal action is needed, but the panel usually imposes a **Compulsory Supervision Order (CSO)**. In 2021–22, children's hearings made 2,283 decisions including 2,012 new CSOs; as of 31 March 2022, there were 7,265 children on CSOs (across all grounds for referral). Conditions of the CSO might include place of residence, including placing in secure care, requiring medical examination or treatment and regulating contact with one or more people. Another is the Movement Restriction Condition (MRC), a rarely imposed measure in which the child's freedom of movement is restricted with compliance monitored by an electronic tag (see Chapter 7). However, while CSOs can be very effective in helping children in other ways, they appear to have little effect on offending (Henderson et al., 2021).

There have been some organisational changes to Children's Hearings since they were set up. The Children's Hearings (Scotland) Act 2011 revised the grounds for referral and created the body **Children's Hearings Scotland**, which has responsibility for recruiting and training panel members. Provision for virtual hearings was introduced during the COVID-19 pandemic, which has raised further concerns about children's ability to meaningfully participate, communication and technological difficulties, and the wider context of digital divides (Porter et al., 2021). Despite these changes, to date, the key elements remain the same.

Further changes are anticipated following the *Hearings for Children* (Hearings System Working Group, 2023) review, which identified problems with the system and sought to better protect child rights. Concerns include children and families' (in)ability to participate meaningfully in these hearings, how the system can be experienced for young people (unfamiliar, distressing, confusing and punitive) and continuity and consistency in decision-making. The review also recommended ensuring that panel members are matched to children and families so that a rapport can be developed, including by ensuring panel members come from the same local communities.

Many proposed changes were accepted by the Scottish Government and were subject to public consultation at the end of 2024, which may have implications for things like panel set-up and the process of establishing grounds. The SCRA website is a useful source of information about the current situation.

9.2.3 Young people in court

Although the CHS deals with the vast majority of cases involving offending by children, criminal courts have an important role in youth justice. This mainly lies in establishing matters of fact, rather than deciding what should happen to the child (as outlined above).

However, while most youth offending in Scotland is dealt with by diversionary measures or children's hearings, *not* courts, prosecutions do still happen, a fact sometimes lost in rhetoric about Scotland's distinctiveness. Children under 16 *can* still be prosecuted and tried in court, though this should only happen for very serious offences, and is now very rare. Until recently, most children 16 and over charged with an offence were excluded from the CHS and usually prosecuted in court, creating a jarring transition from legal 'childhood' to 'adulthood', at which point the same behaviour was responded to very differently.

The Independent Care Review (2000: 41) emphasised that "Traditional criminal courts are not settings in which children's rights can be upheld and where they can be heard". The 2024 Children (Care and Justice) (Scotland) Act extends the use of the CHS to children up until the age of 18. This will at least delay this transition, but since the Procurator Fiscal will retain the discretion to try them in a court, it remains to be seen how often this will continue in practice.

Where young people are prosecuted in court, there are strong arguments for adapting the setting and process through the provision of specialist Youth Courts. A number of problem-solving courts (see Section 4.2.1) for young people have been piloted: Glasgow has a Youth Court while the Aberdeen problem-solving court includes people between 16 and 24.

Since 2008, the **Structured Deferred Sentence (SDS)** has been available in some local authorities in Scotland, with different local schemes working in different ways. The SDS was intended for cases of minor offending involving people with complex needs. It defers sentence after conviction to allow for a period of social work supervision prior to sentencing; in theory, this means that if the person (with support) can address their problems, they may receive a lesser sentence or escape sentence altogether and be admonished instead (there has been discussion of allowing absolute discharge of the case at the end of an SDS). SDS was not designed with young people in mind, and many SDS schemes work with adults. However, the nature of the intended target group, and its diversionary approach, would seem to make the SDS particularly suitable for young people. For this reason, the use of SDS with young people (over 16) in North and South Lanarkshire has recently been piloted in Hamilton and Lanark Sheriff Courts. This has had some success – reoffending rates were very low and most of the young people involved highlighted the value of the programme, particularly the social work support (Miller et al., 2019).

Criminal courts can impose similar sentences on young people as on adults (see Chapter 4), including community sentences (albeit with a more limited range of requirements). In the rare case of a long custodial sentence being imposed, the young person would serve this in secure care until they reached adulthood, at which point they would transfer to a Young Offender Institution (YOI) (and if necessary, an adult prison thereafter). The Scottish Sentencing Council (see Chapter 4) has recently issued guidance on sentencing young people, emphasising their diminished culpability, greater vulnerability and capacity for change. This guideline defines young people as people under 25, informed partly by the scientific opinion that people's brains tend not to reach full maturity until this age, as well as wider developmental arguments. (This idea, although intuitive and straightforward, is also contested among scientists – see Johnson et al., 2009). The guidance states that sentencers must have particular regard to the person's maturity and to rehabilitation and that imprisonment should be a last resort for young people. Nonetheless, children and young people can still be deprived of their liberty.

9.2.4 Deprivation of liberty: secure care, youth and police custody

Secure care is the primary form of deprivation of liberty for children in Scotland. Secure care facilities are operated by charities; they are not prisons and are not intended to punish, but to keep children safe if they are considered to pose a risk to themselves or others. This is often because they have experienced significant trauma and are believed likely either to abscond or to harm themselves or others if left at liberty. Some children in secure care have committed offences, but many are referred for other reasons. Secure care services are staffed by charity staff – not prison officers – and are supposed to be therapeutic environments. Secure care services include private living space, communal spaces for socialising, school-level education provision, and a much higher ratio of qualified staff to young people than found in YOIs.

However, although some 'secured' young people receive nurturing and caring treatment, others may experience secure care as confusing, alienating and punitive – a place to 'do their time' rather than receive assistance (Gough, 2016). The Independent Care Review (2020: 80) heard that it could be "a scary place", with an overuse of restraint, including where perceived as punishment. There are particular challenges in planning transitions in and out of the system due to the vulnerabilities of the children. There are also systemic issues – there are (as of May 2025) only 78 secure care places, mainly in the Central Belt. Pressure on the system has been exacerbated by the use of secure care in Scotland to hold children from England and Wales (where the system is overstretched) (Gibson, 2022). These traumatised children – and those from more rural parts of Scotland – are living far from their families. Aged only 16, William Brown (Lindsay) died in Polmont Young Offenders Institution, having been sent there due to a lack of beds in secure care. Scottish Government now reserves beds so that there is always availability. The **Care Inspectorate** inspects a range of children's services, including secure care but also local authority services for children.

Until 2024, YOIs in Scotland housed young people from 16 to at least 21 years of age. YOIs are very similar to prisons and often on the same site. Like prisons, they are inspected by the HM Inspectorate of Prisons in Scotland. The main YOI in Scotland is Polmont, near Falkirk in central Scotland. A much smaller number of girls and young women were/are held within YOI units. Largely as a result of the Whole System Approach (see below), the population of young people in custody has fallen dramatically, with part of Polmont repurposed to hold adult women prisoners.

YOIs are intended to provide a less painful, more rehabilitative, form of custody through greater emphasis on education and training programmes. However, in practice, young people's experiences are characterised by boredom (often locked in their cells for much of the day), victimisation including bullying and violence, trauma, and mental illness – often exacerbated by other features of life in custody (Goldson, 2005). Ongoing use of and conditions within youth custody were brought sharply into focus by the deaths by suicide of two young people, William Brown (Lindsay, age 16) and Katie Allan (age 21) in 2018. An inspection of Polmont (HMIPS, 2018) found significant problems with mental healthcare in the YOI, while an independent review by Armstrong and McGhee (2019) argued for greater support, less use of isolation, and the need to reduce youth custody. The Fatal Accident Inquiry (FAI) into their deaths found systemic failures contributed to both deaths, which might have been avoided had some reasonable precautions been taken. These high-profile deaths were the catalyst for many subsequent changes, but the FAI highlights that much more remains to be done.

Following a 2020 commitment in *The Promise* (see below), the Children (Care and Justice) (Scotland) Act was passed in 2024, preventing the use of YOIs for under-18s in Scotland. Alternatives to custody must now be explored, including secure care and community alternatives. From September 2024, no children have been held in prison in Scotland, but this came too late for another child who died in Polmont in July 2024 (where there have been a number of other deaths by suicide since 2018).

Finally, it is worth highlighting police custody as another site in which children are deprived of their liberty, which can be a traumatising experience. Children can be subject to strip searches: in 2017–18, this was carried out 788 times by Police Scotland – with nothing found in 96% of cases (Lightowler, 2020). In November 2024, the **Children and Young People's Commissioner** – who has responsibility for upholding children's rights in Scotland – launched an investigation into Police Scotland's use of force, citing much higher use of force against children than adults. The 2024 Children (Care and Justice) (Scotland) Act will require alternative 'places of safety' to be considered for any child, in preference to police custody (Nolan, 2024).

9.3 Scottish youth justice after devolution

We turn now to the historical development of Scottish youth justice. The introduction of children's hearings marked a significant divergence from mainstream UK youth justice. As Scotland 'locked in' welfarism, the UK Parliament (legislating on English/Welsh criminal justice) held back from fully embracing the welfare principle, by failing to bring into force the radical provisions of the 1969 Children and Young Persons Act. However, the Scottish system has been far from immune to pressures from the wider UK.

9.3.1 The UK antisocial behaviour agenda and 'detartanisation'

Across the UK, the second half of the 20th century saw a long-term rise in young people's recorded offending, in the context of a rise in all crime, from the 1960s until about the 1990s. This led to rising concern about young people's offending and perceived moral drift, coming to a head in the reaction to the murder of a very young child by two ten-year-old boys in Merseyside in 1993.

This concern about young people was increasingly framed in terms of 'antisocial behaviour' (ASB), encompassing a broader range of acts than simply criminal offences (see Section 2.1.2). The UK New Labour government (1997–2010) made a political issue of ASB, "recoded as a problem of young people in deprived and marginalised communities and neighbourhoods" (Hughes and Follett, 2006: 157).

Although centred on England, the ASB agenda had a significant impact in Scotland, which at that point was newly devolved but also governed by New Labour. Around the early 2000s, Scottish politics and popular culture became concerned with 'neds' – working-class young people assumed to be at risk of substance misuse, delinquency and antisocial behaviour (reflecting discussions of 'chavs' in the wider UK – see Young, 2012). Language around youth crime became increasingly politicised and more centred on holding young people accountable (Scottish Executive, 2000).

Various new measures were introduced to control young people's behaviour during this period, including Antisocial Behaviour Orders (ASBOs – see

Chapter 2), parenting orders for parents of children involved in ASB, electronic monitoring for 16- and 17-year-olds and powers for the police to stop young people gathering ('dispersal zones'). Reviews of the CHS, while generally supportive, highlighted 'persistent young offenders' as a problem in need of punitive action. To this end, the then-Scottish Executive piloted fast-track 'youth courts' in Hamilton and Airdrie to deal with persistent offending among 16- and 17- (and some 15-) year-olds (different to the 'problem-solving' orientation of more recent youth court pilots).

Concerns were raised by children's rights activists and criminologists who warned that, despite increasing political autonomy, Scottish youth justice was losing its distinct character – referred to as 'detartanisation' (McAra, 2006). The emphasis appeared to be shifting away from welfare and towards justice and governing 'risky' groups. McAra (2006) and Croall (2006) account for this paradoxical development through the political dynamics of Scottish devolution; policy was no longer decided by unelected civil servants, but by elected Members of the Scottish Parliament (MSPs) who had to engage with wider politicised debates about crime to gain favour with voters.

In many cases though, these measures had either limited duration or little impact. Youth courts were found to be ineffective and expensive, as well as punitive and net-widening (Piacentini and Walters, 2006) and were quietly shut down in 2010. Perhaps because of resistance from local government, ASBOs were very rarely imposed on children in Scotland. Children's hearings continued largely unchanged – and as of 2021, they hadn't imposed a single parenting order (CYCJ, 2021). Instead, Scottish youth justice retained its distinctiveness and moved in an altogether different direction.

Post-devolutionary developments largely occurred while recorded offending in Scotland, as well as the wider UK, was falling steadily – and since the late 1980s, recorded offending by young people has fallen *even as a proportion* of crime (Matthews and Minton, 2018).

It is worth bearing in mind however that the relationship between crime rates and criminal justice practice is not straightforward, and crime statistics can anyway only give us a partial picture – most statistics include only those offences that enter the justice system, meaning there is a huge dark figure of youth crime (but self-report surveys, like the Edinburgh Study discussed below, help to shed light on unreported and unrecorded offending).

9.3.2 Reasserting distinctiveness and the Edinburgh Study

Developments around youth justice became connected to wider efforts to improve the lives of children in Scotland. Despite the politicised discourse around young people, the New Labour-led Scottish Government introduced the ambitious **'Getting It Right for Every Child' (GIRFEC)** programme in 2006. This aimed to make Scotland "the best place in the world to grow up" (see Coles et al., 2016 for a general overview). This involved various agencies in promoting the wellbeing of all children in Scotland, so bringing youth justice into connection with child welfare policies. This helped shift the agenda away from the punitive impulses of the early 2000s.

Subsequent Scottish National Party (SNP)-led governments from 2007 onwards enthusiastically took up this agenda. Of course, there was political advantage for a Scottish Nationalist government in emphasising the distinctiveness of Scottish youth justice from England and Wales. However, post-2010s developments in youth justice were heavily influenced by findings from the Edinburgh Study on Youth Transitions and Crime, one of the most important studies on young people's offending. Beginning in the late 1990s, this tracked 4,300 young people in Edinburgh from secondary school well into adulthood, examining their lives and offending careers. It found that infrequent minor offending is common among children, and the few involved in persistent and serious offending are usually also victims of crime, violence and/or abuse, in line with the Kilbrandon philosophy. But contrary to the view of much mainstream criminology at the time, it found that it is very difficult to identify from childhood those who will go on to offend seriously. Not only this, identifying young children as 'high risk' *might make things worse,* since early formal contact with criminal justice agencies was a predictor of *further* offending. Police or courts might be harming these children by stigmatising and labelling them, even if they are trying to help (see McAra and McVie, 2010).

Taken together, these crucial findings offer clear support for **diversionary** approaches to youth justice, and directly inspired the signature youth justice policy of the 2010s – the Whole System Approach.

9.3.3 *The Whole System Approach*

The **'Whole System Approach' (WSA)** was launched in 2011 and seeks to minimise the number of young people dealt with by the criminal justice system. It is so named because it requires a range of agencies, including those beyond typical justice organisations (education, third sector, COPFS, police, Sheriffs, social work, etc.) to work together to minimise the criminalisation and punishment of young people.

It aims to reduce offence referrals to children's hearings, diverting cases out of the system through EEI and away from prosecution (see Section 9.2.1). For those children who are prosecuted, the WSA seeks to put in place support for them in court, and if applicable, during and after their time in custody/secure care to support their reintegration into society, including through targeted partnership support in local authorities. In this way, the WSA seeks to mitigate the stigmatising and labelling effects of justice system contact.

The WSA is organised at the level of local authorities, which can lead to inconsistencies between areas in decision-making practice and in what supports are available for young people (Robertson, 2017). This chimes with similar concerns about community justice, discussed in Chapter 6. However, the WSA has been successful in reducing the number of young people in custody; over the last decade or so, the number of young people (under 21) in custody more than halved, from 864 in 2010–11 to about 325 in 2019–20 – paving the way for the end of children's imprisonment in YOIs in 2024 (Section 9.2.4). Offence referrals to children's hearings have also fallen dramatically, from a high of 17,361 in 2005/06 to 2,398 in 2021–22.

Many people in the Scottish justice system support the diversionary principles of the WSA and see it as chiming with the Kilbrandon philosophy (Murray et al., 2015; Robertson, 2017) and aligning with the wider emphasis on prevention (see Chapter 2).

Box 9.2 The age of criminal responsibility in Scotland

Alongside the debates about what youth justice should look like, there has also been debate about another question: who counts as a child? This is the question behind the **minimum age of criminal responsibility (MACR)** – the lowest age at which a person can be legally capable of committing a crime, and hence the lower age 'boundary' of the youth justice system (the upper boundary being legal adulthood, usually 18). Most jurisdictions around the world have a MACR; a child below that age might do things that are naughty or even harmful, but they *cannot* legally commit an offence. In Scotland, a child below the MACR cannot be referred to a children's hearing on offence grounds (but may be referred on other grounds).

Scotland's MACR was set at eight years old by the 1932 Children and Young Persons (Scotland) Act; it remained there for over 80 years, even through the flourishing of the 'Kilbrandon philosophy', and after England and Wales raised its MACR to ten years old in 1963. By the 2000s, Scotland had the lowest age of criminal responsibility in Europe, well below that of China or Russia (both 16 or 14 for serious crimes). Although prosecutions of very young children were rare, they did sometimes occur (Whyte, 2009).

Following the re-establishment of the Scottish Parliament, there came growing pressure for change, from official reviews (Scottish Law Commission, 2002), the legal profession, criminologists and international bodies. This initially foundered in the punitive 'detartanised' policy climate of the time (see Section 9.3.1, and Sutherland, 2016). The 2010 Criminal Justice and Licensing (Scotland) Act produced an awkward compromise, introducing a 'minimum age of criminal prosecution' of 12 years old. Between the ages of 8 and 12, a child could not be prosecuted but *could* be referred to a hearing on offence grounds and potentially gain a criminal record.

The MACR was finally raised to 12 years old by the Age of Criminal Responsibility (Scotland) Act 2019. This was generally welcomed as evidence that Scotland was willing to treat children who offend in accordance with their age and in some quarters as evidence of a more enlightened attitude than England and Wales (where the MACR remains at ten years old). By international standards, though, Scotland lags behind – the standard in much of Europe is 14 years old. The UN recommends a MACR of *at least* 14 years but argues that 15 or 16 may be more appropriate – a position advocated by the Scottish Children and Young People's Commissioner. The Act required a review of the MACR three years after implementation (reporting by the end of 2025), offering an opportunity for this to be reconsidered.

Questions to consider

- What do you think the minimum age of criminal responsibility should be? Why?
- What might the implications be of changing it further?
- Why do you think the Kilbrandon Report did not recommend raising the MACR? (see Sutherland, 2016).

9.3.4 'Getting it Right' to 'respecting rights'

The GIRFEC-inspired 2015 youth justice strategy, *Preventing Offending: Getting it right for children and young people,* sought to further advance the WSA through strengthening diversionary measures, responding to needs and reducing rates of school exclusion (which the Edinburgh Study identified as a key predictor of future offending).

Despite the progress made in diversion, a remaining problem was that stigmatising convictions from childhood offending (which included offence referrals to children's hearings) could follow someone into adulthood for years or even decades afterwards. This highlights the tensions often inherent in criminal justice, conflicting as it did with the apparent commitment to non-labelling welfare symbolised by the 'Kilbrandon philosophy'. This could affect young people's future life chances, for example negatively affecting future employment prospects, which evidence suggests makes it harder for young people to desist from crime (see Box 6.2). This situation was finally addressed through the Disclosure (Scotland) Act 2020, which means that all childhood convictions (barring some very limited and rare exceptions) will become 'spent' automatically, immediately – meaning they do not usually have to be declared (see Chapter 10 on disclosure).

While the GIRFEC framework and WSA remain central to youth justice, the 2021 and 2024 youth justice strategies – in line with wider efforts to promote child welfare in Scotland – shifted emphasis onto making Scotland a nation that fully respects and upholds the rights of children under the

1989 UN Convention on the Rights of the Child (UNCRC). The need for a rights-based approach to youth justice was highlighted by *The Promise*, the report of the Independent Care Review (2020), which made recommendations for the CHS and secure care, and argued that children should no longer be held in YOIs. This was subsequently made law in the Children (Care and Justice) Act 2024, which also aligns Scottish youth justice with the UNCRC's definition of a child as any human under 18 years old. This finally expanded the CHS to cover all children; previously most 16- and 17-year-olds had been excluded. Commitment to 'rights-respecting' youth justice reflects wider policy towards children in Scotland, with the UNCRC (Scotland) Incorporation Act 2024 integrating child rights as set out by the UNCRC into Scots law, placing duties on public authorities to protect these rights for children.

The emergence of children's rights onto the wider political agenda is only the latest human rights-driven reform to affect children's hearings (Norrie, 2022). Children's rights raise specific issues when the case concerns offending, since children are less likely to comprehend the legal process or the consequences of any punishment, so may need extra support to fully enjoy their rights; conversely, efforts to emphasise the voice of the child in the hearing may create further differences with a court's approach to decision-making.

The adoption of a rights-respecting approach is important, but it does not in itself address deeply rooted patterns of exclusion and deprivation that disproportionately affect children who come into conflict with the law. Lightowler (2020: 29) highlights that it requires "deep soul searching" with the practice implications of rights-based principles, avoiding the risks with mere "technical compliance and bureaucratic box-ticking".

9.3.5 *Recognising childhood adversity and trauma*

Alongside children's rights has come a growing awareness of the long-term impact of stressful or traumatic childhood experiences and concern with how services can better respond to this.

The Scottish Government's Programme for Government in 2017 committed to tacking 'adverse childhood experiences' (ACEs). Originating from American public health research, ACEs usually include: physical, emotional and sexual abuse, physical and emotional neglect, and various household adversities including mental illness in household, incarcerated relative (or 'criminality'), domestic violence, parental separation and substance use in household. ACEs are not the same as trauma, but they are overlapping concepts and are often spoken about interchangeably. ACEs are common in Scotland, with at least half of the Scottish population thought to have experienced at least one. Research has indicated potential links between experiencing multiple ACEs and poor health and social outcomes later in life, including justice involvement (whether as children or adults) (Scottish Government, 2018).

ACEs research has been highly influential – and the concept is often popular with practitioners and students – but there are important critiques of this framework and in particular of how findings have influenced and been interpreted in practice. There is a risk that identifying a child's ACEs is seen as a way to predict their future offending, although the methodologies employed in ACEs research do not support this conclusion (see Anda et al., 2020) and the Edinburgh Study has warned us of the difficulties and dangers inherent in making such predictions. Additionally, the ACEs list frames childhood adversity as a family problem, overlooking other issues such as bullying, community violence, poverty, exposure to pollution, experiences of racism or homophobia, or indeed the harms caused by criminal justice involvement (see for instance Walsh (2020) and the issue in which it appears).

Irrespective of issues with the ACEs framework, few would dispute the importance of preventing childhood trauma and limiting its negative impacts wherever possible. The Scottish Government has repeatedly committed to the development of trauma-informed services across a diverse range of settings (criminal justice, healthcare, education, social work, etc.) which recognise the impacts of trauma and seek to avoid re-traumatisation. Compared to adults, there has been a greater willingness to reckon with the harms of justice involvement for children than adults. Legislating for the introduction of trauma-informed support for children involved with justice services was an overarching aim of the Children's Care and Justice (Scotland) Act 2024, which places a duty to "have due regard to effects of trauma on [a] child"; although some justice settings present serious barriers to doing so (Vaswani et al., 2024)

There has also been an increasing focus on children who have been victims and witnesses of crime. The Scottish Government has stated the ambition of ensuring that all such children around Scotland will have access to 'Bairns' Hoose' (Scots: 'children's house') facilities. The aim is to provide child protection, health, justice and recovery services co-located in a single – more welcoming – building, avoiding the need for child victims to repeatedly tell their stories. This is directly inspired by the *Barnahus* ('children's house') model originally developed in Iceland (conveniently, given the SNP-led Scottish Government's interest in emulating Nordic nations). It is also envisioned that the Bairns' Hoose would provide support for children under the age of criminal responsibility who have committed harmful acts, although not those over this age, despite evidence that child victims and those who offend are frequently the same children (Dyer et al, 2024). The charity Children First has established one Bairns' Hoose in the west of Scotland, while the Scottish Government is supporting further work to test the concept in different contexts. Their development – including the extent to which it remains true to the original model – and impact remains to be seen.

Conclusion

Scottish youth justice is unique, not because it prioritises children's welfare but because it seeks to treat children who have offended as 'children in trouble'. The CHS deals with young people who have offended alongside others in need of care and protection, with an emphasis on promoting the child's welfare rather than punishing them or holding them to account. This 'Kilbrandon philosophy' appears strikingly radical even today and has had an impact well beyond youth justice; it is often seen as culturally emblematic of a more welfare-focused approach to criminal justice in Scotland.

Youth justice is probably the most distinctive element of Scottish criminal justice but has nonetheless been shaped by the shifting political dynamics of Scotland's relationship with England and Wales. The devolutionary settlement produced 'detartanisation' – a partial convergence with English youth justice, including more punitive and actuarial approaches. However, during the tenure of successive SNP governments, Scottish youth justice has been characterised by an emphasis on diversion, particularly the WSA which seeks to minimise the involvement of criminal justice in children's lives, and reforms to the age of criminal responsibility (see Box 9.2). More recent youth justice reforms have taken place alongside efforts to promote children's rights across Scottish society – highlighting the close connection between this area of criminal justice and Scotland's hopes for its children.

Although there have been changes to the details of how they operate, the core of Scotland's youth justice system – children's hearings – has remained essentially the same since they began in 1971. However, a series of reviews in 2020 and 2023 suggest that aspirations for an inquisitorial and not adversarial process, in which children feel able to meaningfully participate, are often not realised in practice. Additionally, the CHS sits within a wider system, many aspects of which emphasise 'justice' instead of welfare or can still feel traumatising or punitive to children. The ending of youth custody for under-18s is an important step. However, it is not clear that the Kilbrandon philosophy has ever been consistently and thoroughly implemented in practice. Similarly, more recent aspirations for a system that protects children's rights and is trauma-informed still have some way to go.

We have alluded in this chapter to reforms to the disclosure of criminal records; we will discuss these in more detail as part of a wider discussion in our next chapter of life after criminal justice involvement.

Critical questions

- Beyond youth justice, the 'Kilbrandon philosophy' has been seen by some in Scotland as a symbol of an approach to criminal justice that is more centred on social welfare than on punishment, especially compared to England and Wales. Do you think this is true?
- According to SCRA stats, most children referred to children's hearings (on any grounds) come from the most disadvantaged areas of Scotland. What do you think might explain this? What should be done about it?
- The adverts used to recruit panel members for children's hearings have provoked controversy. An example from 2018 shows a man dressed normally in a hoodie, but with an angelic halo above his head, with the legend "Be

a Force for Good. I helped protect Mummy's little punchbag from another beating. - Dan, 33, bus driver". What do you think was the intention of these posters, and why do you think they might have been controversial?

- Despite the Kilbrandon principles, children referred to the hearings system on offence grounds are treated differently from other children. Do you think this is a problem, and if so, how would you address it?
- Thinking about the political factors that have affected the development of (youth) justice systems, what expectations or hopes do you have for the future of youth justice?
- Do you think it is useful to think about the Scottish system in terms of 'de-tartanisation' or 'retartanisation'? What kinds of assumptions are implicit in such a view?
- Young Offender Institutions in Scotland are no longer used for people under 18, only for young adults. For people under 18, secure care would be used as the custodial facility. What are some potential implications of this decision for secure care institutions?
- What do you think a fully trauma- or ACE-informed response to offending would look like?

Key resources

Carr, N. and Smith, R. (2023) *Youth Justice: Local and Global*. SAGE.

An essential text for reading more deeply on youth justice policy and practice across the UK and around the world.

Children and Young People's Centre for Justice (CYCJ). https://www.cycj.org.uk/

CYCJ is a research and activist organisation working in youth justice in Scotland, funded by the Scottish Government and based at the University of Strathclyde. Their website is a vital resource for anyone studying youth justice in Scotland.

Dyer, F., Gibson, R., Morrison, P. and Murphy, C. (2024) *Youth Justice in Scotland: Still Fit for the Future?* CYCJ. https://www.cycj.org.uk/wp-content/uploads/2024/11/YJ-in-Scotland.pdf

A guide to recent changes and concerns for the youth justice system in Scotland.

McAra, L. and McVie, S. (2010) Youth crime and justice: Key messages from the Edinburgh Study of Youth Transitions and Crime. *Criminology & Criminal Justice* 10(2): 179–209.

The messages discussed in this article did much to inform youth justice and particularly the development of the Whole System Approach.

References

Anda, R.F., Porter, L.E. and Brown, D.W. (2020) Inside the adverse childhood experience score: Strengths, limitations, and misapplications. *American Journal of Preventive Medicine* 59(2): 293–295.

Armstrong, S. and McGhee, J. (2019) *Mental health and wellbeing of young people in custody: Evidence Review*. SCCJR.

Carr, N. and Smith, R. (2023) *Youth Justice: Local and Global*. Sage.

Children and Young People's Centre for Justice (CYCJ) (2021) *A Guide to Youth Justice in Scotland: Policy, Practice and Legislation*. CYCJ.

Coles, E., Cheyne, H., Rankin, J. and Daniel, B. (2016) Getting it right for every child: A national policy framework to promote childrens' well-being in Scotland, United Kingdom. *Millbank Quarterly* 94(2): 334–365.

Croall, H. (2006) Criminal justice in post-devolutionary Scotland. *Critical Social Policy* 26(3): 587–607.

Donnelly, M. (2019) A tripartite analysis of the grounds of referral to children's hearings. *Juridical Review* 2019(2): 117–135.

Dyer, F., Gibson, R., Morrison, P. and Murphy, C. (2024) *Youth Justice in Scotland: Still Fit for the Future?* CYCJ. https://www.cycj.org.uk/wp-content/uploads/2024/11/YJ-in-Scotland.pdf

Gibson, R. (2022) *What Do We Know about Children From England and Wales in Secure Care in Scotland?* Nuffield Family Justice Observatory. https://www.nuffieldfjo.org.uk/resource/what-do-we-know-about-children-from-england-and-wales-in-secure-care-in-scotland

Gillon, F. (2021) *Grappling with the Complexity of Early and Effective Intervention (EEI): Benevolent Intentions, Negative Consequences in Youth Justice Implications for Scotland*. SCCJR.

Goldson, B. (2005) Child imprisonment: A case for abolition. *Youth Justice* 5(2): 77–90.

Gough, A. (2016) *Secure Care in Scotland: Looking Ahead. Key Messages and Call for Action*. CYCJ. https://www.cycj.org.uk/wp-content/uploads/2016/11/Secure-Care-in-Scotland-Looking-Ahead.pdf

Hearings System Working Group (2023) *Hearings for Children: Hearings System Working Group's Redesign Report, May 2023*. The Promise Scotland.

Henderson, G., Rogon, P., Kurlus, I., Henderson, S. and Woods, R. (2021) *Home Compulsory Supervision Orders – Effectiveness of Decision Making and Outcomes, Report 7: Education and Offending Outcomes*. SCRA and Scottish Government. https://rgu-repository.worktribe.com/preview/1602859/HENDERSON%20 2021%20Educational%20attendance%20and%20offending.pdf

HMIPS. (2018) *Report on Full Inspection of HMYOI Polmont – 29 October to 2 November 2018*. HMIPS. Available at https://www.prisonsinspectoratescotland.gov.uk/publications/report-full-inspection-hmp-yoi-polmont-29-october-2-november-2018

Hughes, G. and Follett, M. (2006) Community safety, youth and the 'Anti-Social'. In Goldson, B. and Muncie, J. (eds.) *Youth Crime and Justice*. Sage. 157–171.

Independent Care Review (2020) *The promise*. Independent Care Review/The Promise Scotland.

Johnson, S.B., Blum, R.W. and Giedd, J.N. (2009) Adolescent maturity and the brain: The promise and pitfalls of neuroscience research in adolescent health policy. *Journal of Adolescent Health* 45(3): 216–221. https://www.ncbi.nlm.nih.gov/pmc/articles/PMC2892678/

Lightowler, C. (2020) *Rights Respecting? Scotland's Approach to Children in Conflict with the Law*. CYCJ. https://strathprints.strath.ac.uk/71808/7/Lightowler_cycj2020_Rights_Respecting_Scotlands_approach_to_children_in_conflict_with_the_law.pdf

Matthews, B. and Minton, J. (2018) Rethinking one of criminology's 'brute facts': The age–crime curve and the crime drop in Scotland. *European Journal of Criminology* 15(3): 296–320.

McAra, L. (2006) Welfare in crisis? Key developments in Scottish youth justice. In Muncie, J. and Goldson, B. (eds) *Comparative Youth Justice: Critical Issues*. Sage. 127–145.

McAra, L. and McVie, S. (2010) Youth crime and justice: Key messages from the Edinburgh Study of Youth Transitions and Crime. *Criminology & Criminal Justice* 10(2): 179–209.

Miller, J., Abercrombie, B. and McLellan, G. (2019) *Evaluation of South Lanarkshire Structured Deferred Sentencing for Young People*. University of the West of Scotland.

Muncie, J. and Hughes, G. (2002) Modes of youth governance: Political rationalities, criminalisation and resistance. In Muncie, J., Hughes, G. and McLaughlin, E. (eds) *Youth Justice Critical Readings*. Sage. 1–18.

Murray, K., McGuinness, P., Burman, M. and McVie, S. (2015) *Evaluation of the Whole System Approach to Young People Who Offend in Scotland*. SCCJR. https://www.sccjr.ac.uk/wp-content/uploads/2015/06/Evaluation-of-the-Whole-System-Approach-to-Young-People-Who-Offend-in-Scotland.pdf.

Nolan, D. (2024) *Children (Care and Justice) (Scotland) Act 2024: Info Sheet*. CYCJ. https://cycj.org.uk/wp-content/uploads/2024/06/Children-Care-and-Justice-Scotland-Act-2024-Info-Sheet.pdf.

Norrie, K.M. (2022) *Children's Hearings in Scotland*. Fourth edition. W. Green.

Piacentini, L. and Walters, R. (2006) The politicization of youth crime in Scotland and the rise of the 'Burberry Court'. *Youth Justice* 6(1): 43–59.

Porter, R.B., Gillon, F., Mitchell, F., Vaswani, N. and Young, E. (2021) Children's rights in children's hearings: The impact of Covid-19. *International Journal of Children's Rights* 29(2): 426–446.

Porter, R., Welch, V. and Mitchell, F. (2016) *The Role of the Solicitor in the Children's Hearings System: A Study Commissioned by the Scottish Legal Aid Board*. Centre for Excellence for Looked After Children in Scotland. https://strathprints.strath.ac.uk/58729/7/Porter_etal_CELCIS_2016_The_role_of_the_solicitor_in_the_childrens_hearings_system.pdf

Robertson, L. (2017) *A Practice-Based Approach to Youth Justice: The Whole System Approach in Scotland*. Unpublished PhD thesis, University of Glasgow.

Scottish Government (2018) *Understanding Childhood Adversity, Resilience and Crime*. https://www.gov.scot/publications/understanding-childhood-adversity-resilience-crime/.

Scottish Law Commission (2002) *Report on Age of Criminal Responsibility* (Scot Law Com No 185). Scottish Law Commission. https://www.scotlawcom.gov.uk/files/5312/7989/6663/rep185.pdf.

Sutherland, E. (2016) Raising the minimum age of criminal responsibility in Scotland: Law reform at last? *Northan Ireland Legal Quarterly* 67(3): 387–406.

Vaswani, N., Moodie, K. and McEwan, D. (2024) Children's experiences of police custody and the implications for trauma-informed policing. *Youth Justice*, 25(1): 108–125.

Walsh, G.M. (2020) The arrival of the ACEs movement in Scotland: Policy entrepreneurship and critical activist responses. *Scottish Affairs* 29(4): 456–474. (See also this entire special issue on ACEs policy in Scotland)

Whyte, B. (2009) Counterblast: Youth 'in Justice' in the UK – Which way for Scotland? *Howard Journal of Criminal Justice* 48(2): 200–204.

Young, R. (2012) Can Neds (or Chavs) be non-delinquent, educated or even middle class? Contrasting empirical findings with cultural stereotypes. *Sociology* 46(6): 1140–1160.

10 Life after punishment in Scotland

Key ideas

- Most convictions result in a criminal record; in Scotland as elsewhere, it is a form of official 'label' with potentially very stigmatising consequences.
- There are rules about disclosure which govern when criminal records have to be revealed; reforms to these rules aim to reduce the number of people who are stigmatised by their past because they are obliged to inform people and organisations about their convictions.
- People on custodial sentences are often released conditionally before the end of their sentence, on some form of 'licence' including parole.
- Decisions about release are generally made by the Parole Board for Scotland; 'throughcare' is then the responsibility of local Justice Social Work teams. Throughcare is intended to support reintegration but necessarily also involves monitoring and control.
- In criminal records and the licence system, as in other areas of criminal justice, there is a tension between efforts to promote reintegration and address stigma, and the management and control of people perceived as 'risky'.
- Structural inequalities that disproportionately affect people in the criminal justice system may intersect in complex ways with criminal records and licence conditions to make desistance extremely challenging.

Introduction

This chapter deals with the ways in which criminal justice can continue to affect a person's life after a period of imprisonment or the completion of a sentence. While imprisonment can have especially long-lasting and serious effects on a person's bonds to family, community and social institutions (see Chapter 8), *any* criminal justice involvement can have long-lasting impacts. The end of the sentence is not always the end of formal criminal justice involvement in a person's life.

Affecting all areas of criminal justice, post-release supervision has been particularly shaped by rising concerns about the 'risk' posed by specific

DOI: 10.4324/9781003372882-10

people and groups and the appealing promise that this risk can be managed effectively in the community. This concept has provided a principal penal rationale for the Scottish criminal justice system, although it is contested (and may sit uneasily or even directly conflict with other rationales such as diversion and reintegration). The apparatus for managing risk has grown in scope and complexity over the past 20 years or so; numerous new laws, institutions and regulations have resulted in a far more pervasive and deeper system of control on certain populations, in the name of managing their perceived risk.

This chapter addresses several different aspects of life after punishment – the system of criminal records, the regime of supervised release from prison 'on licence', and the development of multiagency partnership approaches to managing people thought to be 'risky'. Although this chapter is called 'life after punishment', some of the measures discussed here take place as part of a criminal sentence, while others extend the impact of punishment beyond the end of the sentence. Finally, we reflect on the difficulties of life after punishment: the stigma of a criminalised identity, the practical challenges of accessing employment and services, and sometimes pervasive surveillance by criminal justice.

Key agencies

All of the main justice agencies (police, courts, Justice Social Work (JSW) and prisons) may be involved with a person's life after punishment or on licence, as we will see. However, there are three agencies with specific roles around criminal records, conditional release and supervision after release:

Disclosure Scotland is a government body which processes criminal records data and carries out disclosure checks. It runs the Protecting Vulnerable Groups scheme (Section 10.1.2) and keeps a list of people barred from working with children or protected adults.

The key body involved in decision-making around release from prison is the **Parole Board for Scotland**, established in 1968. The Board, acting on advice from JSW, makes decisions about the release of prisoners on parole licences, life licences, Orders for Lifelong Restriction (OLRs), and extended sentence prisoners where the custodial part of the sentence is over four years. Even where the Board does not make the decision about *whether* a person is released (e.g. non-parole licences), it sets *conditions* on most types of licence – the rules with which the person must comply while released. Finally, where a person on licence is thought to pose a risk, usually because they have breached the licence, the Board considers whether they should be recalled to prison. Victims have been allowed to attend Board hearings since 2021 and may have the right to be notified when the prisoner becomes eligible for parole. Where new information comes to light or where circumstances change, cases can be referred back for further consideration. This includes cases where a person has already been released and may be undergoing their licenced supervision in the community.

The Risk Management Authority (RMA) is a Scottish Government body established by the 2003 Criminal Justice (Scotland) Act. Its key role is in assessing risk for the courts when deciding whether to impose an OLR (Section 10.2.2), and developing Risk Management Plans for people so sentenced. The RMA has a wider advisory role on risk assessment across Scottish criminal justice and validates specific risk assessment protocols – including the LS/CMI system widely used across JSW, as well as specific tools for particular offences or groups of people.

10.1 Criminal records: safeguarding and stigmatising?

To live in a contemporary nation state is to exist as a series of records: passport, driving licence, taxpayer records, employment history, qualifications, etc. This official, administrative version can have significant impacts on life – especially the consequences of one's criminal record. Research from the USA (Miller, 2021) highlights the 'collateral consequences' of criminal records – the ways in which this can affect somebody long after their punishment is (ostensibly) ended. Criminal records are especially powerful labels because they often have to be disclosed when applying for jobs (is it then usually up to the employer to decide whether to hire them) and some other things like adopting a child, applying for insurance or travelling internationally.

10.1.1 Criminal records and data

When a person is convicted or accepts an alternative to prosecution (Chapter 4), they gain a criminal record. The police enter this information into a system of records which includes convictions alongside other information about offending. Scotland has had its own records system since 1979, now known as the **Criminal History System (CHS)**[1] and run by Police Scotland. As well as storing information which can be provided to other agencies, CHS data are used to produce crime and justice statistics.

Police Scotland also uses the **Police National Computer (PNC)** – the main criminal records database serving *the entire UK*. A PNC record contains details of all convictions, reprimands, warnings and arrests (although these are not included in most checks), with links to biometric, DNA and image databases. The PNC is regularly accessed by policing and other organisations, including Disclosure Scotland, though it is now extremely outdated and soon to be replaced.

Another UK-wide database, the **Police National Database (PND)**, records 'soft' information about *suspected* offending and other police intelligence, with no requirement for the person to have been convicted. The PND was set up after the 2004 Bichard Inquiry into the high-profile murder of two children by a man who got a job as a school caretaker despite repeated contact with social services and police for sexual offences against children. These databases hold data on millions of people – many of them never convicted of anything. A person can apply to have their record removed where, for instance, they have been arrested but not convicted (in Scotland, this is handled by the Crown Office).

Despite the promises of seamless computerisation, this technology relies on human labour, and different systems struggle to 'speak' to each other. For example, after a high-profile murder by a prisoner who had breached a Home Detention Curfew (see Chapter 7), an HMICS (2018) report found that relevant information was not shared between agencies. Furthermore, we should not trust blindly in the reliability of 'official' databases or that they will always be used appropriately, given that many convictions under the Computer Misuse Act are of police employees (Hutchings and Collier, 2019).

10.1.2 Disclosure

The effect of criminal records is not limited to a small minority of people – an estimated one in three working-age men, and one in ten women in Scotland have one (McGuinness et al., 2013). This 'label' is enforced by the regime of disclosure – which governs when people must disclose their criminal record. The disclosure regime is shaped by a tension between the need to promote reintegration and reduce stigma for people who have served their sentence, as well as concern about the 'risk' relating to some groups and categories of offence. In Scotland, this has led to the creation of different 'levels' of disclosure.

10.1.2.1 The Rehabilitation of Offenders Act and basic/Level 1 disclosure

The fundamentals of disclosure were established by the 1974 Rehabilitation of Offenders Act (ROA). 'Rehabilitation' here refers not to the penal rationale but a legal concept – the point in time at which a person's previous offending no longer needs to be disclosed when asked, at which point they are said to be 'rehabilitated'. The ROA allows for most convictions (including upheld offence referrals to children's hearings) to become 'spent' after a certain period of time, meaning they do not usually have to be disclosed. Disclosing someone's spent conviction without authorisation is itself an offence.

The length of time it takes for a conviction to become spent (the 'rehabilitation period') depends on *the sentence* (not offence). This reflects the seriousness of the offence, but also the sentencers' decision-making and the discretion they enjoy. For prison sentences, the rehabilitation period does not start until the end of the term (including time served on licence); for others, it starts at conviction. Rehabilitation periods are shorter when the person is under 18 at conviction.

If somebody is convicted of another offence during the rehabilitation period for a previous conviction, the rehabilitation period of the *first* conviction will be extended to the end of the rehabilitation period for the second one.

Table 10.1 Rehabilitation periods in Scotland

Disposal type	*Disposal*	*Rehabilitation period (adult)*	*Rehabilitation period (youth, i.e. under 18 at conviction) (pre-2020 Act)*	*Rehabilitation period (youth) (post-2020 Act)*
Other	*(Rehabilitation periods start at conviction)*			
	Compulsory Supervision Order (children's hearing)	n/a	None	None
	Absolute discharge or admonishment	None	None	
	Police warnings/ FPNs			
	Other alternatives to prosecution	3 months	3 months	
Financial	Fine/compensation order	1 year	6 months	
Community	Community sentence (CPO/ DTTO/RLO)	12 months or length of order (whichever is longer)	6 months or length of order (whichever is longer)	
Custodial	*(Rehabilitation periods start at end of sentence)*			
	Up to 12 months	2 years	1 year	
	12–30 months	4 years	2 years	None, except some sexual offences (2/3 years)
	30–48 months	6 years	3 years	
	Over 48 months	Never (but with possibility for review, yet to be implemented)		
	OLR			
	Life			

This arguably creates an obstacle to reintegration – a person might successfully avoid offending for months or years, but a conviction during the rehabilitation period can cause a 'piling up' of convictions for prior offences. This again demonstrates how the impact of the sentence can extend far beyond the term of the sentence itself.

The ROA applies to the entire UK, but since devolution has been reformed slightly differently on either side of the border (Christensen et al., 2021). The 2019 Management of Offenders (Scotland) Act and the 2020 Disclosure (Scotland) Act have reduced many rehabilitation periods, with the latter eliminating most rehabilitation periods for childhood offences. Rehabilitation periods for sentences discussed in this book are given in Table 10.1.

Disclosure under ROA, often referred to as 'basic' disclosure, is the usual process for ordinary things like job applications. Under the 2020 Act, this has been renamed Level 1 disclosure. There are higher levels of disclosure for a range of situations, which have expanded in the decades since 1974 amid rising concern over specific offences and criminal 'risks'.

10.1.2.2 Higher-level disclosures: Level 2 disclosure and PVG

The key feature of higher-level disclosures is that they include convictions that are spent under the ROA. Higher-level disclosures apply only in some situations, such as for people applying to work as an accountant or a lawyer, run a gambling business or adopt a child; unlike the ROA's rehabilitation periods, they are based on the offence type, *not* the sentence (Weaver, 2018). There were previously two levels above 'basic' disclosure ('standard' and 'enhanced'), but the 2020 Act simplified these into a single 'Level 2'. It also placed strict limits on when a person's childhood offending can be disclosed, allowing some offences to become 'non-disclosable' even in Level 2/enhanced disclosure.

A person can still apply to a Sheriff to have spent convictions 'disregarded' – removed so that they never have to be disclosed, even under higher-level disclosures. Under 2018 legislation, a small number of Scottish men convicted of offences connected with same-sex sexual activity while this was criminalised, were pardoned – but they still have to apply to have the conviction disregarded, otherwise it may show up on disclosure checks as a (very stigmatising) sexual offence.

The 2020 Act maintains the **Protecting Vulnerable Groups (PVG)** scheme, which provides ongoing information about people working with children or vulnerable adults. Alongside this, Disclosure Scotland maintains a list of people who are 'barred' from this sort of work.

Measures like PVG (and its English/Welsh counterpart the Disclosure and Barring Service) were vigorously criticised when introduced, on privacy grounds – particularly given the inclusion of 'soft' information, the outward creep of disclosure into situations where this might not be required, the stigmatisation of legally innocent people as (potential) sex offenders and, arguably, contributing to a growing atmosphere of mistrust (Baldwin, 2017).

10.1.3 Community notification

Alongside the system of disclosure for all criminal records, developments in the last few decades provide for information on specific types of offending to be disclosed to people in the community. The 1997 Sex Offenders Act introduced notification requirements for sexual offences, subsequently outlined in the 2003 Sexual Offences Act. Formally called **Sex Offender Notification Requirements**, these are known in everyday life as the 'sex offenders' register'. This implies a centralised list, which is slightly misleading; rather, the requirements are for people convicted of these offences to notify police of where they live, any change of address or name, and international travel plans. People subject to these requirements also constitute the bulk of those supervised (and surveilled) under Multi-Agency Public Protection Arrangements (MAPPA) (see Section 6.1.5).

Unlike in the USA (and despite campaigning by British tabloids during the 2000s), the UK has no general public right of access to information about people with sexual offence convictions living in one's local area. However, '**community disclosure**' allows parents or guardians in Scotland to request and receive information about a person who has or will have contact with their child, similar to a scheme in England widely known as 'Sarah's Law'. Similar to the disclosure regime, notification requirements become 'spent' after a certain period, though these tend to be longer than for ordinary criminal records disclosure. Failure to comply with notification requirements is itself an offence which can attract up to five years in prison.

Another scheme, the **Disclosure Scheme for Domestic Abuse Scotland**, can be used to disclose a person's history of domestic abuse. Concerned relatives and friends can ask about a person's partner, and Police Scotland have the power to tell people if they are at risk, similar to 'Clare's Law' in England. However, it has been argued that the Scottish scheme is ambiguous about what constitutes 'domestic abuse' and what the police consider an appropriate basis for action – a significant problem given the privacy implications of schemes like these (McMillan and Tickell, 2024).

Beyond the stigma of criminal records, many of those processed by the criminal justice system will be subject to ongoing conditions in the community which can affect their ability to work, where they live, and who they see.

10.2 The licence regime in Scotland

It is rare for prisoners to spend their entire sentence in prison; most qualify for some form of release to supervision in the community. This is a conditional freedom, however – prisoners released 'on licence' are supervised by JSW and must abide by certain conditions, such as informing JSW about their movements, staying in particular accommodation, completing certain programmes and (usually) refraining from further offending. They are liable to be recalled to prison for *any* breach of their conditions (not just offending) and sometimes for other reasons as well.

Media tends to frame supervised release very negatively, but there are important arguments in its favour. It is well-established that imprisonment severely damages people's connections to their communities and families, and their ability to do essential, everyday tasks. Supervised release is intended to mitigate these and enable a managed, supported transition back to ordinary life ('reintegration'). It also creates incentives for compliance: for people in prison (the potential reward of early release) and those supervised in the community (the threat of recall). A managed system of early release is attractive to justice agencies and policymakers, since this 'back door' sentencing (Weaver et al., 2012) offers a comparatively low-profile way of managing high prison populations, without the more difficult task of reducing the numbers of people entering prison or the lengths of their sentences.

As with many other areas of criminal justice, the Scottish system has developed organically into a complex patchwork of eligibility and requirements across various stages (for further details, see Grant et al., 2020). The key agencies involved are JSW (Chapter 6), in their role as providers of 'throughcare' for people released from prison; the courts (Chapter 4) who can impose various licences at sentence; and the Parole Board for Scotland, who make decisions about release and recall and about conditions on some types of licence. The various forms of supervised release are summarised in Table 10.2.

10.2.1 Determinate sentences

Determinate sentences are those of a set length. In addition to the sentences and licences discussed below, some prisoners may be released earlier by the Scottish Prison Service on Home Detention Curfew (HDC) to be monitored electronically (see Section 7.2.2).

10.2.1.1 Short sentences

The Prisoners (Early Release) (Scotland) Act 2025 changed the automatic release point for those serving these sentences from 50% of their sentence to 40% (with exceptions for domestic abuse and sexual offences).

With some exceptions (see Table 10.2), there is no compulsory engagement with JSW on release, but these prisoners can apply for voluntary throughcare support. Perhaps understandably, uptake of voluntary throughcare is low – only about a quarter to a fifth of cases. This could be due to the association of JSW in particular with surveillance and sanction as well as support (and reported breach of licence conditions could result in being returned to prison). Furthermore, if every prisoner entitled to voluntary throughcare requested it, it would place enormous additional burdens on already stretched services. In an attempt to remedy this problem, a new National Voluntary Throughcare Service was launched in April 2025 as a partnership of eight third-sector organisations. Funded by the Scottish Government, the new service aims to provide coordinated support across prison and the community and across justice and other agencies. It replaces and expands on previous third-sector reintegration partnerships, one of which was specifically for women – raising questions about efforts to embed 'gender-responsive' justice (Cleary, forthcoming).

10.2.1.2 Long sentences: parole and non-parole licences

The term 'parole' has a specific legal meaning, though it is often used informally to mean any supervised release from prison. Prisoners on long sentences (a determinate sentence of four years or more) are eligible to apply for

Table 10.2 Supervised release in Scotland

Custodial sentence type	*Offence type*	*Order*	*Throughcare*
Short (<4 years)	Most (not including sexual or domestic violence convictions)	Automatic release on licence 40% through sentence	Voluntary (can be requested by the individual) – often provided by third sector
Any	Significant sexual aspect (not necessarily a sexual offence)	Extended sentence (at court's discretion on advice from JSW)	Statutory (the individual *must* engage with JSW as a form of both support and supervision)
>6 months	Sexual offences	Statutory throughcare as Short-Term Sex Offender (STSO) *Unlike other supervised release, conditions are set by Parole Unit, SPS.*	
Short (<4 years) determinate sentence	People judged 'high risk', *excluding* sex offences	Supervised Release Order (at court's discretion on advice from JSW)	
Long (4 years +) determinate sentence	Any	Parole (at discretion of Parole Board)	
	Any (sentenced before 1 Feb 2016), if parole not granted	Automatic non-parole licence two-thirds through sentence	
	Any (sentenced after 1 Feb 2016), if parole not granted	Automatic non-parole licence 6 months before end of sentence	
	Some violent and terrorism offences	Extended sentence (at court's discretion on advice from JSW)	
Order for Lifelong Restriction (OLR)	Offences and/or pattern of behaviour which suggest the person poses a risk of serious harm	OLR (at court's discretion after RMA risk assessment)	
Life	Murder (mandatory) Other serious offences (at judge's discretion)	Life Licence	

release on **parole licence** from the halfway point onwards. Applications are heard by the Parole Board for Scotland, who take advice from JSW to make their decision. If unsuccessful, the prisoner must wait another year before applying again.

Long-term prisoners sentenced before 2016 who are not granted parole, are released automatically on a **non-parole licence** two-thirds of the way through the sentence. Legislation then changed the release date for those sentenced after February 2016 to occur only six months before the end of the sentence. Regardless of the type of licence, throughcare after release is mandatory for all long-sentenced prisoners until the end of their sentence.

10.2.1.3 Extended sentences and Supervised Release Orders

As the risk management agenda began to take hold in the 1990s, the courts were given new powers to impose two types of supervision at sentencing for cases where the person is considered high risk. These allow the court to attach extra compulsory supervision to the end of a period of imprisonment, where it might not otherwise be required. The **extended sentence** extends the period before a person can apply for parole and may last as long as ten years beyond the end of the original custody period. The **Supervised Release Order (SRO)** adds supervision lasting a maximum of 12 months from the release date. In 2021–22, 403 of these orders were made.

10.2.2 Lifelong supervision: life licences and the Order for Lifelong Restriction

Since the abolition of the death penalty in the 1960s, a life sentence is mandatory for murder, in Scotland as elsewhere in the UK. They can also be imposed in other cases; in Scotland, these 'discretionary' life sentences almost always take the form of the **Order for Lifelong Restriction (OLR)**.

In both life sentences and OLRs, the judge sets a minimum period (known as the '**punishment part**') that must be served in prison before release can be considered. If released, the person spends their remaining life on licence and is always liable to be recalled to prison for any suspected breach of licence conditions. So even though they may not spend their entire life in prison, they *are* punished for their entire lives.

The OLR was established to manage people thought to pose a continuing high risk of further harm, evolving from concerns about the supervision of people who were considered high risk, but whose conviction(s) would not themselves result in the extensive supervision felt to be required (Ferguson, 2021). The OLR is in effect a form of supervision – arguably punishment – based on views about what someone might do in the future, rather than what they have done in the past. Everyone on an OLR is subject to a Risk Management Plan developed by the RMA, for the rest of their lives.

There are similarities between the OLR and the Imprisonment for Public Protection (IPP) sentence in England and Wales, which remains controversial long after its abolition in 2012. The OLR has been used less frequently and requires specialist evaluation by RMA forensic psychologists, rather than relying on the court's judgement. However, contrary to traditional criminal legal norms, that assessment can consider *any* allegation of 'criminal behaviour' whether or not this ever came to the attention of criminal justice (van Zyl Smit and Morrison, 2020). The OLR has avoided the level of controversy found with IPPs – notably, cases of people imprisoned indefinitely on very short minimum tariffs have been a less prominent issue than with IPPs. However, whereas England and Wales did (belatedly) set a minimum tariff for IPPs, OLRs have no minimum punishment part. Several people a year receive OLRs with a 'short' (under four years) punishment part (Scottish Government, 2024b); indeed, there are examples of people on OLRs with 18-month tariffs or for offences which might usually attract a community sentence (such as fire-raising). The relative lack of controversy around OLRs is probably not because they are 'better' than IPPs, but because of the veneer of legitimacy conferred by risk assessments and a general lack of scrutiny (but see Nicola Ceesay's forthcoming PhD research). In 2024, the organisation NO-LR (https://nolr.org/) was established to campaign for the abolition of this sentence.

After the 'punishment part', the prisoner is eligible for release on licence at the discretion of the Parole Board for Scotland. This does not mean they *will* be released; in 2021–22, only about a sixth (63 of 388) of life prisoner cases resulted in release, and the proportion has often been closer to a tenth (Parole Board for Scotland, 2024). For OLRs, release is extremely rare: as of 2023, 257 OLRs had been issued but only 17 OLR prisoners had been released into the community – of whom five had since died and six had been recalled. Therefore, OLR-sentenced people may serve the rest of their natural lives in prison, even if their index offence was one which would usually attract a much shorter sentence.

For life-sentenced prisoners on licence, there is significant stigma attached to the sentence. Licence conditions are likely to be especially onerous, with the constant threat of recall even for minor technical (i.e. non-offence) breaches. RMA (2023) research suggests that for the few people on OLRs who do achieve release, integration into the community is extremely difficult – characterised by extreme social isolation arising from the stigma of the sentence and the requirement for new relationships and activities to be reported.

Despite a long decline in violent crime and a stated commitment to welfare and rehabilitation, Scotland has an exceptionally high rate of life-sentenced prisoners, with OLRs accounting for an increasing proportion of these (van Zyl Smit and Morrison, 2020). The OLR sentence highlights the pervasive, and deep, encroachment of risk management into Scottish punishment, which keeps people imprisoned not for what they have done but for what they might do in the future.

10.2.3 Decision-making, throughcare and recall

Most prisoners who come before the Parole Board are unsuccessful in their applications for release. In Scotland in 2023–24, release on licence (including parole, SRO and HDC) accounted for about a thousand departures (10% of the total) from prison. The Board's decision is intended not to be about *punishment* – that is decided by the court – but about the *risk* they believe the person may pose. But for the person, the result of a negative decision is the same: time in prison, with all its associated harms (Chapter 8). This may be due to factors entirely outwith the person's control, e.g. the very long waiting lists for offending behaviour programmes (Section 8.3.2), the result of which means the Board is very unlikely to recommend release.

As well as supervising people on community sentences (Chapter 6), JSW supervises people released on licence ('**statutory throughcare**') and works with prisoners to plan for release, in collaboration with the Scottish Prison Service (SPS). Around 1,000 cases of supervision on licence are commenced annually within custody and another thousand within the community. At the end of March 2023, there were around 5,400 people on statutory throughcare, the lowest in a decade; two-thirds were supervised within prison in preparation for release. Throughcare is intended to help prisoners reintegrate into the community on release, but also to manage and reduce the possible risks of further offending. However, people on statutory throughcare of any sort still experience the 'pains of supervision' outlined in Chapter 6.

If someone is judged to have broken their licence conditions they can be **recalled** to prison. SPS data suggest that recalled prisoners account for about 4% of the average prison population (around 500 people), with current pressures in prisons (Chapter 8) renewing concerns about how to reduce these numbers (Care Inspectorate, 2021). The factors driving rates of recall are complex, however, and relate both to actual numbers of breaches and to criminal justice decision-making.

The power to recall rests at various points, depending on the situation. A person released on licence may be recalled by the court if convicted of an imprisonable offence during the 'unexpired period' of their sentence, while for prisoners on HDCs, the decision lies with SPS. For most forms of licence, the decision to direct recall or not rests with the Parole Board. In practice, this would usually follow a breach referral from the supervising social worker. JSW *must* refer a case to the Parole Board if the person has been charged with a further offence while on licence. However, recall can occur for *any* breach of conditions, such as failing to attend appointments, moving out of appointed accommodation or failing to inform JSW of a change of employment. JSW has wide discretion for dealing with non-offence breaches, but an increasingly risk-focused approach has likely increased their willingness to refer them (Weaver et al., 2021), indeed, many of those recalled to prison have not committed any further offence.

Box 10.1 A Blether with … James Smith, solicitor specialising in parole

What are your views on licence conditions that are placed on people after they're released? Do you think that they're realistic? Are they fair?

There's been a journey that the Parole Board has gone on in terms of licence conditions. I think that during my time, they've become clearer [but also] they have possibly become more restrictive. There used to be a condition that you must for example tell your supervising officer about new and emerging relationships. Domestic [violence] backgrounds, for example. And because they are wanting to protect any new partner, you then found yourself [for] many years arguing about what 'a relationship' was, the dictionary definition. But now the condition [is] written in such a way that … there's no doubt about it. Actually, the people we want to know about are everybody. So, [we] want to know who your friends are. Want to know who your family [are]. Our relationships are no longer necessarily just intimate relationships, they're now about all of your relationships. So, there's an example of how we've come from a condition which was really just to protect [a new] partner or intimate relationship to now actually getting a whole host of things.

But is that overly restrictive? Possibly.

Does it hopefully foster a bit of openness and honesty between the individual on licence and supervising officer? Hopefully.

Does it allow the supervising officer to have a better knowledge of who they're spending the time with and what they're doing in order to ensure that risk can be managed? Probably does. Is that proportionate [and] necessary? It's helpful.

Proportionate in some cases might not be necessary, but it would seem reasonable enough.

And are there any problems with these conditions in practice then?

My concern about licence conditions is the policing of them. There needs to be a uniformity of how it is done. And this isn't a criticism of social work, but some maybe stick to the conditions to the absolute letter. I think [social work] sometimes need to be reminded that in fact there is a discretion in the licence conditions that they can do certain things. So, for example, if there is a curfew in place, the social worker doesn't need to be rigid [about that]. They can say well; actually, I can say the curfew is something different because the licenced condition actually allows me to do it – I don't need to go back to ask the Parole Board.

10.3 Criminalisation, reintegration and stigma

We have outlined the development of the criminal records and disclosure regime which affects almost everyone who is dealt with by criminal justice, and the complex system of supervision after release from prison. Here we discuss the effects these may have on efforts to achieve a successful 'life after punishment'.

10.3.1 Stigma and identity

Symbolic interactionist sociologists, especially Goffman (1963), advanced the notion of '**stigma**' to refer to any attribute of a person that is seen as discrediting or devaluing. The concept of stigma has entered everyday usage, and the label of 'offender' or 'criminal' has retained its power to stigmatise. The shame attached to these labels can affect how people see themselves and their possibility for change, as well as how this is seen by others. Many of the things that people need to put previous offending and criminalisation behind them are made substantially harder by a criminal record (Anderson, 2020).

Aside from the potential impact of the offence itself, it is not unusual for relationships with partners, family and friends to break down during imprisonment, leaving the prison leaver lonelier and more vulnerable than when they entered. While families can be an important source of support, this may be a lot to ask, particularly since prisoners' families are generally affected by the same overlapping disadvantage as prisoners themselves (Jardine, 2018). Even if relationships are maintained successfully, imprisonment may still have complex emotional impacts on all concerned, as well as practical impacts on families, e.g. of long-term unemployment. These issues may be exacerbated in various ways by licence conditions or other features of the crime, the community or the people involved.

Desistance from crime is typically seen as the successful outcome for involvement in criminal justice and as indicative of a successful life after punishment, but this may be a painful and frustrating process in which the stigma of offending interacts with wider social inequalities and discrimination (Box 6.2; Nugent and Schinkel, 2016).

10.3.2 Employment and access to services

There is significant empirical support for the role of employment in promoting desistance from crime; as well as a legitimate income, it can supply a structured routine, new social relationships and sometimes a source of meaning and purpose. However, a criminal record can make seeking employment very difficult – especially if the person has been imprisoned. Prison sentences attract longer rehabilitation periods, and even where the rehabilitation period has expired, periods of imprisonment continue to stigmatise as suspicious 'gaps' in a person's employment history.

Aside from the requirement to disclose unspent convictions, the complex legal framework may mean people disclose offences they don't have to or that employers may (accidentally or otherwise) break the law by requesting disclosure beyond what is required. Convictions may also become known by other ways, not least the internet. The fear of being 'found out' and stigmatised further ('anticipated stigma'), can itself be a factor in the further marginalisation of people with convictions and hence a potential obstacle to their desistance; even where they can get jobs, people with convictions are more likely to be in low-paid or insecure work with little prospect of advancement (Weaver and Jardine, 2022).

By shortening or eliminating rehabilitation periods, recent reforms (Section 10.1.2) have sought to reduce the range of situations in which records must be disclosed, and improve employers' attitudes towards criminalised people. This has been driven partly by the success of the international 'Ban the Box' movement (the name refers to a tick-box question about convictions common on application forms); and some employers (e.g. Timpson and Virgin Trains) make a point of recruiting people with convictions. A person's life is also affected by the *quality* of their employment.

Older UK statistics (MoJ/DWP, 2011) suggest at least half of released prisoners must claim benefits to survive, at least until they find a job but often while employed. Some people under criminal justice supervision will face benefit deductions (Chapter 5), and people become ineligible for many benefits while in prison. Universal Credit (now the main UK unemployment/low-income benefit) is paid in arrears, meaning no money is received until five weeks after the first claim. People cannot apply from prison – extensive preparation ahead of release can mitigate this but only to some extent.

Homelessness affects people released from prison and secure care particularly badly. People often leave prison without stable accommodation, reliant on 'sofa surfing' with friends and family, in short-term hostel accommodation and/or living on the street. Social housing providers may be reluctant to house someone with convictions, and even if the person is rehoused, their reputation (i.e. stigma) may affect their dealings with neighbours. Ex-prisoners are overrepresented among the homeless population; in 2023–24, 4% of people registered as homeless are listed as coming from prison, but this refers only to those coming *direct* from prison (as opposed to those staying first with family or friends) *and* registering as homeless – so represents a very partial picture (Scottish Government, 2024a). Justice agencies, particularly SPS, have attempted to address post-prison homelessness through coordinating support in local partnerships. However, such arrangements cannot by themselves address the wider problems with housing provision.

When a person is released from prison, they must navigate several systems at once, which even on their own would be challenging for anybody to engage with, let alone someone just released from prison (and thus disproportionately likely to be affected by various learning difficulties, educational disadvantage and health inequalities). These systems are not just complex bureaucracies, they are also experiences – of struggling with impenetrable forms and systems, waiting for inadequate money that may not come, bouncing between precarious short-term contracts and living arrangements, and dealing with staff who are likely to be, at best, sympathetic but overstretched and, at worst, indifferent or hostile.

Under the *Unlocking Potential, Transforming Lives* agenda (Section 8.2.3), the SPS provided additional training for 41 officers to begin working as Throughcare Support Officers to support people after release. However, in 2019, the programme ceased due to operational challenges in SPS (increases in prison population and levels of staff absence). Research on the programme (Maycock et al., 2020) gives a sense that prison officers accompanying people on licence in the community were brought face to face with challenges they had not previously appreciated, and illustrated the acute need for more service support in this area.

Arnal and McNeill (2023), discussing ex-prisoner experiences of engaging with a homelessness service, describe long and tedious waiting (wasting time that could be used attending to other urgent concerns) in unpleasant environs for help that rarely comes, arguing further that the process deepens disadvantage and stigma, in a way that is not reintegrative but *dis*-integrative – a form of social '*de*-habilitation'.

Much of the work of 'throughcare' centres on addressing the damaging effects of criminalisation on efforts to achieve stable housing and employment. However, the criminal justice system can simultaneously work *against* attempts to stay out of trouble and out of prison.

10.3.3 Criminal justice and surveillance

Findings from research on compliance with probation/JSW supervision among people supervised on licence, as well as under community penalties – in line with the wider literature on desistance (Section 6.3.4) – consistently support an emphasis on person-centred approaches that address a wide range of issues: developing motivation and hope, working *with* rather than *on* people, supporting strengths, maintaining hope and attending to the complexity of desistance and identity (McNeill, 2012; Weaver et al, 2021). However, with limited resources and in a risk-averse climate, justice agencies may 'default' to surveillance.

While ostensibly centred on supporting a person to reintegrate, throughcare by JSW also necessarily involves a high degree of surveillance and control – and may lead to recall to prison, which remains a constant threat. For a person on licence, even minor offending can lead to disproportionate punishment, as one person interviewed by Anderson (2019) described:

> I get busted one day. [...] Automatically, cause of my licence, I went to Barlinnie [prison]. Any normal guy would've been kept out. They'd have been took to the polis station and charged and let out that night.

> Because of my licence I was taken straight to Barlinnie. And when you go back in again, you're back doing your life sentence automatically.
>
> (Unpublished interview extract)

Importantly, a person does not need to have committed a crime to be recalled. Recall may be immediate and where the person has been accused of an offence, happens before a trial (at which the person may be acquitted).

Police Scotland may have a formal role in surveilling and supervising people released on licence – but surveillance by police goes beyond this. Police Scotland's 'intelligence-led' policing approach focuses on the detection, arrest and disruption of 'known' criminals. This means that those regarded as persistent offenders (with 'well-kent' faces) experience regular police stops and are viewed negatively by police during these encounters (Schinkel et al., 2019). These encounters not only lead to the person feeling labelled and targeted, but as frustrations escalate within these interactions, they can also lead to further arrests.

When people do not comply with supervision, it is often because of structural reasons that may not be within their control – such as the cost of travelling to appointments, the impact of dependent substance use or time commitments (which may disproportionately affect women – see Box 10.2). However, people may also refuse to comply – or engage in begrudging 'instrumental' compliance – if they feel they have been treated unfairly, stigmatised, ignored or misjudged as 'risky'. This point raises significant questions of legitimacy and fairness (Weaver et al., 2021).

For people supervised by the regional MAPPA partnerships (see Section 6.1.5), the emphasis on prevention, control and surveillance sits uneasily with the stated intention of supporting desistance and participation, which has implications not only for the people supervised but also for the effectiveness of these arrangements. Weaver and Barry (2014) found that while some supervisees experienced MAPPA as supportive and actively cooperated in reducing their own risk, others saw it as a regime of surveillance, illogical restrictions and pervasive mistrust which had to be complied with, but did not inspire cooperation. In Barry's (2021) study, even where probation/JSW thought a person's risk could be managed safely in the community, police were likely to see their role in terms of surveillance, arrest, and advocating recall to prison *when* (not if) the person breached their conditions.

Box 10.2 Gendered experiences of life after punishment

We have discussed in Chapter 6 (Section 6.3.4, Box 6.2) the prominence of 'desistance' narratives in Scottish criminal justice, and the ways in which gender inequalities may affect women's experiences of desistance. Compared to men, women are more likely to breach community sentences for reasons to do with inability to comply, not further offending (Barry and McIvor, 2010) – since their domestic commitments (such as single parenthood) are more likely to get in the way of attending appointments. These issues are likely to apply to throughcare supervision as well as community sentences, although the 2012 Commission on Women Offenders report (see Box 8.1) led to the creation and funding of several services specifically to support women's reintegration after imprisonment (but see Cleary, forthcoming).

Nonetheless, Crowley (2022) highlights that despite the aspirational language of support for reintegration, women who leave prison/secure care in Scotland may be particularly vulnerable to housing insecurity (for instance, young women are less often able to return to the family home after prison). There are also gendered aspects of criminal records which intersect with wider sexism in society, such as the job market (Collett, 2022). For instance, women are (for complex reasons) over-represented in social care and related roles. These roles tend to make more use of (enhanced) disclosure checks, while the types of jobs most available to people with criminal records tend to be in male-dominated sectors and/or have conditions (such as particular working hours) that conflict with the caring responsibilities disproportionately borne by women.

In these ways and others, the stigma of criminalisation may bear particularly heavily on women, beyond the additional shame from having violated social expectations of womanhood (the 'double deviance' thesis of classic feminist criminology). Gender-specific services for women in the community are intended to address these issues, but arguably also serve to extend carceral practices of (gendered) social control into the community without addressing underlying patterns of gender, socioeconomic and other inequalities (Malloch et al., 2014).

Questions to consider

- How do you think women involved in criminal justice should be supported to reintegrate into the community?
- How do concerns about women's experiences of life after punishment intersect with other gendered aspects of criminal justice already discussed? (Boxes 6.3 and 8.1).

We have measures intended to support people in the transition from prison to the community, but we are left with questions – whether these forms of supervised release achieve their aims and whether they even *can* do so, given the pervasive structural inequalities which affect people in prison. Box 10.2 considers this in relation to sexism and women's experiences of life after punishment. In supporting people to 'reintegrate' after prison, charitable projects may be less degrading and more effective, but since they lack the financial security of the public sector, they are vulnerable to gaps in funding and to short-notice closures (Arnal and McNeill, 2023). Furthermore, these organisations may also act as agents of state social control, while appearing to be 'community' oriented (Malloch et al., 2014).

Conclusion

This chapter is about the various institutions and procedures which govern the continued involvement of criminal justice in a person's life as their formal punishment (or time in prison) comes to an end. There are several themes and ideas that cut across these. The first is the way in which information about a person's offending can be labelling and stigmatising, particularly through the use of official criminal records and other information held by criminal justice agencies. For almost everybody convicted of an offence, the offence is recorded somewhere as a criminal record. This can affect how people see themselves and their possibility for change, and how they are seen by others, and reduce access to the supports and opportunities that people need to stay out of the criminal justice system. This all makes change much harder.

Efforts to promote (legal) rehabilitation for the very large number of people with criminal convictions have developed alongside the rise of actuarial and risk-focused approaches to criminal justice, as well as an extremely emotive social and political discourse about mental disorder, violence and sexual offending. As will have been apparent from reading this book so far, the theoretical and contested concept of 'risk' has become enmeshed across the structure of criminal justice.

Numerous new laws, institutions and regulations have resulted in a far more pervasive and deeper system of control on certain populations, in the name of managing their perceived risk. Whether the 'weight' of this apparatus is justly balanced according to the 'risk' it seeks to manage, is a question that is difficult to answer. These efforts also rest on the premise that risk is something that can be accurately measured and reduced. While this is a tantalising promise, the evidence base for our current risk assessment tools and practices has been challenged (Prins and Reich, 2021), with serious questions about the ability of such tools to predict individual behaviour (Hart et al., 2007) with an over-emphasis on assessing individuals for their risks, rather than situations. Even the best system cannot eliminate risk altogether; failures of these sorts of preventive measures are extremely harmful and attract significant attention, while success is essentially invisible. We will never know how much harm has been prevented due to implemented measures and whether this exceeds the harms caused. However, it is easy to mobilise often quite repressive forms of punishment and control, in the name of preventing potential harm in the future.

This is arguably particularly prominent in the management of people after punishment or in the community as part of a longer custodial sentence. The result is an extraordinarily complex, confusing regime at the 'edges' of the criminal justice system, which may actively hinder rather than promote desistance from offending – both for the small number of people considered to pose the highest risk and for the very large number who have any sort of criminal record at all. The next chapter will focus on another aspect of Scottish criminal justice that is not the exclusive preserve of any single agency – the ways in which Scotland deals with crime, policing and punishment beyond its own borders.

Critical questions

- Thinking about the different 'penal rationales' (rehabilitation/deterrence/incapacitation/retribution/denunciation/reparation – Box 4.3), how do you see these operating in the systems of criminal records, licences and post-release supervision?
- If you were involved in making decisions about a person's release from prison, what would you want to know? Why do you think this information is important?
- Do you think 'community notification' (e.g. for domestic abuse or sexual offences) is helpful? What are some arguments in favour of and against it?
- Rosser, in Christensen et al. (2021) suggest that recruiting people with convictions is "not just about business doing good, it's good for business". What are some possible advantages of recruiting people with convictions? If you were in charge of recruiting people for a job, what (if anything) would you want to know about their convictions? Is there anything you think would or should be disqualifying? How do you think this might change across different types of jobs?
- The discussion of criminal records often centres on the idea of striking a 'balance' between the protection of the public and the reintegration of people with criminal records. Are there any issues or problems with thinking about it in this way?
- EXERCISE: Imagine you have been released from prison on licence. What sort of challenges might you face in trying to return to the community? What would help you to avoid further offending? What would 'life after punishment' look like?

Key resources

Henley, A. (2018). Mind the gap: Sentencing, rehabilitation and civic purgatory. *Probation Journal* 65(3): 285–301.

Parts of this relate specifically to England and Wales, but key arguments are relevant to Scotland as well.

The charity Unlock supports people with criminal records to move on with their lives and advocates for their rights: https://unlock.org.uk/

Probation Journal Volume 69(3) – Special Issue: Criminalisation, criminal records and rehabilitation: From supervision to citizenship?

This special issue only includes one article about Scotland, but the issues raised throughout are relevant to Scotland.

Nugent, B. and Schinkel, M. (2016) The pains of desistance. *Criminology and Criminal Justice* 16(5): 568–584.

A key source that uses Scottish research with people living after punishment to challenge the widely accepted narrative of 'desistance'.

SCCJR Podcast – Just Talk: Is There Life After State Punishment? https://sccjr.libsyn.com/just-talk-is-there-life-after-state-punishment

A podcast in which experts from Scotland and elsewhere discuss the issues covered in this chapter.

Note

1 Not to be confused with the Children's Hearings System.

References

Anderson, S. (2019) *Punishing Trauma: Narratives, Desistance and Recovery*. Unpublished PhD thesis, University of Glasgow.

Anderson, S. (2020) Frustrating desistance: Stigma as a barrier to change. In Best, D. and Colman, C. (eds) *Strengths-Based Approaches to Crime and Substance Use: From Drugs and Crime to Desistance and Recovery*. Routledge. 159–177.

Arnal, A.R. and McNeill, F. (2023) Exploring social re/habilitation and developing a new conceptualisation of re/integration. In Coppola, F. and Martufi, A. (eds) *Social Rehabilitation and Criminal Justice*. Routledge. 251–267.

Baldwin, C. (2017). The vetting epidemic in England and Wales. *The Journal of Criminal Law* 81(6): 478–496.

Barry, M. (2021) 'Walking on ice': The future of parole in a risk-obsessed society. *Theoretical Criminology* 25(2): 325–342.

Barry, M. and McIvor, G. (2010) Professional decision making and women offenders: Containing the chaos? *Probation Journal* 57(1): 27–41.

Care Inspectorate (2021) *Community Justice Social Work: Throughcare Review*. Care Inspectorate.

Christensen, E., Jardine, C., Kennedy, A., Mabon, K., Taylor, E. and Weaver, B. (2021) *The Collateral Consequences of Criminal Records*. https://strathprints.strath.ac.uk/76456/1/Christensen_etal_2021_The_Collateral_Consequences_of_Criminal.pdf

Collett, N. (2022) Accounting for the gendered nature of 'collateral consequences' of a criminal record. In Masson, I. and Booth, N. (eds) *The Routledge Handbook of Women's Experiences of Criminal Justice*. Routledge. 475–486.

Cleary, J. (forthcoming) Scottish community justice and women: Progress or peripheral concern? *British Journal of Community Justice*.

Crowley, A.R. (2022) "She has nothing really when she goes out of Prison": Community-based practitioners' perceptions of young women's pathways through the criminal justice system in Scotland. In Masson, I. and Booth, N. (eds) *The Routledge Handbook of Women's Experiences of Criminal Justice*. Routledge. 548–560.

Ferguson, E. (2021) *'A Sentence of Last Resort': The Order for Lifelong Restriction and the Sentencing of Dangerous Offenders in Scotland*. PhD thesis. https://theses.gla.ac.uk/82066/7/2021FergusonEAPhD.pdf

Goffman, E. (1963) *Stigma: Notes on the Management of Spoiled Identity*. Prentice-Hall.

Grant, S., Buchan, J. and O'Donnell, A. (2020) Scotland. *Probation in Europe* (updated online chapter). Confederation of European Probation. https://www.cep-probation.org/wp-content/uploads/2020/11/Scotland-chapter-final-version.pdf

Hart, S. D., Michie, C. and Cooke, D. J. (2007) Precision of actuarial risk assessment instruments: Evaluating the 'margins of error' of group v. individual predictions of violence. *British Journal of Psychiatry* 190(S49): s60–s65.

Her Majesty's Inspectorate of Constabulary in Scotland (HMICS) (2018) *Strategic Review – An Independent Assessment of Police Scotland's Response to a Breach of Home Detention Curfew (HDC)*. https://www.hmics.scot/sites/default/files/publications/HMICS20181025PUB.pdf

Hutchings, A. and Collier, B. (2019) Inside out: Characterising cybercrimes committed inside and outside the workplace. *2019 IEEE European Symposium on Security and Privacy Workshops*. https://ieeexplore.ieee.org/stamp/stamp.jsp?arnumber=8802445

Jardine, C. (2018) Constructing and maintaining family in the context of imprisonment. *British Journal of Criminology* 58(1):114–131.

Malloch, M., McIvor, G., Burgess, C. (2014) 'Holistic' community punishment and criminal justice interventions for women. *Howard Journal of Criminal Justice* 53(4): 395–410.

Maycock, M., McGuckin, K. and Morrison, K. (2020) 'We are "free range" prison officers', the experiences of Scottish Prison Service throughcare support officers working in custody and the community. *Probation Journal* 67(4): 358–374.

McGuinness, P., McNeill, F. and Armstrong, S. (2013) *The Use and Impact of the Rehabilitation of Offenders Act (1974): Final Report*. Scottish Centre for Crime and Justice Research.

McMillan, L. and Tickell, A. (2024) Lawful, proportionate and necessary? A critical examination of the domestic abuse disclosure scheme for Scotland. *Feminists@law* 13(1): 1–27.

Miller, R.J. (2021) *Halfway Home: Race, Punishment and the Afterlife of Mass Incarceration*. Little, Brown.

Ministry of Justice and Department for Work and Pensions (2011) *Provisional Estimate of Benefit Claims by Recently Released Prisoners*, May 2011. https://assets.publishing.service.gov.uk/media/5a7ce260ed915d36e95f0406/prov-estimate-benefit-claims-prisoners-may11.pdf

Nugent, B. and Schinkel, M. (2016) The pains of desistance. *Criminology and Criminal Justice* 16(5): 568–584.

Parole Board for Scotland (2024) *Parole Board for Scotland – Annual Report 2021–2*. Parole Board for Scotland. https://scottishparoleboard.scot/wp-content/uploads/2024/01/AnnualReport2021-22.pdf

Prins, S.J. and Reich, A. (2021) Criminogenic risk assessment: A meta-review and critical analysis. *Punishment & Society* 23(4): 578–604.

Risk Management Authority (2023) *Initial Insights into Experiences of Release, Community Integration and Recall for Individuals on the Order for*

Lifelong Restriction. Risk Management Authority. https://www.rma.scot/wp-content/uploads/2023/11/2023-24-Initial-Insights-Full-Version.pdf

Schinkel, M., Atkinson, C. and Anderson, S. (2019) 'Well-kent faces': Policing persistent offenders and the possibilities for desistance. *British Journal of Criminology* 59(3): 634–652.

Scottish Government (2024a) *Homelessness in Scotland: 2023-24*. Scottish Government. https://www.gov.scot/publications/homelessness-in-scotland-2023-24/

Scottish Government (2024b). *Order for Lifelong Restriction and Custodial Sentences: FOI Release*. Scottish Government. https://www.gov.scot/publications/foi-202400395707/

van Zyl Smit and Morrison (2020) The paradox of Scottish life imprisonment. *European Journal of Crime, Criminal Law and Criminal Justice* 28: 76–101.

Weaver, B. (2018) *Time for Policy Redemption?: A Review of the Evidence on Disclosure of Criminal Records*. University of Strathclyde. https://www.sccjr.ac.uk/wp-content/uploads/2019/01/Weaver_SCCJR_2018_Time_for_policy_redemption_a_review_of_the_evidence.pdf

Weaver, B., Tata, C., Munro, M. and Barry, M. (2012) The failure of recall to prison: Early release, front-door and back-door sentencing and the revolving prison door in Scotland. *European Journal of Probation* 4(1): 85–98.

Weaver, B. and Barry, M. (2014) Managing high risk offenders in the community: Compliance, cooperation and consent in a climate of concern. *European Journal of Probation* 6(3): 278–295.

Weaver, B. and Jardine, C. (2022) Citizenship on probation: Understanding the labour market exclusion of criminalized people in Scotland. *Probation Journal* 69(3): 296–317.

Weaver, B., Piacentini, L., Moodie, K. and Barry, M. (2021) Exploring and explaining non-compliance with community supervision. *British Journal of Criminology* 61(2): 434–455.

11 Crime control in Scotland in a transnational context

Key ideas

- Although Scotland is not a nation state and does not have an official foreign policy, its activities (including criminal justice) can still have significant international impacts.
- Transnational crime control may involve specialist expertise and a range of formal and informal partnerships working across domestic as well as international policing agencies (notably, the NCA and Europol, respectively).
- Scotland is affected by international norms around the criminal justice process and conditions. This has been complicated by Brexit, which has also posed challenges to UK's transnational policing arrangements.
- Transnational criminal justice, prisoner transfers and extraditions raise various issues of diplomacy as well as justice, exemplified in one of the highest-profile controversies surrounding Scottish criminal justice – the release of Abdelbaset al-Megrahi.
- Immigration to the UK is a UK (not Scottish) government responsibility; the increasingly heated political rhetoric about migration raises challenges for Scottish criminal justice generally, including efforts to address human trafficking.
- Working with criminal justice agencies transnationally raises important questions about the complicity of Scottish criminal justice in human rights violations elsewhere and about international commitments to human rights in general.

Introduction

We began this book by considering Scotland's place within the UK and how this has shaped our approach to criminal justice. We now examine the place of Scottish criminal justice beyond the borders of the UK, as well as Scotland's relationship with international and transnational developments in offending and crime control in a globalised world.

The first section of this chapter discusses the place of Scottish criminal justice in the world and its interaction with other justice systems. This includes

DOI: 10.4324/9781003372882-11

processes of extradition, the treatment of foreign nationals in the system, and the connection between the (Scottish) criminal justice and (UK) immigration systems. We then consider the role of international treaties and norms, particularly around human rights, in shaping Scottish criminal justice and the involvement of Scottish institutions in less formal networks of international cooperation (with potentially problematic consequences).

The second part of this chapter considers Scotland's response to forms of transnational crime, a key beneficiary of globalisation. Any of the agencies discussed in Chapters 3–10 may be involved in matters that cross borders as part of their ordinary business, but there are bodies for Scotland and the wider UK that specialise in transnational crime – particularly the National Crime Agency (NCA). We conclude by reflecting on the implications of Scotland's uncertain constitutional position for its transnational crime control arrangements.

11.1 Scottish criminal justice across borders

Some borders (like that between the UK and Europe) are visibly marked and heavily securitised, while others, like the border between England and Scotland, are barely noticeable and little policed. Some borders are more porous than others to different groups of people, and national borders can be socially produced and performed in what Soliman (2024) describes as 'borderisation'.

We begin by looking at two ways in which 'ordinary' criminal justice processes may cross borders to interact – the process of extradition, and the position of foreign nationals in our criminal justice system. We then consider how Scottish criminal justice is shaped by international norms and how it participates in international professional networks. Concerns about human rights become particularly challenging and important in these contexts.

11.1.1 Extradition

'**Extradition**' refers to the process by which a person who is suspected or convicted of a crime in one country, and is currently in another, can be arrested and legally returned to the first country to face trial and punishment. The ruling about whether and where to extradite someone is made by a special type of hearing, which are not trials, but share certain features with them (Arnell, 2018) – the court decides whether the person's conduct would be an offence in the UK and whether it meets a certain threshold of seriousness.

The UK has extradition agreements with many countries, but not all extradition requests are granted. The European Arrest Warrant (EAW) scheme allows streamlined extradition for its signatory European states; members are required to arrest people subject to an EAW and extradite them unless there is a specific objection. After its withdrawal from the EU in 2020 ('Brexit'), the UK left the EAW but streamlined extradition arrangements have been organised under the EU–UK Trade and Cooperation Agreement (TACA). The EU's cross-border Schengen Information System is also used to circulate information about warrants.

People *should* only be extradited where there are assurances that their human rights will be respected. Considerations include seeking assurances that extradited people will not face capital punishment, and, where the person to be extradited has children in their country of residence, the right to family life. However, human rights abuses and miscarriages of justice are features of criminal justice systems worldwide, indeed, including in Scotland. In 2023, an Irish court refused to extradite a man for trial in Scotland on the grounds of a "real and substantial risk of inhuman or degrading treatment", due to concerns about conditions in Scottish prisons, including overcrowding and inability to care for the man's mental health needs and neurodevelopmental disorders (a later ruling found that the latter point had been adequately addressed, and the man was extradited to Scotland the following year (*The* Journal, 2024)).

In high-profile cases, extradition may be not only a legal procedure but also a matter of international diplomacy. While legal aspects of Scottish extraditions are the business of Scottish courts, diplomatic aspects are for the *UK* government. The Scottish/American dual national Kenny Richey spent 21 years awaiting execution in Ohio after conviction for murder (which most evidence suggested was in fact a tragic accident), until he was freed after lengthy lobbying by British politicians, diplomats and activists. Box 11.1 discusses the diplomatic implications of a controversial episode in Scottish history – the release of the convicted Lockerbie bomber Abdelbaset al-Megrahi.

Box 11.1 The release of Abdelbaset al-Megrahi

One of the biggest controversies in Scottish criminal justice centred on the release from prison, on compassionate grounds, of Abdelbaset al-Megrahi, a Libyan national convicted of the 1988 bombing of an American airliner (Pan Am Flight 103) over Lockerbie, Dumfries and Galloway. The bombing killed 270 people (including all passengers and crew, and 11 residents) and remains the deadliest terrorist attack on British soil, although most victims were American. A joint investigation between the FBI and Dumfries and Galloway Constabulary identified two Libyan suspects including al-Megrahi.

From 1969 to 2011, Libya was under the authoritarian rule of Colonel Muammar Gadaffi, and diplomatic relations with the UK were poor, particularly following the murder of a Metropolitan Police officer, Yvonne Fletcher, by gunfire from within the Libyan embassy in

London. In 1991, al-Megrahi was indicted by a US grand jury and the Lord Advocate of Scotland; after lengthy negotiations and under pressure from economic sanctions, Libya agreed to hand over the suspects. They were tried at a special session of Scotland's High Court, held (at Gadaffi's insistence, under a deal brokered by the International Court of Justice) in a neutral country, the Netherlands. Al-Megrahi was convicted and sentenced to life imprisonment – which, as a matter of diplomatic agreement between the USA and the UK, would be served in Scotland. The other suspect was acquitted. These events formed part of a normalisation of relations between Libya and the West, in the wider context of Libyan cooperation with the USA in the War on Terror and with the EU in policing Mediterranean migration.

In 2009, with terminal cancer and given three months to live, al-Megrahi was freed on compassionate release and allowed to return to Libya. The exact reasoning for this decision is contested, but pressure from Libya for his return had been building over the late 2000s, as part of negotiations over a Prisoner Transfer Agreement between the UK and Libya.

Kenealy (2012) argues that the release was motivated, at the UK government level, by British commercial interests in Libya, and at the level of the (then Scottish National Party (SNP)-led) Scottish Government by the opportunity to engage in 'paradiplomacy', articulating a distinctive *and compassionate* Scottish identity on the world stage. The release of US diplomatic cables via Wikileaks in 2010 suggested that the UK government, having leaned on Scotland to release al-Megrahi, then succeeded in deflecting the blame onto Scotland, when Megrahi would likely have been transferred to Libya anyway under the UK–Libya Prisoner Transfer Agreement. In 2011, the Libyan Civil War concluded with Gadaffi's assassination by rebel forces; al-Megrahi died the following year, significantly outliving his original three-month prognosis. In 2020, American authorities charged another suspect, also a Libyan national; when his trial takes place (this time under US jurisdiction) it is likely to stir memories of the controversy over al-Megrahi.

Questions to consider

- What are the non-legal and non-criminal justice factors which affected the punishment and release of al-Megrahi?
- What are all the different ways in which the planning, commission and effects of the Lockerbie bombing make this a transnational crime?
- How does this textbox relate to other issues discussed in this chapter?

11.1.2 Foreign nationals in the justice system

There are well-established frameworks for sentences imposed by courts to be served in other parts of the UK; where a person under (for instance) an English community sentence moves to Scotland, the Scottish system can take over their case; likewise, a fine imposed by a Scottish court can be passed to the English system for enforcement.

The picture is more ambiguous for people involved in the criminal justice system who are not British citizens (often called **'foreign national offenders'** in the literature). It is important not to conflate foreign nationals in the criminal justice system with irregular (sometimes called 'illegal') migration. The former are often in the country legally at the time of the offence and may have established lives here, including families. Some people who came to the UK when they were very young – even some who were born here – may not realise that they do not have British citizenship until they encounter the criminal justice system (Godshaw, 2020).

Foreign nationals form a particularly vulnerable group, especially in prison – they may be far from sources of support and lack the language skills needed to navigate rules, socialise and receive care and support (Ugelvik, 2014), and it may be challenging for the prison system to get information on the person from their home country.

Foreign nationals make up a smaller proportion of the Scottish prison population than in England and Wales and much smaller than in some Western European jurisdictions. However, this population appears to be growing. Data on foreign nationals in Scottish prisons are not routinely published, but information from various sources illustrates this rise. This mirrors similar patterns across Western Europe (Ugelvik, 2014), which may be explained partly by changing patterns of European migration but also by racist discourses associating immigration with crime, which have become increasingly politically 'mainstream'.

In 2005, there were just under 100 foreign nationals in prison (1% of the prison population) (Aebi et al., 2015), but by 2023–2024 this proportion had risen to 9% (Scottish Prison Service, 2024).

The Scottish Prison Service (SPS) have only very recently begun publicising nationality data, and there is little information on the experiences of foreign nationals in prison; the only information available from SPS (Downie and Carnie, 2018) surveyed ethnic minority *and* foreign national prisoners, making no distinction between them.

Arrangements can be negotiated with foreign governments to transfer some prisoners back to their home country to serve their sentence (and for British prisoners abroad to serve their sentence in the UK). In addition, the Early Removal Scheme allows short-term prisoners to be released up to 180 days early for **deportation** from the UK. Other foreign national prisoners can be deported at the end of their sentence.

In 2006, the foreign national prisoner 'crisis' – in which there was media outcry about the release of foreign national prisoners without considering them for deportation – led to stricter measures aimed at ensuring the deportation of foreign nationals at the end of their sentence, resulting in foreign national prisoners serving sentences of a year or more being deported, unless this breaches their rights under **European Convention on Human Rights (ECHR)**, especially the right to family life (Article 8). Subsequent immigration rules outlined that where someone has received a sentence of over four years, "very compelling circumstances" would be needed for deportation to be considered a breach of Article 8. Even without imprisonment, someone can be deported for persistent offending or when deemed to have caused serious harm.

The experience and process for people without British citizenship in the Scottish criminal justice system is affected by devolved Scottish criminal justice and reserved UK immigration policies and legislation; while Scots law determines the sentence someone receives, UK law (including, where relevant, post-Brexit agreements with the EU) determines whether they will be deported. Given that policy around deportation is reserved (Chapter 1), the 'foreign criminal' has featured less prominently within Scottish media and political discourse, although in 2024 the Scottish Conservatives argued for greater efforts to transfer these prisoners back to their home countries to alleviate Scottish prison overcrowding (Chapter 8).

The UK government may wish to deport someone after their sentence, but may not be able to do this immediately. There may be legal challenges to the decision, conditions in the country of origin may mean that the government is unable to return them, or their presumed country of origin may not be willing to receive them. As with extradition, this process may require diplomatic negotiations.

While awaiting deportation, the person may be detained in immigration detention facilities – unlike in many European countries, without a time limit. Dungavel House, a former open prison that is privately operated but under contract to the Home Office, is the only such facility in Scotland, but people can be transferred to other immigration removal centres (IRCs) in the UK. Immigration detention sits outwith the criminal justice system. As well as people being deported following a crime, Dungavel IRC holds those being removed from the country simply because they do not (or no longer) have permission to stay in the UK. Immigration is described as 'administrative' rather than 'punitive' – but while not officially a 'punishment', it may well be experienced this way. Bosworth and Turnbull (2015) highlight the stark similarities between IRCs and a penal environment. Detention and deportation can be experienced as a double punishment for foreign nationals, who are denied the possibility of reintegration, in practices which are highly gendered, racialised and classed (Turnbull and Hasselberg, 2017: 137).

This raises important questions about what constitutes a punishment, what types of infringements should warrant detention against someone's will, whether there should be different responses to crimes committed by non-British citizens, and whether it matters that the people affected are often already oppressed or marginalised.

11.1.3 International norms, treaties and human rights

Scottish criminal justice is shaped by international treaties and norms, particularly around human rights. As well as the Universal Declaration of Human Rights (UDHR) and ECHR, there are treaties focused on standards of treatment in criminal justice systems, including the 2015 UN Standard Minimum Rules for the Treatment of Prisoners (known as the Mandela Rules), the 2010 UN Rules for the Treatment of Women Prisoners and Noncustodial Measures for Women Offenders (the Bangkok Rules) and the UN Convention Against Torture and other Cruel, Inhuman or Degrading Treatment or Punishment. The UN Convention on the Rights of the Child (UNCRC) has inspired significant work across Scottish children's services and youth justice (Chapter 9).

The UK is a signatory to the UN Convention Against Torture; under the Optional Protocol to that Convention, several bodies form part of the UK's **National Preventive Mechanism (NPM)**, which connects domestic inspection regimes with international bodies to prevent torture and ill-treatment and promote human rights in criminal justice. Scottish organisations within the NPM include HM Inspectorate of Constabulary in Scotland (HMICS) and independent custody visitors (Chapter 3), the Care Inspectorate (Chapter 6) and HM Inspectorate of Prisons for Scotland (HMIPS) (Chapter 9).

The Council of Europe (CoE) is charged with promoting human rights and upholding the ECHR in Europe; even after Brexit, the UK remains a member of the CoE, so must follow the ECHR. Much of the Scottish Parliament's early activity centred on writing ECHR into Scots law, and this has brought the issue of human rights to prominence in political rhetoric about Scotland's place in the world. The ECHR (and the 1998 Human Rights Act) enshrine in law the right to a fair trial and legal representation (see Chapter 4 and Section 3.3.2).

The European **Committee on the Prevention of Torture and Inhuman or Degrading Treatment or Punishment (CPT)**, run by the CoE, visits member countries to inspect conditions in police custody and prisons, sometimes alongside NPMs. A report by the Scottish Human Rights Commission (2024) found many CPT recommendations had not yet been enacted and one had been outstanding since 1994. The CPT has no power to compel national governments to do anything – its only 'sanction' is publicity, although critical reports may exert significant political pressure.

The CoE also set out **European Prison Rules** and **European Probation Rules**. These are legally non-binding but set norms around what is expected of criminal justice institutions, and compliance is increasingly expected for non-EU countries seeking to join.

The European Prison Rules were first adopted in 1973 and revised in 2020 to include more detail on segregation and solitary confinement; they follow UN rules on imprisonment and are also used to inform the work of the CPT. One basic principle, Rule 4, states "Prison conditions that infringe prisoners' human rights are not justified by lack of resources". In practice, though, a lack of resources routinely prevents full compliance with the Rules across Europe (Spolverato, 2021) – a concern notable in respect of progression through the Scottish prison system (Chapter 8).

While Scottish community justice fits well with the European Probation Rules, they are little discussed, even though reforms to probation in England and Wales and Northern Ireland have explicitly emphasised alignment to these norms (Buchan and Grant, 2021).

These Rules have traditionally centred on human rights standards and reducing imprisonment, but with successive revisions has come an increasing emphasis on matters of process, organisational aspects and 'what works' (van Zyl Smit et al., 2015); a broad range of critical perspectives on criminal justice (and indeed on the EU) might take issue with the use of international agreements to entrench criminal justice processes internationally.

A wide range of other (especially European) instruments may also impact on Scottish criminal justice. For instance, the EU Directive 29/2012 on victims' rights (enacted in Scots law as the 2014 Victims and Witnesses (Scotland) Act) has promoted the development of restorative justice. However, this has been a very 'institutionalised' model in which restorative justice is used as a tool of the criminal justice system, provoking significant critique from those who argue restorative justice should remain separate from (and critical of) mainstream criminal justice (Gavrielides, 2016). Other international conventions centre on recognising and addressing specific forms of crime – e.g. the Palermo Protocol and the Budapest Convention (Sections 11.2.3 and 11.2.4).

Following Brexit, the Scottish Government (2024) under the SNP has repeatedly emphasised its interest in future EU membership as an independent state; if this occurred, Scotland would gain full access to European transnational agencies (Section 11.2.1). The Scottish Government and Parliament increasingly use the European phrase 'Justice and Home Affairs' rather than 'Justice' (e.g. the relevant minister is now called the Cabinet Secretary for Justice and Home Affairs) and passed legislation (Criminal Justice (EU Exit) (Scotland) (Amendment etc.) Regulations 2020), which allows Scottish courts some discretion to take EU convictions into account, in alignment with practice amongst EU member states. Much of this, however, is moot while Scotland remains part of the UK.

11.1.4 *Training and professional networks*

Scottish criminal justice interacts with other systems not only through formal and legal mechanisms. Scottish justice practitioners might share learning with their counterparts in other countries through study visits, secondments and international conferences. These exchanges are one way in which 'policy transfer' between jurisdictions can occur; an example of this in Chapter 2 is the adoption of American approaches by the Scottish Violence Reduction Unit (later adopted, and adapted, in England and Wales).

Police Scotland has institutionalised these arrangements through its **International Development and Innovation Unit (IDIU)**, which predates the national service. IDIU began by facilitating visits to and from other countries' forces but has become increasingly involved in training. These activities are overseen by part of the UK's Foreign, Commonwealth & Development Office and are often targeted towards the Scottish Government's international development partners.

This training is intended to promote good practice in policing worldwide and support Scotland's role as a 'good global citizen' that upholds human rights (see Scottish Government, 2021). However, there has been controversy over the provision of training to police in countries where there are significant concerns about police involvement in human rights violations.

In 2010, the Scottish Police College, with financial support from the Scottish and UK Governments, established a scheme to train police officers in Sri Lanka. At this time, the Sri Lankan Civil War had just concluded with the crushing of the Tamil insurgency by government forces; since the police had been complicit in the repression of the Tamil minority, trust in policing was very low. The intention of the Scottish project was to promote the development of community policing and hence the establishment of a stable democracy in Sri Lanka (Milne and Thomson, 2012). However, the country soon descended into further violence and the project itself proved controversial. It emerged that the Scottish training included not only ordinary officers but also the paramilitary Special Task Force, which had been involved directly in the brutal repression of political dissent, ostensibly to prevent terrorism. Furthermore, the initial training had begun before 2010, while the civil war was still ongoing. As the situation in Sri Lanka deteriorated further, the attention of UK government, diplomats, and both Parliaments was drawn to the scheme (BBC News, 2016), leading to it being ended in 2021.

Sri Lanka is the most prominent controversy, but there have been criticisms by activist groups since the 2000s of Scottish police involvement in training police forces in countries where violations of human rights by police and other justice agencies, including the use of torture and the death penalty, are routine. These include Saudi Arabia and Bahrain, (Scottish Legal News, 2016), UAE, South Sudan, and the Maldives (Carrell, 2012 and see Police Scotland, n.d.). The IDIU also works with police from jurisdictions including Norway and the USA, on projects which have attracted less controversy (though American policing and criminal justice, in particular, are far from unproblematic).

International training activities like this are in line with a longstanding self-conception of British policing as the envy of the world – quintessentially civilian, democratic and community-facing, especially compared to policing elsewhere in Europe – which may be at least as much myth as reality (Emsley, 2012). Such activities raise echoes of colonialism, a historical context which did much to shape the history of British policing – particularly since many of the countries in which IDIU provided training are former British colonies.

11.2 Globalisation, transnational crime and Scotland

Having outlined ways in which Scotland's criminal justice system may interact with others, we turn to other aspects of globalisation. **Globalisation** is enabled by communication technologies such as the internet, but also economic policies which aim to promote 'free trade' between nations by relaxing regulations and border controls. This has created opportunities for a range of transnational crimes. Telecommunications technologies have enabled cybercrime, and efforts to facilitate international trade have created opportunities for trafficking. The combination of international demand for exploitable labour, displacement created by conflict and climate change, and efforts by nations to restrict immigration have encouraged people smuggling and human trafficking. Alongside this, however, has come an increasingly interconnected and international approach to criminal justice and the establishment of various transnational crime control institutions and practices (Franko, 2020).

11.2.1 Transnational policing in Scotland

In the 1980s, Scotland had a regional crime squad, similar to other regions of the UK, for dealing with organised and transnational crime. (In England and Wales, this role is now performed by Regional Organised Crime Units (ROCUs)). Devolution brought the first distinctively Scottish arrangements. The Scottish Crime and Drug Enforcement Agency (SCDEA) was established in 2001 (as the Scottish Drug Enforcement Agency – renamed and expanded in 2006–07) to address serious organised crime, including drug trafficking, working alongside Scotland's (then) eight ordinary police forces (Scott, 2008). SCDEA was folded into Police Scotland in 2013.

Police Scotland is unusual, as a national force for a country that is not a nation state – and which has no checks or security at the border with England. It has therefore had to engage with a range of international policing agencies. Elements of the Specialist Crime Division centre on forms of offending that are (or may be) transnational – the Organised Crime and Counter Terrorism Unit uses local teams to target organised crime and a national approach to dealing with terrorism, linking to the wider UK Counter Terrorism Policing network. Border Policing Command focuses on the prevention of crime (including terrorism) at airports and seaports. Police Scotland also operates the Fugitive Action Search Team to track down people who are fugitive in other countries and seek to return them to Scotland.

Much transnational crime control in Scotland involves the **National Crime Agency (NCA)**, which (as discussed in Section 3.1.1) is essentially a UK-wide policing organisation specialising in serious and organised crime. The NCA work in an Organised Crime Partnership (OCP) with Police Scotland; their approach emphasises disruption of organised crime groups, including through seizing the proceeds of crime (see Section 5.1.4); it also highlights an increasing focus on online and technology-enabled forms of crime. More generally, the NCA provides specialist investigative support for Police Scotland as well as liaising with UK government and international organisations. The NCA has a presence at the Scottish Crime Campus, which was opened in 2014 at Gartcosh near Glasgow to coordinate the policing of transnational crime between Police Scotland, the Crown Office, the Scottish Police Authority Forensic Service, the NCA and His Majesty's Revenue and Customs (Atkinson, 2019).

Alongside this, the Scottish Government operates a Serious Organised Crime Taskforce which includes Police Scotland and the NCA alongside a range of other justice, local government and third sector agencies (Cavanagh et al., 2016). NCA (2024) data show that hundreds of NCA investigations a year disrupt Serious Organised Crime (SOC) in Scotland, although this includes many cases not centred on Scotland, but which would have had impacts in Scotland (for instance, drugs intercepted in England but bound for sale in Scotland).

Some of the NCA's work targets the infrastructures and services that support or facilitate organised crime. A particularly high-profile international operation targeted Encrochat, a secure messaging service used on special encrypted smartphones to coordinate organised crime activity, with tens of thousands of users. Encrochat was compromised by French and Dutch police in 2020, with support from the NCA via Europol; authorities collected huge quantities of messages leading to numerous convictions, including 31 in Scotland, many relating to drug trafficking between England and Scotland via the M74.

Various international organisations have been set up to facilitate cooperation between nation states in criminal justice matters and to deal with transnational crime. The NCA is the key point of contact between these international agencies and Police Scotland, including **Interpol** (more an intelligence-sharing service than a police agency proper) and **Europol** (an EU agency that works more like a police service to coordinate investigations between police forces in primarily EU countries). The EU also has an online database for holding criminal records data, the **European Criminal Records Information System (ECRIS)**, which can be queried by UK police. EU law requires member states to consider convictions in other member states when sentencing.

After Brexit, the UK left Europol and ECRIS, as well as other important international cooperation mechanisms including the European transnational prosecution agency Eurojust, creating considerable uncertainty for the UK's and Scotland's international criminal justice arrangements. The subsequent TACA with the EU has reinstated similar arrangements, albeit at the cost of significant disruption. The UK now has a liaison (from the NCA) with Europol and a liaison prosecutor within Eurojust, with access to the shared criminal records data on ECRIS. Much of this transnational institutional development has been justified in terms of tackling specifically transnational criminal threats, such as serious organised crime, cybercrime and human trafficking – all of which (as with other globalised phenomena) play out in Scotland in locally specific ways.

11.2.2 *Serious and organised crime*

Much of the development of transnational policing has centred on '**Serious Organised Crime**' (SOC; sometimes 'Serious and Organised Crime'). This language is found in the name of the NCA's predecessor agency, the Serious Organised Crime Agency (SOCA, established in 2006), and the passage of the 2015 Serious Crime Act in the UK Parliament. The official definition of SOC in the Scottish Serious Organised Crime Strategy is:

> crime which involves more than one person; is organised, meaning that it involves control, planning and potentially use of specialist resources; causes, or has the potential to cause, significant harm; and involves financial or other benefit to the individuals concerned.
>
> (Scottish Government, 2022: 5)

This could however include a wide range of offences; what constitutes *organised* crime is notoriously ambiguous. In terms of the justice response, SOC is considered an especially harmful form of offending not just because of the potential for direct and obvious harms (e.g. the use of violence to enforce debts) but also because of its capacity to infiltrate and corrupt legitimate activities, while remaining hidden behind or within them. For instance, SOC may use ordinary businesses as fronts to launder money, engage in modern slavery under the guise of legitimate employment (see Section 11.2.4) and use bribery to compromise the public sector (including the criminal justice process itself). Furthermore, the organised aspect tends to imply a degree of premeditation, sophistication, and persistence that is likely to lead to cases being treated more harshly by the system.

These factors arguably make SOC a threat not merely to those victimised, but to the infrastructure and functioning of significant parts of the economy or even to the security of the state itself; hence efforts to tackle SOC may combine elements ordinary policing and specialist intelligence-led practices. While SOC may be transnational, it is not necessarily so – and even where it is, as with other aspects of globalisation, the impacts and effects still play out at a local level, shaped by local circumstances (Graham et al., 2018).

Over the 2000s, the focus of Scottish organised crime policing shifted from identifying and arresting 'kingpins' to a more intelligence-focused approach centred on gathering intelligence, 'mapping' organised crime networks, disrupting networks and embedding preventive approaches more widely (Kirby and Snow, 2016), including by raising awareness among the wider public. The emphasis on disruption implies a tacit acknowledgement that it may not always be possible to arrest, prosecute and punish the perpetrators – a point particularly relevant in cases of transnational crime where perpetrators may not be accessible to police. This is also reflected in Police Scotland's adoption of the Home Office's 4P approach (Pursue, Protect, Prepare and Prevent) in discussions of both SOC and cybercrime policing (SPA, 2024).

Lavorgna and Sergi (2016) suggest that the 'SOC' formation increasingly draws together and conflates two separate descriptors – 'organised' and 'serious'. Thus organised crime is defined as serious, and vice versa, and this is used to justify the involvement of national security organisations and tactics (such as covert and electronic surveillance), in what have traditionally been matters for ordinary policing. All of this has occurred in the wider context of an increasingly securitised UK state in the context of the War on Terror.

11.2.3 Policing cybercrime in Scotland

Cybercrime is a term that lacks a consistent definition. Yar and Steinmetz (2024:10) summarise it as "computer-mediated activities that are illegal". Although cybercrime is often associated with highly skilled hackers, in fact, it is increasingly linked to older crimes, such as fraud, and organised around large-scale illicit businesses. This captures a large range of offences (credit card fraud, ransomware, image-based sexual abuse etc.) and in some cases is strongly linked to nation state conflict – becoming a national security concern – as well as organised crime. It *may* be transnational in character, involving perpetrators and victims thousands of miles from each other; however, cybercrime can also be local, taking place between people who know each other offline. It relies, in either case, on international communications infrastructure, so may require specialist expertise to investigate (as well as being deeply connected to globalisation). These aspects create challenges for traditional policing (Yar and Steinmetz, 2024).

Elsewhere in the UK, Action Fraud (run by the City of London Police) is the main centre for reporting cybercrime and fraud. In Scotland, this responsibility is currently held by Police Scotland, but this requires significant resources from Police Scotland. As of January 2025, it is anticipated Police Scotland may rejoin Action Fraud.

Police Scotland has specialist provision for cybercrime investigation, alongside 'digital forensics' – the examination of digital devices for evidence, whether investigating cybercrime or other offences. Some of this is contracted out; a recent Police Scotland trial of 'cyber-kiosks' to quickly extract this evidence attracted controversy for its data protection implications (particularly since crime victims' data were also gathered) and the involvement of the Israeli surveillance company Cellebrite as the provider (Daly et al., 2023).

Cybercrime policing also engages with businesses through the **Cyber and Fraud Centre Scotland**, a social enterprise providing advice to businesses on (among other things) preventing cybercrime and fraud. There may also be liaisons with specific platforms (for instance, if an offence involves social media, the police may request removal of content or user data). The UK's 2023 Online Safety Act, which applies in Scotland, requires major social media platforms including Meta and X (formerly Twitter) to take action against harmful and illegal content – thus enlisting these companies in the policing of Scottish cybercrime.

As with other aspects of criminal justice (Section 11.1.3), there are international conventions to consider – the UK is a signatory to the 2001 Budapest Convention on Cybercrime. This Convention, developed by the CoE and now ratified by 78 countries, seeks to harmonise criminal law and procedure in cybercrime cases between these countries and facilitate cooperation (including information sharing and extradition proceedings). In 2024, the UN approved a new Convention on Cybercrime, but as of January 2025, it is not yet clear how many countries will sign it, particularly given concerns about the impact of its provisions on human rights (Tropina, 2024).

The systems and infrastructure we use every day depend on digital systems, which are increasingly 'cloud-based', contracted out by service providers to major corporations, and hold large quantities of data about us. Attacks that compromise or damage this infrastructure therefore arguably cross into questions of national security; responses and preventative interventions typically involve the NCA and the intelligence services via the **National Cyber Security Centre (NCSC)**, as well as private sector specialists and governmental support. Major attacks like these are crimes, but in the level of disruption created, they may start to resemble natural disasters. The Scottish Government and most large organisations have 'resilience' strategies and certification programmes in place to ensure they can mitigate the operational impacts of cyber-attacks, while bodies such as the NCSC and EU cybersecurity agency ENISA work to develop security standards and promote best practices internationally. Box 11.2 discusses a prominent Scottish case study – the 2020–21 cyber-attack on the Scottish Environmental Protection Agency.

Box 11.2 The SEPA cyber-attack

Several public institutions in Scotland have been subject to major cyber-attacks in recent years. One example is the Scottish Environment Protection Agency (SEPA) – Scotland's environmental regulator, which also coordinates responses to floods and can act as a specialist reporting agency for environmental crime. At midnight on Christmas Eve 2020, a SEPA employee at home received an automatic alert and logged on to check the system. SEPA had been hit by a ransomware attack, a form of cyber-attack that targets sensitive or essential data and 'holds it hostage' – stealing, encrypting and/or deleting it. The data are returned if a ransom is paid, usually in cryptocurrency. The attack started from a phishing email – an employee had clicked on a link that enabled the attackers to gain access to SEPA's systems.

Under arrangements developed by the Scottish Government and NCSC, SEPA reported the attack to the Scottish Government's Cyber

Resilience Unit and the data breach to the Information Commissioner's Office. Unlike many organisations that are victimised by cyber-attacks, SEPA openly acknowledged the attack and has published a number of reviews (see https://beta.sepa.scot/about-sepa/cyber-attack/).

SEPA was able to resume most critical activities (especially flood warnings) within a day of the attack, but the effects were long-lasting. The quantity of stolen material was relatively small – 1.2GB of data comprising about 4,000 files – but included permits, corporate plans, commercially sensitive information and staff data. The attackers published this online when SEPA – in line with police guidance – refused to pay the ransom. However, a lot more SEPA data were encrypted or destroyed, including tens of millions of pounds worth of financial records, which had to be recreated from scratch (Audit Scotland, 2022). Even unaffected systems had to be taken offline during the recovery to avoid contamination, and the hackers are thought to have tried again to compromise SEPA systems while the recovery effort took place.

At the time of the attack, SEPA had been accredited with the Cyber Essentials programme and was described as having strong defences, including regular backups of data. The attack was able to compromise the backups and prevented online access to SEPA's incident response plans; COVID-19 restrictions meant only a few people could access the hard copies kept at SEPA offices.

The recovery entailed a joint effort to rebuild most of SEPA's core IT systems; this took months and is thought to have cost £5.5m of public money. The investigation led by Police Scotland's Cybercrime Investigations Unit determined the attack was the work of an international organised crime group. Suspicion fell on Conti, a Russian group that provided its ransomware 'as a service' to other groups, possibly with Russian state support. It was therefore not possible to bring them to justice in the usual way, although the police were able to gather evidence and contribute to the recovery effort.

Conti has attacked many other institutions and is thought to have extorted a total of £27m from 149 victims in the UK (NCA, 2023); the total cost (including recovery) is far higher. In 2022, Conti's support for the Russian invasion of Ukraine led someone (possibly a former member) to leak a huge trove of private messages between members. This made it possible for the NCA and US Government to identify seven members of the group and place economic sanctions on them, prohibiting property ownership or engaging in business activity in the UK or the USA and restricting their travel. These tactics can disrupt organisations and reduce the rewards of these offences, but within Russia, the perpetrators remain free; operating in this way, some ransomware attackers have made fortunes which remain inaccessible to Western authorities.

Questions to consider

- Who is harmed by this incident, and how?
- In what ways is globalisation relevant to this story?
- What should the role of criminal justice be in incidents like this, and what are the limitations of a criminal justice approach?

11.2.4 Human trafficking

Human trafficking in Scotland was little discussed until the late 2000s (Lebov, 2010) but is now a significant concern in policing and community safety (Atkinson and Hamilton-Smith, 2022). The UN's Palermo Protocol – another international agreement – defines human trafficking as:

> the recruitment, transportation, transfer, harbouring or receipt of persons, by means of the threat or use of force or other forms of coercion, of abduction, of fraud, of deception, of the abuse of power or of a position of vulnerability or of the giving or receiving of payments or benefits to achieve the consent of a person having control over another person, for the purpose of exploitation.
>
> (United Nations 2000: Article 3(a))

Human trafficking is often called an 'invisible' crime since its victims may be working in ordinary jobs, apparently legitimately, while actually being exploited. They may be marginalised by their ethnicity, nationality, language skills, and/or gender and may not wish to report or even be aware that a crime has occurred. They may be fearful of police and other authorities and particularly concerned about the possibility of being deported. Remote rural contexts, of the type common in northern Scotland, can be particularly isolating for victims, but exploitation may be more likely to raise suspicion in a village where residents know each other than in a large city (Atkinson and Hamilton-Smith, 2022).

In 2015, the Human Trafficking and Exploitation (Scotland) Act created a single offence of human trafficking with a maximum penalty of life imprisonment. Victims may have committed offences themselves, by breaking immigration rules, being coerced into committing offences (e.g. drug production, shoplifting, even assisting in human trafficking), or offences in attempting to escape – so may be reluctant to report. Hence, the Act follows established good practice in understanding the victims *as victims* rather than offenders and introduces a presumption against prosecuting victims of human trafficking.

Immigration is reserved to Westminster and since 2009, in order to comply with the UN Convention, the UK Home Office has operated a National Referral Mechanism (NRM), a framework for identifying potential victims of human trafficking and modern slavery and referring victims for support and to police for investigation. Various organisations in Scotland and the wider UK can refer cases to the NRM, but the 'Single Competent Authority' which judges whether trafficking has occurred is part of the Home Office. Where the NRM establishes that human trafficking has occurred, it refers the case back to Police Scotland for investigation; recent reports show a steady rise in these referrals to around 200 people every quarter.

Protection and support for victims in Scotland is devolved, as it takes place under Scottish institutions (Thomson, 2016). The Scottish Government has its own Trafficking and Exploitation Strategy. Police Scotland operates a National Human Trafficking Unit at the Scottish Crime Campus which coordinates with the NCA; in cases centring on specific countries, they may also cooperate with international police forces. Gaitis (2023) suggests that the Scottish Government's approach is more victim-focused, while the UK government continues to see human trafficking at least partly as an immigration problem. Borders and migration remain reserved to Westminster; the emphasis on understanding human trafficking victims *as victims* sits uneasily with the use of criminal justice measures including deportation as an increasingly prominent part of *UK* (not Scottish – but applying to Scotland) migration policy.

Any effort centred on recognising victimisation and exploitation pulls against prevailing anti-immigration narratives which stigmatise immigrants as criminals. Claims that modern slavery protections were being abused to facilitate irregular immigration led to the UK's 2023 Illegal Migration Act, which would severely restrict the right to claim asylum and protections for human trafficking victims. The Law Society of Scotland (Sirel, 2023) suggested that this would not only contravene international conventions but may force Scotland to break its own human rights obligations. However, following a Labour victory in the 2024 UK general election, these controversial provisions have not been brought into force; for now (May 2025), some protections remain for human trafficking victims.

Preventive measures emphasise raising awareness and encouraging ordinary people – especially those who may encounter potential victims in their work – to report signs of human trafficking (e.g. movement of people at strange times, overcrowded homes whose occupants change often). Aside from more conventional public information channels, this includes a mobile anti-trafficking reporting app developed by the charity Unseen, provided to all Scottish police officers.

Critical perspectives highlight the limitations of a policy that centres on raising awareness, suggesting that such measures create the impression of action while drawing attention away from the structural contexts which enable trafficking to occur (see Franko, 2020). The use of the 'anti-trafficking' label may draw law enforcement responses towards, and collect data on, already marginalised people and groups; Mendel and Sharapov (2023) suggest that responses centred on 'awareness-raising' may be most beneficial for an 'anti-trafficking industry' which benefits from sensationalising and simplifying the issue, in a way that may itself perpetuate racist 'white saviour' assumptions. Again, narratives of globalised transnational crime are inseparable from local and global ethnic, gender and socioeconomic inequalities.

Conclusion

In this book, we have already seen various ways in which Scottish criminal justice has been shaped by international examples through processes of 'policy transfer' – for instance, the Scottish Violence Reduction Unit (SVRU)'s borrowing of American examples (Chapter 2). We have also seen how international events in Scotland (e.g. the 2014 Commonwealth Games, or protests around COP26 – see Chapters 2 and 3) have affected criminal justice practices.

In this chapter, we have examined how the dynamics of globalisation have played out in a Scottish criminal justice context, including various forms of cooperation and interconnection between governments and justice agencies, and the increasingly transnational character of both crime and policing. It is important to bear in mind that the benefits and harms of globalisation are not distributed equally. Patterns of social, economic, gender and ethnic inequalities intersect with inequalities at the global level. It is no coincidence that these patterns reflect earlier patterns of colonisation, with formerly colonised countries disadvantaged and often still in subordinate economic relationships with their former colonisers (Bhambra, 2021).

The discussions here highlight ways in which Scottish criminal justice requires cooperation with agencies overseas. However, this chapter has also highlighted how Scotland is reliant on decision-makers in Westminster for its ability to shape its own responses to questions of international and transnational responses to crime. Being a devolved jurisdiction with distinct criminal justice arrangements, within a larger nation state, makes Scotland's position with respect to transnational criminal justice particularly complex. Whatever its eventual future – in or out of the UK and/or EU – the issues raised here will figure significantly in Scotland's future. Our next final chapter summarises this book's key ideas and considers the possible futures of Scottish criminal justice.

Critical questions

- Thinking about your recent life, consider some ways in which globalisation has affected you. How might these be relevant to criminal justice?

- Think about the different types of transnational crime discussed here and how Scotland responds to them; what are some key similarities and differences?
- What are the potential challenges posed for Scottish criminal justice by transnational forms of offending not discussed here?
  - Drug trafficking;
  - International terrorism;
  - Trafficking in cultural property.
- From a criminal justice perspective, what are some potential advantages and disadvantages of Scotland rejoining the EU as an independent state?
- Are international norms and human rights frameworks sufficient to ensure decent criminal justice conditions? If not, what could be done to strengthen them?
- Should criminal justice agencies cooperate with agencies in countries where there are concerns about human rights or due process? What are some implications of this for Scotland? You may wish to think about this in relation to police investigations, the provision of training and equipment, and deportations/extraditions.

Key resources

Franko, K. (2020) *Globalization and Crime*. 3rd edition. SAGE.

Although not focused on Scotland, this book is a key criminological text on global crime and crime control.

Malloch, M. and Rigby, P. (eds) *Human Trafficking: The Complexities of Exploitation*. Edinburgh University Press.

A recent edited collection on human trafficking, with a discussion of Scottish contexts.

Scottish Government (2024) *Serious Organised Crime Taskforce*. Scottish Government. https://www.gov.scot/groups/serious-organised-crime-taskforce/

Official SOC Taskforce website with progress reports and links to partner organisations.

References

Aebi, M., Berger-Kolopp, L., Burkhardt, C., Chopin, J., Hashimoto, Y.Z. and Tiago, M.M. (2015) *Foreign Offenders in Prison and on Probation in Europe: Trends from 2005 to 2015 (Inmates) and Situation in 2015 (Inmates and Probationers)*. Council of Europe.

Arnell, P. (2018) What an extradition hearing is and why it matters. *Juridical Review* 4: 250–268.

Atkinson, C. (2019) Where were you while we were getting high policing? The consequences of co-location for broader partnership working in tackling organised crime and terrorism. *Policing and Society* 29(8): 922–935.

Atkinson, C. and Hamilton-Smith, N. (2022) Still an 'invisible crime'? Exploring developments in the awareness and control of human trafficking in Scotland. *European Journal of Criminology* 19(5): 911–931.

Audit Scotland (2022) *The 2020/21 Audit of the Scottish Environment Protection Agency.* https://audit.scot/publications/the-202021-audit-of-the-scottish-environment-protection-agency

BBC News (2016) *Police Scotland's Overseas Training Work Is 'Hypocrisy'*, 25 May. https://www.bbc.co.uk/news/uk-scotland-36378490

Bhambra, G. K. (2021) Colonial global economy: Towards a theoretical reorientation of political economy. *Review of International Political Economy* 28(2): 307–322.

Bosworth, M. and Turnbull, S. (2015) Immigration, detention, and the expansion of penal power in the United Kingdom. In Reiter, K. and Koenig, A. (eds) *Extreme Punishment.* Palgrave Macmillan. 50–67.

Buchan, J. and Grant, S. (2021) Community justice: An opportunity to 'Re-integrate'? *SCCJR Blog.* https://sccjrblog.wordpress.com/2021/03/22/community-justice-an-opportunity-to-re-integrate/

Carrell, S. (2012) Maldives police accused of civil rights abuses being trained by Scottish police. *Guardian*, 17 December. https://www.theguardian.com/world/2012/dec/17/maldives-training-scottish-police-college

Cavanagh, B., Hamilton-Smith, N. and Mackenzie, S. (2016) Organised crime in Scotland and the criminal justice response. In Croall, H., Mooney, G. and Munro, M. (eds) *Crime, Justice and Society in Scotland.* Routledge. 115–130.

Daly, A., Mukushi, T., Quiroz, D., Schafer, B., Hamill, D., Alexander, A., Aston, L., Brotchie, J., Stevenson, B., Oswald, M. and Ferguson, S. (2023) *Independent Advisory Group on Emerging Technologies in Policing: Legal Frameworks and Ethical Standards Workstream Report – Final Report.* Scottish Government.

Downie, D. and Carnie, J. (2018) *Ethnic Minority & Foreign National Prisoners Survey.* Scottish Prison Service. https://www.sps.gov.uk/sites/default/files/2024-02/16thPrisonerSurveyEthnicMinorityBulletin_2017_Research.pdf.

Emsley, C. (2012) Marketing the brand: Exporting British police models 1829–1950. *Policing: A Journal of Policy and Practice* 6(1): 43–54.

Franko, K. (2020) *Globalization and Crime.* Third edition. Sage.

Gaitis, K.K. (2023) *How Is Human Trafficking Regulated in the UK? A Critical Examination of the UK's Anti-Trafficking Response: A Research Policy Brief.* SCCJR. https://www.sccjr.ac.uk/wp-content/uploads/2023/12/Dr-Konstantinos-Kosmas-Gaitis_FINAL.pdf

Gavrielides, T. (2016) Repositioning restorative justice in Europe. *Victims & Offenders* 11(1): 71–86.

Godshaw, D. (2020) Becoming an immigrant? Border harms and "British" men with previous convictions in British Immigration Removal Centers. *Critical Criminology: An International Journal* 28(2): 225–241.

Graham, W., Atkinson, C., Hamilton-Smith, N. and Fraser, A. (2018) *Community Experiences of Serious Organised Crime in Scotland.* Scottish Government. https://www.gov.scot/binaries/content/documents/govscot/publications/research-and-analysis/2018/06/community-experiences-serious-organised-crime-scotland-research-findings/documents/00536114-pdf/00536114-pdf/govscot%3Adocument/00536114.pdf

The Journal (2024) Man whose surrender to Scotland was refused last year to be extradited after new request, 29 April. https://www.thejournal.ie/man-to-be-extradited-scotland-richard-sharples-6367578-Apr2024/.

Kenealy, D. (2012) Commercial interests and calculated compassion: The diplomacy and paradiplomacy of releasing the Lockerbie bomber. *Diplomacy & Statecraft* 23(3): 555–575.

Kirby, S. and Snow, N. (2016) Praxis and the disruption of organized crime groups. *Trends in Organized Crime* 19: 111–124 (2016).

Lavorgna, A. and Sergi, A. (2016) Serious, therefore organised? A critique of the emerging "cyber-organised crime" rhetoric in the United Kingdom. *International Journal of Cyber Criminology* 10(2): 170–187.

Lebov, K. (2010) Human trafficking in Scotland. *European Journal of Criminology* 7(1): 77–93.

Mendel, J. and Sharapov, K. (2023) Expanding circles of failure: The rise of bad anti-trafficking, and what to do about it. In Vasilyeva, A. (ed) *Issues in Modern Slavery*. Durham University. 21–40.

Milne, B. and Thomson, G. (2012) *Scottish Policing and Policy Transfer: Developing a Sustainable Model of Community Policing in Sri* Lanka. SIPR Briefing No 11, March 2012. https://www.sipr.ac.uk/wp-content/uploads/2024/01/SCOTTISH-POLICING-AND-POLICY-TRANSFER-DEVELOPING-A-SUSTAINABLE-MODEL-OF-COMMUNITY-POLICING-IN-SRI-LANKA-.pdf

National Crime Agency (2023) *Ransomware Criminals Sanctioned in Joint UK/US Crackdown on International Cyber Crime*. NCA. https://www.nationalcrimeagency.gov.uk/news/ransomware-criminals-sanctioned-in-joint-uk-us-crackdown-on-international-cyber-crime

National Crime Agency (2024) *Scotland Report: NCA Summary October 2023–March 2024*. https://www.spa.police.uk/spa-media/qckf55kc/item-9-nca-performance-in-scotland-report-oct-23-march-24.pdf

Police Scotland (no date) *International Development Unit*. Police Scotland. Archived via https://web.archive.org/web/20161114025313/https://www.scotland.police.uk/about-us/police-scotland/scottish-police-college/international-development-unit

Scott, K.B. (2008) The Scottish Crime and Drug Enforcement Agency: From common police service to 'MacFBI'. *The Police Journal* 81: 154–164.

Scottish Government (2021) *Scotland: A Good Global Citizen. A Scottish Perspective on Climate, Defence. Security and External Affairs*. Scottish Government. https://www.gov.scot/publications/scotland-good-global-citizen-scottish-perspective-climate-defence-security-external-affairs/

Scottish Government (2022) *Serious Organised Crime Strategy*. Scottish Government. https://www.gov.scot/publications/serious-organised-crime-strategy/

Scottish Government (2024) *Building a New Scotland: Justice in an Independent Scotland*. Scottish Government. https://www.gov.scot/binaries/content/documents/govscot/publications/research-and-analysis/2024/04/building-new-scotland-justice-independent-scotland/documents/justice-independent-scotland-paper-13/justice-independent-scotland-paper-13/govscot%3Adocument/justice-independent-scotland-paper-13.pdf

Scottish Human Rights Commission (2024) *Review... Recommend... Repeat... An Assessment of where Human Rights have Stalled in Places of Detention*. Scottish Human Rights Commission.

Scottish Legal News (2016) *Police Scotland trained Saudi and Bahraini Forces without Making Human Rights Checks, FOI Reveals*, 23 December. https://www.scottishlegal.com/articles/police-scotland-trained-saudi-and-bahraini-forces-without-making-human-rights-checks-foi-reveals

Scottish Police Authority (SPA) (2024) *Policing in a Digital World – Annual Report 2024*. SPA.

Scottish Prison Service (2024) *Scottish Prison Population Statistics 2023-24*. Scottish Government.

Sirel, A. (2023) Broken words: The Illegal Migration Act. *Journal of the Law Society of Scotland* 68(8): 22–23. https://www.lawscot.org.uk/members/journal/issues/vol-68-issue-08/broken-words-the-illegal-migration-act/

Soliman, F. (2024) *Social Harm at the Border: The Case of Lampedusa*. Routledge.

Spolverato, G. (2021) The implementation of the European Prison Rules regarding education in Belgium and Ireland. *European Journal of Crime, Criminal Law and Criminal Justice* 29(1): 47–65.

Thomson, K. (2016) International and European standards in relation to victims and survivors of human trafficking. In Malloch, M. and Rigby, P. (eds) *Human Trafficking: The Complexities of Exploitation*. Edinburgh University Press. 63–83.

Tropina, T. (2024) 'This is not a human rights convention!': The perils of overlooking human rights in the UN cybercrime treaty. *Journal of Cyber Policy* 9(2): 1–21.

Turnbull, S. and Hasselberg, I. (2017) From prison to detention: The carceral trajectories of foreign-national prisoners in the United Kingdom. *Punishment & Society* 19(2): 135–154.

Ugelvik, T. (2014) The incarceration of foreigners in European prisons. In Pickering, S. and Ham, J. (eds) *The Routledge Handbook on Crime and International Migration*. Routledge. 107–120.

United Nations (2000) *Protocol to Prevent, Suppress and Punish Trafficking in Persons, Especially Women and Children, Supplementing the United Nations Convention against Transnational Organized Crime (Palermo Protocol)*. United Nations.

van Zyl Smit, D., Snacken, S. and Hayes, D. (2015) 'One cannot legislate kindness': Ambiguities in European legal instruments on non-custodial sanctions. *Punishment & Society* 17(1): 3–26.

Yar, M. and Steinmetz, K. (2024) *Cybercrime and Society*. Fourth edition. Sage.

12 Interrogating Scottish distinctiveness

Key ideas

- Discussions about Scottish criminal justice are sometimes characterised by an emphasis on Scotland's distinctiveness, particularly from England and Wales. This long-running narrative aligns well with a Scottish nationalist political agenda but does not necessarily match the reality.
- Scottish criminal justice intersects with patterns of structural inequality (socioeconomic, gender and others) in terms of who is punished and how they experience punishment; arguably, the criminal justice system serves to reinforce these inequalities.
- Scotland's criminal justice system does not consistently adhere to any specific model or paradigm but reflects multiple different logics. In the messy reality of everyday practice, these logics may align or conflict with each other.
- Although the scrutiny of criminal justice was much improved with devolution, it is arguably still insufficient in places, and the accountability of the system (as in, its ability to change in response to critique) is poor.
- There remains a deep-rooted institutional and cultural resistance to change, and a gradual 'creep' of criminal justice functions out into other areas of social life.

Introduction

In our final chapter, we reflect on some themes that cut across institutions of Scottish criminal justice – the intersection of criminal justice with deep-rooted structural inequalities across Scotland, its apparent resistance to substantive reform, the outward creep of punishment and control beyond the formal institutions of criminal justice, and the coexistence of different and conflicting paradigms within the same system. In doing so, we hope to encourage reflection on these themes and on the possible futures of criminal justice in Scotland. We begin by evaluating one of the most persistent claims in rhetoric about Scottish criminal justice – the idea that Scottish criminal justice is distinctive or 'exceptional', especially relative to the wider UK.

DOI: 10.4324/9781003372882-12

12.1 Interrogating Scottish distinctiveness

Scottish criminal justice is often understood as 'distinctive', but throughout this book, we have sought to question this narrative.

One way in which this narrative has been prominent has been in descriptions of **'Scottish exceptionalism'** – the idea that Scotland is an exception to wider trends in criminal justice (Brangan, 2019). This has echoes of other 'exceptionalist' arguments in the sociology of punishment, particularly the Scandinavian or Nordic exceptionalism thesis. Despite the similarity in these descriptions and a political desire to present Scotland as more like our Scandinavian neighbours than our English ones, the Scottish imprisonment rate is more similar to the latter.

Imagining Scotland as distinctive or exceptional immediately raises the question of what we claim to be distinctive or exceptional *from*. Many political discussions in Scotland (not just in criminal justice) emphasise its distinctiveness from the wider UK, especially from the punitive practices of England and Wales – an argument that chimes neatly with 'nation-building' politics and Scottish Nationalist agendas. There is *some* truth to this, both prior to devolution but also driven by the post-devolution political will for Scotland to be different.

Some of Scotland's institutional arrangements are markedly different from those found elsewhere, notably institutions established under the 1968 Social Work (Scotland) Act – justice social work and the Children's Hearings System (Chapters 6 and 9). Both these features are distinctive of Scotland not only within the UK but within both Europe and the Anglophone world. Across courts, prosecution (Chapter 4), prisons (Chapter 8) and elsewhere, Scotland has its own agencies, some of them (especially the Crown Office) long predating their English equivalents.

Also distinctive is Scotland's extremely limited embrace of criminal justice privatisation – except for electronic monitoring (Chapter 7), where an Anglo-American privatised model (as opposed to the emphasis on state institutions found in continental Europe) has been adopted with seemingly little consideration or controversy.

Narratives of distinctiveness predate devolution; however, these narratives have become far more prominent with both devolution and the ongoing debate about independence. The early devolutionary years brought a series of new criminal justice organisations, which McAra (2008) described as 'hyper-institutionalisation' in an exercise in building political capital for the new institutions of a new polity. This era was characterised by narratives of a specifically 'Scottish approach' to policing, especially the policing of protest, supposedly typified by egalitarianism, openness and an emphasis on policing by consent and community relations (Gorringe and Rosie, 2010). The reality of Scottish policing does not always match up to this (Section 3.4.2), nor is any success in this area necessarily distinctive of Scotland.

Paradoxically, by introducing a new set of policy actors electorally accountable to the public (MSPs), devolution also arguably produced some apparent convergence with English and Welsh models initially. This 'detartanisation' (McAra, 2006) was particularly notable in the proliferation of punitive and actuarial measures in youth justice, such as Antisocial Behaviour Orders (ASBOs) (Chapter 9) – but ultimately, uptake of these measures was limited, efforts to promote child wellbeing took prominence, and the distinctive core of Scottish youth justice remains.

The ascendancy of the Scottish National Party (SNP) in 2007 brought further emphasis on narratives of Scottish distinctiveness since these would align well with a pro-independence political agenda. Thus, the SNP could show both that Scotland was distinctive in its approach to criminal justice and that it was competent to govern itself autonomously (MacLennan, 2016).

The period in which the SNP held an overall Parliamentary majority (2011–16) brought numerous institutional and structural reforms across the justice system, most prominently perhaps in the replacement of Scotland's eight regional forces with the single national service Police Scotland (Chapter 3). The fact of a single national police service itself differentiates Scottish policing from that of England and Wales (though not Northern Ireland; national forces are also the norm in many other countries). Narratives of distinctiveness surfaced in various other ways: a dramatic fall in violent crime was credited to the activities of the Scottish Violence Reduction Unit and more generally to a 'public health approach' to preventing violence (Chapter 2; Fraser and Gillon, 2024). Discussions of efforts to reduce imprisonment following the Scottish Prisons Commission (2008) report and the Scottish Prison Service (SPS) (2013) organisational review *Unlocking Potential, Transforming Lives* fuelled claims of Scottish exceptionalism.

More substantive change was achieved in youth justice, where measures including the diversion-oriented Whole System Approach have led eventually to the abolition of imprisonment for children (Chapter 9). Another important reform was the increase in the minimum age of criminal responsibility from 8 to 12 years old (it remains at 10 elsewhere in the UK). However, 12 is still low by European standards, the ending of youth imprisonment came too late for a number of children who died in custody, and there remain overall, significant problems with how children are dealt with by criminal justice.

There have been repeated policy aspirations to reduce imprisonment – and there has been real success in nearly eliminating imprisonment for fine default, ending the imprisonment of children and reducing the number of very short-term prison sentences. Yet, the *overall rate* of imprisonment has remained similar if not higher to that of England and Wales (Northern Ireland's is much lower) and very high by Western European standards (Sections 6.2.4 and 8.3.1). This is despite significant rises in the numbers of people supervised under community penalties, leading to a situation in which Scotland has been estimated as having the highest 'combined correctional rate' (combined imprisonment and community supervision) in Europe (McNeil, 2019); within prisons, there are serious and persistent problems with overcrowding, progression, solitary confinement, and high rate of deaths in custody (Chapter 8). In such a context, Scottish exceptionalist narratives begin to look less like a description and more like a 'performance', politically convenient for nation-building narratives (Buchan and McNeill, 2023).

Scotland has been far from immune to the late modern 'punitive turn'; beyond this, Scotland continues to be affected by wider trends. Rising concern about international crime has led to an expectation of international cooperation in criminal justice, and Scotland remains in a complex position with respect to the UK's institutions of international crime control and Westminster's foreign policy (Chapter 11). The dominance of human rights treaties in the latter part of the 20th century is apparent in Scotland too, with the Scottish Parliament recently embracing the UN Convention on the Rights of the Child, with implications for youth justice as well as child welfare (Chapter 9). However, not only are there numerous examples of the Scottish criminal justice system violating human rights, but the accountability bodies intended to respond to, and prevent these, have extremely limited powers.

In sum, while Scotland and its criminal justice system are distinctive in important ways, we have outlined a number of ways in which it conforms with or exceeds England and Wales in punitiveness.

12.2 Cross-cutting themes

In writing this book, we have tried to convey a sense of the institutional and procedural complexity of Scottish criminal justice, but balanced with a sense of the 'bigger picture'. With this in mind, we now consider some of the major themes that cut across much of Scottish criminal justice.

12.2.1 Inequalities

Scotland is a very unequal country within another, larger very unequal country, and this has implications for criminal justice.

Throughout this book, we have shown how criminal justice disproportionately affects people from poorer backgrounds. The causal connection between poverty and crime (as opposed to criminalisation) is disputed, but such a connection could not fully explain the relationship, which is notable in the enormous overrepresentation of people from the most disadvantaged postcodes in prison (Houchin, 2005) and of working-class young people among those stopped and searched (Murray, 2014) (Chapters 8 and 3). Criminal justice not only reflects but reinforces inequalities – as we see when we consider the pervasive impacts of financial penalties on the poorest in society, or the financial impacts of imprisonment on prisoners' families (Chapters 5 and 8).

Furthermore, it is essential to understand social inequalities as *intersecting* with each other. Thus, Scottish women, despite accounting overall for much less (and less serious) crime than men, may be especially severely affected by experiences of punishment (Boxes 6.3, 8.1, and 10.2), due to an increased likelihood of having histories of dependent drug use, mental illnesses, head injuries, various forms of trauma and victimisation, and gendered healthcare needs.

At present, women (as with young people) constitute a group of prisoners for whom it is more acceptable in policy circles to show sympathy. It is not that they don't deserve sympathy (or – less paternalistically – empathy), but we do seek to problematise the ways in which the justice system extends its 'helping' hand to women. Not only is provision very limited within the system, but this casts carceral spaces as places of healing. Furthermore, the (limited) push to improve conditions for women has not been accompanied by a similar attention to groups (such as adult men serving long sentences) who might be rather less outwardly 'sympathetic' to the public but may also have experienced a range of personal and structural challenges and who, at the very least, warrant safe and healthy conditions, fair treatment and support towards reintegration.

We suggest that there is cause for concern about racism in Scottish criminal justice, e.g. in the ways in which foreign national prisoners are disadvantaged within the system and concerns about police racism following the deaths of Sheku Bayoh and Badreddin Abdalla Adam Bosh. It is difficult to say much more than this with any certainty, since the assumption that there is 'no problem here' with racism has been, until recently, so pervasive that we are missing the data on ethnicity needed to fully investigate the issue. Other forms of identity and inequality have been touched on more briefly (see for instance Box 3.1, 8.3).

12.2.2 *Competing logics of criminal justice*

Taking a sociology of punishment approach, we can understand the development of criminal justice in Scotland as being shaped by a number of (often competing) logics including penal welfarism, desistance, neoliberalism and risk management, rights, and public health approaches.

The ascendancy of **penal welfarism** and associated ideas of **rehabilitation,** in the mid-20th century, led to a number of developments in Scottish criminal justice, most notably in the 1968 Social Work (Scotland) Act (see Chapters 6 and 9). These created some distinctive Scottish institutional arrangements which have persisted despite a widespread loss of faith in rehabilitation and commitment to social welfare across the UK and much of the West. In Scotland, the language of rehabilitation shifted somewhat to the language of **desistance** (see Chapter 6), which became commonplace across many parts of Scottish criminal justice (see Chapters 6 and 8) in the 2000/2010s. However, the implementation of desistance-based policies was done so in ways more compatible with other competing logics of welfarism and risk management than the more radical insights from desistance research which emphasised the role of communities, social structures and criminal justice agencies in the co-creation of reoffending and desistance (see Section 6.3.4; Box 6.2).

Neoliberalism has been another driving force within Scottish criminal justice, with managerialism evident throughout the system (see e.g. Chapters 6 and 8). Despite limited privatisation (but see Chapter 7 for an exception), this has included an increase in partnership working to increase efficiency. However, an emphasis on management structures and efficiencies runs the risk of diverting attention away from deeper concerns about the purposes of punishment and appropriate responses to crime and harm. In contemporary Scottish criminal justice, the logic of desistance is often commingled with actuarial practices of frequent **risk assessment** (Chapter 10), but labelling someone 'high risk' can arguably hinder desistance.

Scottish criminal justice has also been influenced by various '**rights**' discourses including the UN Convention on the Rights of the Child (Chapter 9) and the 'Mandela Rules' (Chapter 8). However, human rights are routinely not upheld in Scottish prisons (Chapter 8) while other Scottish criminal justice agencies have been potentially complicit with human rights violations overseas (Chapter 11). Logics including rehabilitation or risk management can be used to in effect exclude certain groups as subjects deserving of rights (Armstrong, 2020), despite the supposed universality within human rights discourse. In parallel, there has also been an emphasis on the rights of victims through the Victims' Rights (Scotland) Regulations 2015 and with a Victim's Code for Scotland published in 2016, with recognition of the frequently poor experience of victims in the system (see especially Chapter 4). Victims' rights are sometimes, unhelpfully, pitted against the rights of people with convictions (despite the overlap between these groups).

A relatively recent logic is that of public health, which has been embraced over recent years in Scottish criminal justice policy, most notably in the narrative of the Scottish Violence Reduction Unit as a 'success story' of **public health** approaches (Chapter 2, Fraser and Gillon, 2024). Closely related is the growing awareness of the impact of trauma on the lives of people in the criminal justice system, and an expectation that criminal justice services can and should be 'trauma-informed' (Box 8.1, Sections 4.3.5 and 9.3.5) particularly services for women and young people, a selectiveness of which we are critical. Similar developments have occurred within policing, although with more of an emphasis on 'vulnerability', despite concerns (among police officers as well as activists) about the appropriateness of using police to respond to mental distress (Section 3.4.3). However, these approaches individualise trauma and vulnerability, failing to see trauma as structural, and they are based on an assumption that criminal justice can protect and even heal vulnerable people – even though these institutions are deeply implicated in rendering people 'vulnerable' and perpetuating inequalities more widely (Anderson, 2025).

12.2.3 Under-scrutiny in a small polity

Although small spaces can offer opportunities for debate, there are also dangers that **scrutiny** and debate are stifled in a small polity where those working on criminal justice issues frequently know each other and where diversity in civil society institutions is more limited. Many of the chapters in this book attested to problems with arrangements for scrutiny and accountability in criminal justice. One recurring problem was a paucity or lack of public availability of data (see e.g. Chapter 3 on stop and search and investigation and complaints, Chapter 4 on race and ethnicity in relation to court procedures, and various prison data issues, such as foreign national prisoner data in Chapter 11). There continues to be little data on financial penalties in Scotland; the exception being COVID FPNs which briefly brought this area of criminal justice into the spotlight. However, there has been a notable increase in the political focus on policing as well as other areas of criminal justice, particularly centralised institutions most closely linked with central government (Murray and Harkin, 2017).

Although democratic accountability and political 'heat' in criminal justice can be problematic (see McAra, 2006 for this in the Scottish context), this has also arguably brought with it the positive benefit of greater challenge and accountability to Scottish criminal justice agencies. We hope that this book will contribute to that scrutiny by bringing attention to Scotland's justice system as a system in its own right in a very specific social and cultural context.

12.2.4 *The inertia and creep of criminal justice*

This leads us to another recurrent theme through the chapters of this book: the inertia of the criminal justice system, with its resistance to change, and the creep of criminal justice outwards, numerically, temporally, and institutionally – with more agencies being brought into the implementation of investigation, surveillance and punishment activities, but also with some extension outward of its logics and technologies apparent in other areas of public policy.

Several chapters of this book testified to concern about the high Scottish prison population and political intentions to decarcerate. This was particularly prominent in discussions of community sentences (Chapter 6), electronic monitoring (Chapter 7), and prisons (Chapter 8), yet the prison population has nonetheless grown alongside a growing population of people subject to community sentences. As in some other European jurisdictions, Scotland saw an expansion of those under penal control (that is, in prison and/or under supervision in the community), from less than 8,000 people in 1980 to over 30,000 in 2013–14 (McNeill, 2019), a rise that dramatically outstrips the growth in the general population in Scotland over this time. This means that Scotland is subjecting a greater proportion to criminal justice punishment and surveillance, which cannot be fully explained by rises in recorded crime.

Despite the dominance of the prison in public imaginaries of criminal justice, much punishment and surveillance happens beyond the prison walls. There has been a rise in post-release supervision for different sentences, the number of people on an Order for Lifelong Restriction (OLR) (see Chapter 10) also exceeds the 'small number' they were initially introduced to serve, and there has been the expansion of surveillance and risk and carceral logics into the community, for example through Multi-Agency Public Protection Arrangements (MAPPA) (Chapter 6), electronic monitoring (Chapter 7) and licence conditions (Chapter 10).

These examples also demonstrate the institutional expansion of Scottish criminal justice, with additional institutions and organisations being brought into criminal justice activities, e.g. community safety activity (see Chapter 2), and some diversification of providers (as discussed briefly in Chapter 3, and Chapters 5 and 6). The use of the welfare system to claw back unpaid fines through benefits deductions (see Chapter 5) offers another example of institutional creep, and how systems of welfare have been coopted to enforce criminal justice punishments. Finally, in Chapter 11, we saw the ways in which the rise of anti-immigration political rhetoric and public sentiment, particularly in England, has led to the increasing use of immigration enforcement as a response to offending and of the criminal justice system to respond to immigration infractions. The 2021 Kenmure Street incident, where Police Scotland in effect tried to facilitate immigration enforcement against community opposition, created political tensions between the Scottish and UK governments at the time. Finally, the outwards sprawl of the system can also be seen in the attempts to implement restorative justice within Scotland, which (as in other European jurisdictions) has sought, albeit with limited success so far, to incorporate it within criminal justice rather than to position it as an alternative way of addressing harm (Box 6.1); this is an example of a wider issue, the ability of the criminal justice system to absorb ideas intended to challenge it.

As has been seen in other Western jurisdictions, the welfare and immigration system also offer examples of where the technologies and logics of criminal justice have been incorporated into other public policy areas within Scotland, for example, the use of prison-like detention at Dungavel House immigration removal centre or the use of benefits sanctions to penalise those who are deemed not to have met the stringent conditions of accessing employment-related financial support. This form of creep has been particularly facilitated through UK government policy, but nevertheless plays out in Scotland.

This inertia and creep of the criminal justice system in Scotland are important when we look ahead, to think about the future of Scottish criminal justice.

Conclusion: possible futures

In 2008, *Scotland's Choice* reflected on two possible futures for Scotland's criminal justice system. In one, punishment would move wherever possible from prison to the community, and Scottish prisons would be held up internationally as positive examples. The alternative posited future was one in which there are more overcrowded prisons, staff with low morale and public distrust.

Since then, Scottish criminal justice has undergone much change. Ensuring no children are sent to prison (Chapter 9), the ending of slopping out within prisons (Chapter 8), and changes to police stop and search practice and accountability (Chapter 3) are notable examples of developments with clear positive consequences. For other changes, the outcomes are more ambivalent or contested – the shift away from imprisonment and towards benefits deductions to deal with fine default (Chapter 5), the institution of mandatory Fatal Accident Inquiries to investigate deaths in custody (Chapter 8), the continued institutional restructuring of community justice (Chapter 6).

Scotland's Choice presented a moment of hope for advocates of reform, but nearly two decades later, it is hard not to see the state of Scottish criminal justice – with its overcrowded prisons, high rate of imprisonment alongside mass expansion of community supervision, and human rights concerns – as more closely resembling the negative alternative future outlined. McLeish had emphasised that: "A negative future is not inevitable and a positive one is not unattainable" (Scottish Prisons Commission, 2008, p.1), but the former resulted from doing the same while the latter required thinking differently. It is unfair to say that there has been no attempt to think differently in Scotland, but we have certainly seen little evidence of concerted efforts to disentangle ourselves from the very embedded carceral thinking that underpins the tendency of the system to reassert itself in the face of challenge. Projecting forward, the negative future depicted in *Scotland's Choice* is still not inevitable, but thinking *a little bit* differently is not enough.

Attempts to reduce the reliance on criminal justice, and in particular imprisonment, have coexisted alongside attempts to *improve* the system; to make it work 'better'. Abolitionist critiques have long argued that many such reforms end up reinforcing the system (through better resourcing and a rehabilitated image), resulting in greater use. Proponents of reform argue instead for improvements in the system while simultaneously striving to reduce its reach and depth, arguing that reform has not been the reason for penal expansion over the decades. Either way, centering the harms of criminal justice can yield positive results, as the current absence of any children in prison in Scotland shows.

As we complete this book, much about the Scottish context of criminal justice seems in flux. The next Holyrood election in May 2026 is likely to result in a different looking Scottish Parliament than any seen over the past two decades, with consequent effects on criminal justice policy, a common battle ground within elections – and possibly the end of an era for the SNP's current nation-building project and its associated narratives. That said, narratives of Scottish distinctiveness are likely to remain influential irrespective of the election outcome. Challenging economic conditions will also be influential; potentially playing out in more austere conditions or alternatively focusing attention on reducing the use of costly justice interventions (e.g. imprisonment).

While there have been some reforms aimed at penal reduction, these have so far been relatively minor and / or affected a relatively narrow range of people. Challenge therefore remains important to counter the inertia and creep of the criminal justice system outlined above. While formal scrutiny arrangements have an important part to play (and where improvement is needed), challenge must also come from outside this system, from civil society. However, punitive voices within civil society can be a powerful brake on progressive change, so it must also be shaped in such a way as to be receptive to political courage in this area if and when that occurs. However, attempts to meaningfully engage the public and civic society in matters of criminal justice have been rather limited in Scotland, though the 2008 Scottish Prisons Commission was a notable exception. Nonetheless, the public cannot be left out of these debates, for questions of legitimacy if for nothing else. We see the need for further similar conversations to that of the Commission; for example, an increase in the use of citizen assemblies for contentious areas of public policy could offer an opportunity here.

Other solutions come from a number of nascent grassroots groups and coalitions consisting of those with direct experience of the justice system, racial justice and/or left-wing activists, who work together with academics and human rights observers to collect evidence of harms and argue for better access to data. These groups are frequently fragile and can be short-lived (especially given the toll that campaigning can place on those directly harmed by the criminal justice system), but they do constitute small but important voices, challenging dominant narratives that frame the Scottish criminal justice system as a source of safety. The continued existence and emergence of these and other dissenting voices will be important to try and reshape public discourse about safety, accountability, justice and harm, shining a spotlight on what the Scottish criminal justice system does or does not have to play in achieving these.

One thing we can be certain of is that in criminal justice as elsewhere, debate will continue between those who advocate reform of existing institutions about what those reforms should look like, and between advocates of reform and those who believe they should be replaced or abolished altogether. Indeed, we have often discussed these debates between ourselves while writing this book – and we hope it will support students of the Scottish criminal justice system to take part in them in an informed and critical way.

Critical questions

We leave you with some last critical questions:

- How distinct really is the Scottish criminal justice system?
- Discuss the different logics of the criminal justice system: what do these do and how do they interact?

- Find the political parties' manifestos for the most recent or next Scottish election. What does each manifesto say about criminal justice? What are key similarities and differences? What would criminal justice look like in each of these visions of the future?
- What would 'better' look like for the Scottish criminal justice system, and are there risks of such a focus?
- This book took the *Scottish criminal justice system* as a starting point. How different would it have looked if it had set out to discuss *responses to serious harm to people, communities and environments in Scotland* instead?

References

Anderson, S. (2025) The trouble with trauma: Interconnected forms of violence in the lives of repeatedly criminalised men. *Howard Journal of Crime and Justice*. 64: 24–43.

Armstrong, S. (2020) At risk of rights: Rehabilitation, sentence management and the structural violence of prison. *Critical Criminology* 28: 85–105.

Brangan, L. (2019) Civilizing imprisonment: The limits of Scottish penal exceptionalism. *British Journal of Criminology* 59(4): 780–799.

Buchan, J. and McNeill, F. (2023) Progressive penality as performance. *Howard Journal of Crime and Justice* 62(3): 325–340.

Fraser, A. and Gillon, F. (2024) The Glasgow miracle? Storytelling, violence reduction and public policy. *Theoretical Criminology* 28(3): 328–345.

Gorringe, H. and Rosie, M. (2010) The 'Scottish' approach? The discursive construction of a national police force. *The Sociological Review* 58(1): 65–83.

Houchin, R. (2005) *Social Exclusion and Imprisonment in Scotland: A Report*. Glasgow Caledonian University.

MacLennan, S. (2016) Safer and stronger? The decline of managerial competence and liberal welfarism in justice policy. *Scottish Affairs* 25(1): 62–82.

McAra, L. (2006) Welfare in crisis? Key developments in Scottish Youth Justice. In Muncie, J. and Goldson, B. (eds) *Comparative Youth Justice: Critical Issues*. Sage. 127–145.

McAra, L. (2008) Crime, criminology and criminal justice in Scotland. *European Journal of Criminology* 5(4): 387–504.

McNeill, F. (2019) Mass supervision, misrecognition and the 'Malopticon'. *Punishment & Society* 21(2): 207–230.

Murray, K. (2014) *Stop and Search in Scotland: An Evaluation of Police Practice*. SCCJR. https://www.sccjr.ac.uk/wp-content/uploads/2014/01/Stop_and_Search_in_Scotland1.pdf

Murray, K. and Harkin, D. (2017) Policing in cool and hot climates: Legitimacy, power and the rise and fall of mass stop and search in Scotland. *The British Journal of Criminology* 57(4): 885–905.

Scottish Prisons Commission (2008) *Scotland's Choice: Report of the Scottish Prisons Commission*. Scottish Prisons Commission.

Scottish Prison Service (2013) *Unlocking Potential, Transforming Lives: Report of the Scottish Prison Service Organisational Review*. Scottish Prison Service.

Index

Note: Page numbers followed by "n" refer to end notes.

Printed in Dunstable, United Kingdom

73892072R00161